HOW TO OPERATE
YOUR HOME

Tom Feiza
Mr. Fix It

Published
by
Mr. Fix It Press

PO Box 510724
4620 South Raven Lane
New Berlin, WI 53151
Phone: (262) 786-7878
Fax: (262) 786-7877
E-mail:Tom@misterfix-it.com

NOTICE:

This book is available at special discounts for bulk purchases, sales promotions, premiums, fund raising, or educational use. For details, write, phone, fax or email the publisher.

First Edition

ISBN 0-9674759-1-0

Library of Congress Catalog Card 00-093196

Printed in the United States of America

BE SAFE

The information in this book has been carefully assembled to ensure that it is as accurate as possible. However, the book provides general information only, and it is sold with the understanding that the publisher and author are not rendering legal or professional services.

This book does not provide product-specific information and you should consult the manufacturer of the product or equipment for specific information. The operation and maintenance information is provided for general understanding only. Consult the reference section in the rear of the book to contact manufacturers or consult with local contractors and professionals.

When attempting a home repair project, always consult professionals and always follow label directions. Companies that manufacture equipment and home repair products are the ultimate authorities. Follow their instructions.

Many home repair, operation, and maintenance projects involve a certain degree of risk and should be approached with care. You should only attempt repairs if you have read and understood the instructions for the product, equipment, or tool that you are using. If questions or problems arise, consult a professional or the manufacturer.

Due to the variability of local conditions, construction materials, and personal skills, neither the author nor the publisher assumes responsibility for any injuries suffered or for damages or other losses that may result from the information presented.

DEDICATION

Who made me Mr. Fix-It?

I owe a lot to Uncle Nick and Uncle Joe in Virgil, Illinois, who put me on the road to being a real fix-it guy. I worked at their dairy farms, racetrack and motorcycle shop and on their many construction projects.

I was nine years old when Uncle Nick began paying me 50 cents a day to work on his farm. When I graduated from Marquette University Engineering School, I was still working for and learning from Nick and Joe and their crews.

They taught me you "learn by doing" and that the real education takes place working in the trade. From Uncle Nick and Uncle Joe, I learned the value of hard and honest effort.

My mom was also a great fix-it lady who taught me a lot about painting and refinishing. We still share information today.

What is my house like?

Ask Gayle, my wife and best friend. She will tell you we have a lot of fix-it projects waiting for me. Just like every other couple, we operate with a "honey-do" list—you know, "Honey, you need to do this." And when the list gets too long, we talk about hiring a contractor. Our home is just like every other home.

So this book is dedicated to:

My wife, Gayle, and my kids, Lindsay and Tom III, for putting up with all my fix-it projects and my basement full of stuff; and to my mom, Uncle Nick, and Uncle Joe.

ACKNOWLEDGMENTS

Special thanks go to all the people who listen to my radio show, watch my television appearances, attend my seminars, use my home inspection service, and read my newspaper column. Your questions, answers, and tips made this book possible.

Many manufacturers have provided me with excellent technical information, and I value their help.

My editor, Leah Carson, took my rough copy and made the information much more useful and user-friendly. Lynn Eckstein designed my Mr. Fix-It logo years ago, and she is responsible for the great cover design. Tonya Schoemperlen at Hot Dot designed the wonderful interior layout.

Artwork came from product manufacturers and graphic artist/architect, Justin Racinowski. Justin took my rough drawings and produced the easy-to-understand computer-generated drawings. Tom Feiza III spent a summer gathering and organizing artwork for the book.

Most importantly, I owe a lot to my wife, Gayle, and our kids, Lindsay and Tom. They helped me keep things in proper perspective by dragging me out of the office for vacations and family time.

Please enjoy my book and have a great Fix-It day!

Tom Feiza – "Mr. Fix-It"

Author:	Tom Feiza
Editor:	Leah Carson
Artwork:	Justin Racinowski
Assistant:	Tom Feiza III
Layout:	Tonya Schoemperlen
Cover Art:	Lynn Eckstein

The author gratefully acknowledges and thanks many individuals and companies that helped with this book. Companies that contributed artwork include:

1st Alert, Honeywell, American Air Filter, 3M, Aprilaire, Oatey, Genova, Reliance, Wayne Dalton, Mastergas, Zinsser, B&K Industries. Kohler, Squeak Relief, Squeek No More, Herr, In-Sink-Erator

ABOUT THE AUTHOR

Tom Feiza, Mr. Fix-It, is a "recovering" mechanical engineer and a real life fix-it guy. He personally tests home-related products and evaluates home construction problems.

Tom worked on a dairy farm through grade school, high school and college. After graduating from Marquette University as a mechanical engineer, Tom became licensed as a Professional Engineer and later a Home Inspector. After college, Tom worked for over 20 years in the construction, maintenance and operation of large facilities. He shifted from engineering to become Mr. Fix-It, helping people with their home operation, maintenance and repair problems.

Tom now combines his hobby, his passion and his profession into his unique enterprise—Tom Feiza, Mr. Fix-It, Inc.

Tom hosts a live radio call-in show on AM 620 WTMJ in Milwaukee, Wisconsin. More than 80 newspapers carry his question-and-answer column, and he often appears on television, providing home repair tips.

Tom presents unique and entertaining how-to seminars at home shows, association meetings, and retail events. He also gives entertaining keynotes at dinner meetings and professional conventions.

In another venture that helps him stay in touch with homes, people, and their related problems, Tom provides home inspection services and engineering investigations and evaluations for residential construction problems.

CONTENTS – SHORT LIST FOR QUICK REFERENCE

CONTENTS

INTRODUCTION

So you have a new home—and no idea what to do next. It's like bringing your first baby home from the hospital. Throughout the pregnancy, everyone was helpful and encouraging. You read all the books and went to all the classes. But now you are home alone with the baby. What do you do next?

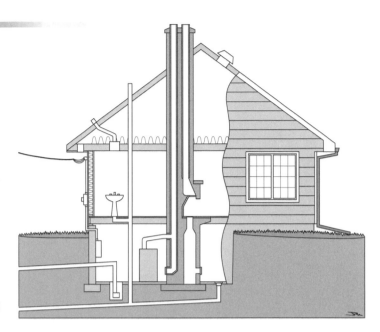

Sure, you have that home improvement "Honey Do" list for the painting and decorating tasks that will make the house your home. But what about the furnace, the roof, the garage door opener, the hose bibs, the everything? A home is the most complicated thing you have ever bought. It has more than 5,000 parts and components. Now you own it, and you need to run it.

So where is that operating manual? You didn't get one?! You got one with the new car—and driving a car isn't complicated. For a new home, you're lucky if you get instruction manuals for major systems. For a used home, don't plan on receiving any instructions.

Everyone who owns a home has faced all the same questions and concerns. We never had an operating manual. Most of us just muddled through and eventually got things right. We learned through trial and error and corrected our mistakes. Lucky buyers had a dad, mom or Uncle Nick who was a great resource and would explain what to do and how things work. This book fills the void. It's an operating manual for your new or older home. It won't replace Uncle Nick—but it will come close. The book shares my 35 years of experience around homes, fixing or breaking the complicated stuff that fills them up.

You see, I am a mechanical engineering graduate of Marquette University and a registered professional engineer. I have over 25 years of experience working as an engineer on the maintenance and construction of buildings and equipment. Big deal! Actually, I know stuff about houses because I'm a hands-on guy. My Uncle Nick took me under his wing when I was 9 years old. He was a great teacher with the patience of a saint. Since Uncle Nick, I've regarded homes as a great learning experience.

I have not included all the answers. That is impossible. But all the basic information is here. There are even clues to the mysterious sounds and smells in your home. This book also provides great references in case you need to do a little research on your own.

Enjoy your home. It is the biggest and best investment you have ever made. This book will certainly make your home a little easier to understand, operate and enjoy. Congratulations on your purchase!

Tom Feiza

"Mr. Fix-It"

Walk Through Before Closing

Just before closing, walk through your new home to observe its condition and contents. This will help avoid surprises and misunderstandings. Your real estate broker may arrange the walk-through and help you make sure everything is in order. Bring your purchase agreement and any related documentation so you can refer to all items that are included in your home purchase.

In addition to the home purchase agreements, check the following:

- Documentation on equipment and utility systems: instruction books, service information, contractor information

- Appliances

- Heating and air conditioning operation

- Potential water leaks in ceilings, basement, water heater, plumbing

- Garage door opener operation and controls

- Home construction documents, if available

- Warrantees or guarantees that may transfer with your home

- Any natural gas smells or sewer odors

- Any physical damage inside and out

- Septic and well maintenance information

- Instruction manuals for equipment and appliances

Have the owner explain all the features of the home and its systems. Only he or she will know about that special key for the basement storage…..the interior switch that turns off the power to the garage….the emergency release for the garage door.

Utility Services

Prior to closing, arrange a transfer of all utility services to your name. Be ready to answer questions about budget payment or monthly payments. Ask about special electrical controls on air conditioning and water heaters that save you money and reduce utility demands. This is a good time to ask the utility companies for any home operating tips or instructions they may have.

Also, ask the utilities for emergency procedures and phone numbers. Often, they will mail you this information.

Most telephone companies now connect their lines to a junction box at the exterior of your home. This will usually activate the internal jacks that the owner had connected. Any changes inside your home will be your responsibility, and you can hire either the phone company or private contractors to set up the inside wiring.

Garbage, Recycling

In some municipalities, garbage and trash removal is provided by private companies. Arrange this in advance. Your new neighbors will be your best resource for information on private trash contractors that service the area.

You will also need to learn local rules on recycling paper, metal, cardboard, plastic, aerosol cans, and glass. Ask about separation of trash and requirements for containers. Your local municipality and neighbors will be a big help. Also ask about rules on disposal of hazardous materials such as paint, solvents, chemicals, and oil.

Insurance

Prior to closing on your home, you will need a homeowner's insurance policy in force. Your mortgage company will require this, and you should understand all the details of the policy. When you set up this policy, be ready to answer questions about the size of the home, type of construction, security and fire alarm systems, local fire department, wood-burning appliances and other details.

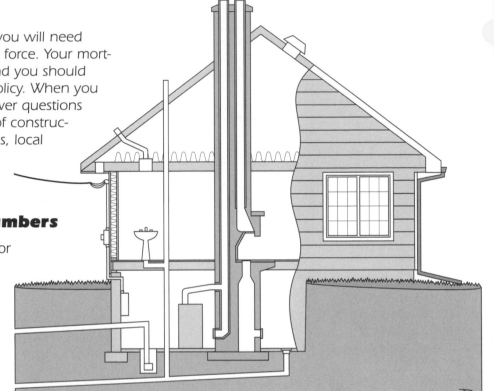

Post Office / Phone Numbers

Remember to plan in advance for a change of address and phone number(s). A quick note to family and friends will take care of the important people. File a change of address form with your current post office.

Keys and Locks

When you take occupancy of your new home, you should receive all keys and security codes. Plan on re-keying all locks. Consider keying all exterior door locks to the same key. Find a trusted neighbor or friend who can keep a spare key for an emergency, but don't put your name and address on the key; use a code, first name, or initials only.

For your garage door opener, change the security code on the transmitters and receiver. Most door openers installed in the past 20 years have a security code that can be changed easily; check the instruction manual.

Welcome Wagon / Local Government and Service Groups

Take time to contact your local government office for information on the community. Also, contact the Welcome Wagon and any other local service organizations. They can provide useful information about your new neighborhood.

Safety and Security Your First Priority

Local Fire, Police and Emergency Numbers

By your first day in your new home, have on hand all local emergency phone numbers for fire, police, ambulance, family physician, poison control center, hospital, eye doctor, utility companies, Mom and Dad at work, schools, and relatives. Keep these listed next to your phone, and make sure your kids know where to find this information. Also, carry a copy of the list with you. Accidents and problems can occur in new and unfamiliar places, so be ready.

Kids—Safety Information and Practice

Take some time with the kids to identify emergency telephone numbers. Walk through the exits and make sure everyone knows how to operate all locks and doors. Test your carbon monoxide, smoke and fire alarms so you all know where they are, how they work, and what they sound like.

It is wise to place smoke and fire detectors on all levels, in sleeping areas, in utility rooms, and at the top of stairs. Test smoke detectors periodically after you move in. **See Figure 1-1**

Establish an escape plan. All family members should know how to exit your home in an emergency and where to meet outside. Be sure your kids know that they must leave immediately and not return for pets or possessions. Use a sketch of your home's floor plan to identify all escape routes, utility shut-offs, and meeting points. Include your emergency numbers with the plan.

In some homes, a window may be the alternate exit from a second story or lower level. Identify such windows, and practice opening and using them.

Consider adding some battery-powered lights that come on during a power outage. Always have a few flashlights available.

Practice your escape plan with your kids. Activating an alarm helps the kids take a drill seriously. When practicing, keep in mind that emergencies can occur in the night, during a storm, when you are sound asleep, and/or when the power is off.

Fire Extinguishers

Equip your home with a fire extinguisher on each level and in the garage, basement and kitchen. Fire extinguisher have different ratings; select one that's rated "ABC," which means it's good for all common household fires. Contact your local fire department for more information.

Flammable Storage

The best advice for storing flammable materials is "just don't do it." When such storage is necessary, keep it to a minimum. Of course, we all need to store some gasoline for the lawnmower and solvents for household chores, so learn to store and use flammables safely. Use the original container or a container designed for that purpose. Keep flammable materials away from open flames and sources of combustion.

When using flammable solvents or cleaners, follow all safety precautions on the container. Never use a solvent cleaner or finish in a closed area without ventilation or near a source of combustion such as a gas furnace, gas water heater, or electric heater.

Use a spillproof container when storing gasoline. Gasoline should never be stored indoors. Vapors from gasoline are extremely flammable and must never be allowed to accumulate. If gasoline is stored in your garage, the entrance into your home should be up at least one step. Since gasoline vapors are heavier than air, they will settle in low areas. If you have a gas-fired heater or a water heater in the garage, do not store gasoline there.

Tags for Main Utility Valves and Shutoffs

In the event of an emergency, you may need to turn off a utility service to your home. It is important to identify the main shutoffs with tags telling how to turn them off. **See Figure 1-2** Make sure

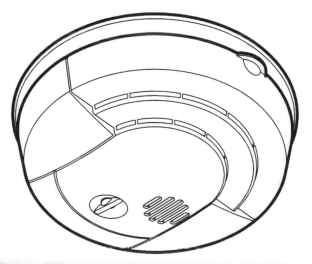

Figure 1-1.

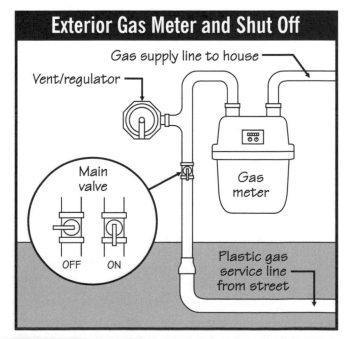

Figure 1-2.

everyone in your family knows where to find and how to operate these shutoffs. **(See the chapters on utilities for information and illustrations on the types of shutoffs and their operation.)**

Identify the following:

- Main electrical disconnect: fuse block, breaker or switch

- Main water valve

- Main gas valve or propane valve

In addition, identify shutoffs for individual parts of systems:

- Furnace disconnect switch (electrical)

- Furnace gas or fuel valves

- Air conditioning disconnect switch

- Gas valves for appliances

- Hot water shutoff

- Individual breakers or fuses for branch circuits

- Plumbing valves for appliances and main distribution connections

Garage Door Safety

All garage door openers should have an automatic reverse that stops the door's downward motion if there is an obstruction in its path. This feature helps prevent injury to people or pets beneath the door. **See Figure 1-3.**

The first day in your home, test the garage door reverse. After that, test it once a month. **(For testing instructions, see the section on windows and doors in the "General Home Systems", Chapter 6.)**

If your garage door opener does not reverse, take it out of service until it is repaired or adjusted. Look for adjustment instructions on the housing of the opener or in the instruction manual. If you are confused or unsure about how to make these adjustments, consult a professional.

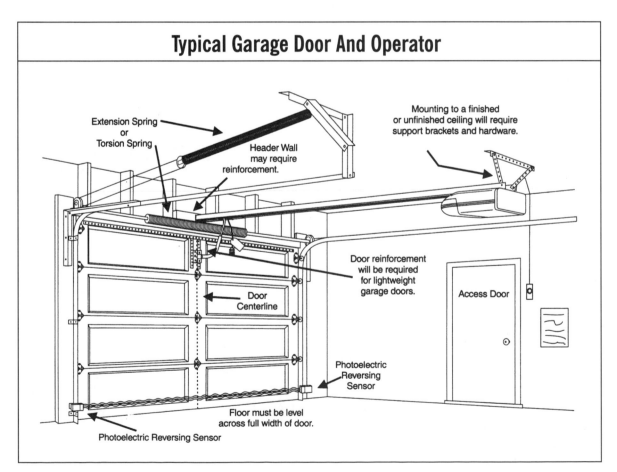

Figure 1-3.

Check the location of the garage door operator button(s). The button should be located at least 5 feet above the floor so children can't reach it. **See Figure 1-4.** Since these control buttons are low voltage, you can easily relocate them as needed.

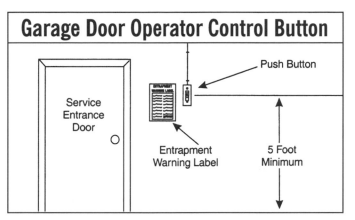

Figure 1-4.

Lighting Controls and Exterior Security

A brightly lit entrance is always a welcome sight on a dark evening. Consider adding motion sensor lights to entrances and garage door areas. These inexpensive fixtures replace the existing light fixtures. When anyone drives up or walks up, the unit senses motion and turns on the light.

For further information: Your local fire and police departments can be excellent sources of safety information. You could also contact the National Safety Council, the National Fire Protection Association (NFPA), and/or Underwriters Laboratories, Inc. (UL). See the References chapter for addresses and phone numbers.

Lead

Starting in 1996, federal regulations required landlords and sellers of single family homes built before 1978 to notify renters and buyers about potential lead hazards. This requirement has raised concerns for everyone.

The regulation affects homes built before 1978 because that is when the manufacture of lead-based paint was banned. Lead-based paint was used almost universally in homes until the 1950s and was used to a lesser degrees in the 1960s and 1970s. If you buy a home built before 1978, you will be given an excellent booklet, "Protect Your Family from Lead in Your Home."

The main concern with lead is that exposure can harm young children, babies, and even unborn children. People can get lead in their bodies by breathing or swallowing lead dust or by eating soil or paint chips with lead in them. If you think your home may have lead hazards, call the National Lead Information Clearinghouse at 1-800-424-LEAD to obtain free information.

Lead-based paint that is in good condition is usually not a hazard, but peeling, chipping, chalking or cracking lead-based paint is a hazard that needs immediate attention. Friction and rubbing points on windows and doors raise the biggest concern. Remodeling and paint removal can increase the risk if the lead-based paint is not handled properly.

Good housekeeping techniques can help reduce the risks of existing lead-based paint surfaces. Clean up paint chips immediately. Clean floors, window frames, windowsills and other surfaces weekly. **See Figure 2-1.** Use a mop or sponge with warm water and a general all-purpose cleaner or a cleaner made specifically for lead. Thoroughly rinse sponges and mop heads after cleaning.

Wash children's hands often, especially before they eat and before naps and bedtime. Keep children from chewing windowsills or other painted surfaces.

Lead can also be present in drinking water. Call your local health department or water supplier to find

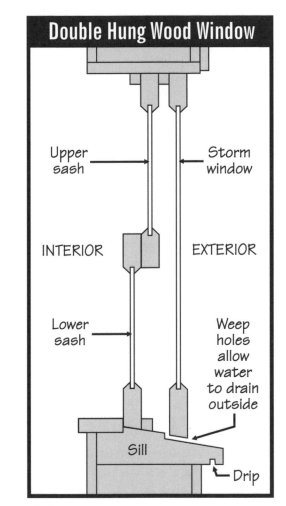

Double Hung Wood Window

Upper sash

Storm window

INTERIOR

EXTERIOR

Lower sash

Weep holes allow water to drain outside

Sill

Drip

Figure 2-1.

out about testing your water. If your water supply does have lead, follow the recommendation of the local water supplier.

For more information, contact:

- The National Lead Information Center at 1-800-LEAD-FYI

- Your local health department

- The Consumer Product Safety Commission

- The Environmental Protection Agency (EPA)

Also, see the References section for additional contact information.

Asbestos

Asbestos was often used in building materials until the 1970s. However, the mere presence of asbestos in your home is not hazardous. The danger is that asbestos materials may become damaged over time; damaged asbestos may release asbestos fibers that present a health hazard.

Studies show that people exposed to high levels of asbestos fibers have an increased risk of cancer and asbestosis. The risk increases with the number of fibers inhaled. Smokers are also at increased risk.

You may find asbestos fibers in pipe and duct insulation, resilient floor tiles, cement sheeting and shingles, soundproofing, joint compounds, and many fireproof or fire-resistant materials. The only way to determine whether a building material contains asbestos is to have it sampled and tested by a qualified lab.

If you think you have asbestos in your home, don't panic. Usually the best thing you can do with asbestos materials in good shape is to leave them alone. Repairs or remodeling must be done properly to avoid disturbing these materials. Do not sweep, dust or vacuum debris that may contain asbestos; these steps may release asbestos fibers into the air.

For more information, contact:

- Consumer Product Safety Commission
- Environmental Protection Agency
- American Lung Association
- Your state and local health departments

Also, see the References section for additional contact information.

Radon

Radon is a radioactive gas that has been found in homes all over the U.S. It comes from the natural breakdown of uranium in soil, rock and water, and it gets into the air we breathe. Typically, radon moves up through the ground and enters a home's foundation through cracks and holes. Your home can trap this radon.

Testing is the only way to know whether you and your family are at risk from radon. You cannot see, smell or taste it. Breathing air containing radon increases your risk of getting lung cancer. If you smoke and your home has high radon levels, your risk of lung cancer is especially high.

You can conduct a radon test using a small charcoal canister or alpha-track detector. Test kits are available through hardware stores, and the cost usually includes lab analysis. The most accurate testing procedure follows EPA testing requirements. You can also hire a professional testing firm, but make sure it is registered with the EPA and that it follows EPA guidelines. A professional test will cost about $100.

A short-term test over two to four days provides only a quick snapshot of the radon levels in your home. A much better test is a long-term test conducted over more than 90 days.

Radon can also be present in your drinking water Contact your water supplier for specific information. You can receive more information on radon from several local and federal sources.

For more information, contact:

- The Environmental Protection Agency
- State or local health departments
- The American Lung Association

Carbon Monoxide

Carbon monoxide (CO) should be a concern for all homeowners. The government estimates that 300 people are killed by CO in their homes each year. CO is called a silent killer because it has no taste, color or odor. Almost all CO problems are caused by poor maintenance or improper use of fuel-burning equipment **See Figure 2-2.**

You can take simple precautions to protect your family by understanding CO and by properly maintaining combustion equipment in your home.

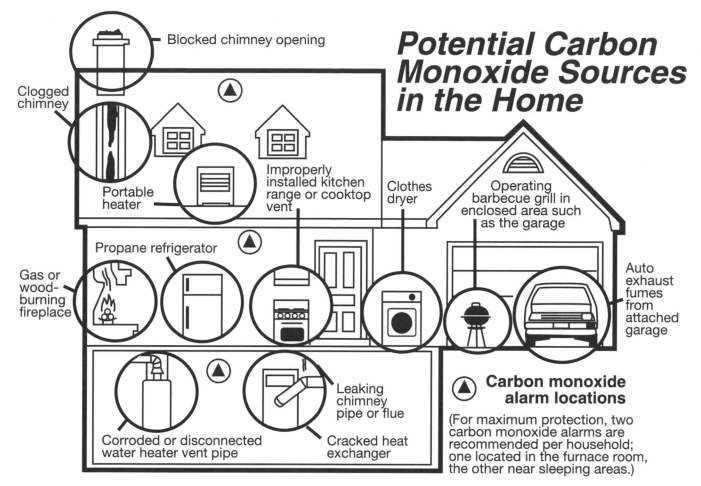

Information provided by BRK Electronics.

Figure 2-2.

CO is produced when fuel is burned. Fuel-burning appliances such as your furnace are potential sources. Properly maintained appliances produce very little CO and will not cause a problem. However, improperly operating appliances, your auto, or any non-vented indoor fire can cause CO poisoning.

Proper maintenance of fuel-burning appliances is essential. This includes the furnace, water heater, gas clothes dryer, fireplace, and even a gas range or space heater. All of these appliances should be used as designed, and all need periodic servicing.

Pay particular attention to furnaces and water heaters. Have them serviced regularly, and routinely inspect the flue connections and chimney. Flue pipes should not have holes, rust or soft areas. Flues should not show signs of water streaking or sooting; this indicates that combustion gas is not flowing up the flue into the chimney.

Also, know the symptoms of CO poisoning. Initial symptoms are similar to the flu without fever: dizziness, nausea, fatigue, headache and irregular breathing. If you have these symptoms at home and then feel better when you go outside your home, suspect a problem. If all the members of your family have similar symptoms at similar times, suspect a problem.

You can also help protect your family with a CO detector. **See Figure 2-3.** Buy one similar to a smoke detector. It should have a loud audio alarm. Do not rely on detectors with small dots that turn black when exposed to CO—how often will you look at the dots? Select a top-of-the-line alarm with a digital CO readout so you can monitor the level in your home.

The best location for a CO detector is on a wall in your sleeping area, about 5 feet from the floor. Place it where you will see it every night before you go to bed so you will remember to check the level.

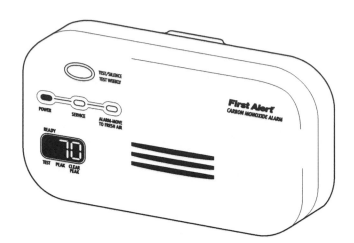

Figure 2-3. Carbon Monoxide Detector

For sources of safety information, see the References section.

Utility and General System Notes

This is where your homework starts. Take time to read these chapters. They contain important information about the many systems in your home. The explanation of each system includes operating information, terminology, sketches, main shutoffs, and part names. **See Figure 3-1.** If you need more specific information, check the References section.

Since some systems are very complicated, they need to be serviced routinely by contractors. Look in the Service Checklists chapter for specifications you can copy and use with service contractors. You can do simple maintenance yourself; this information is provided in utility systems chapters and in the chapter on Service Requirements by the Calendar.

Your home will not have all of the systems shown in this book. For instance, you may have a warm air furnace or a hot water furnace, but not both. You may have either a central air conditioner or a heat pump. As you read, walk around your home to determine the type of equipment you have and identify important valves and switches. If some systems or parts are confusing, ask a professional service contractor or a knowledgeable friend to walk you through the system.

The chapters on emergencies will help you solve problems and perhaps avoid a service call. Many emergencies, strange noises, leaks and smells have simple solutions. I have attempted to include all common problems.

Heating and Air Conditioning

Most homes are heated with a warm air furnace (also called a forced air furnace) because this type of system provides heating and cooling through the same air distribution ducts. **See Figure 3-2.** A warm air system requires supply grills in most rooms. Some homes are heated with a hydronic (warm water) system that uses radiators, baseboard (convector) elements, or heating pipes buried in walls or floors.

The energy source for heating can be natural gas, propane, or oil. In warmer climates, electrical resistance heating elements may be used in a warm air furnace. Usually, the energy source for air conditioning is electricity, but gas-powered engine systems can also provide cooling.

Some homes have separate heating and cooling systems. One common system combines hydronic heating with ducted air conditioning.

As you review the information on heating and air conditioning, identify the system used in your home.

As with all systems in your home, you must understand the basics of heating and air conditioning so you can perform basic maintenance and operate the system properly and efficiently.

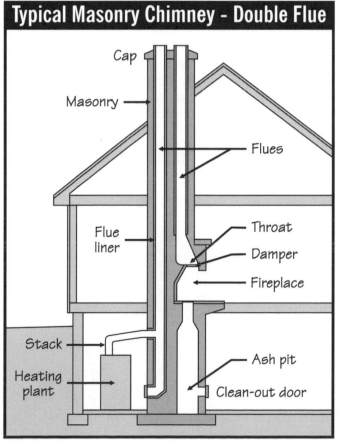

Typical Masonry Chimney - Double Flue

- Cap
- Masonry
- Flues
- Flue liner
- Throat
- Damper
- Fireplace
- Stack
- Heating plant
- Ash pit
- Clean-out door

Figure 3-1.

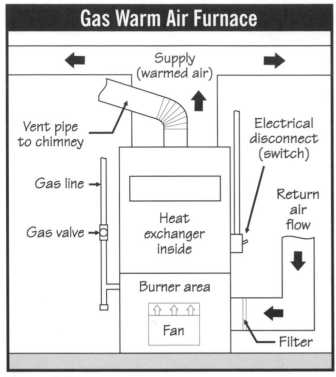

Gas Warm Air Furnace

Supply (warmed air)

Vent pipe to chimney

Gas line →

Gas valve →

Heat exchanger inside

Burner area

Fan

Electrical disconnect (switch)

Return air flow

Filter

Figure 3-2.

Must Know / Must Do— Heating and Air Conditioning

- Understand how your heating and cooling system works and whom you can call for service.

- Understand the control (thermostat) for the heating and cooling system.

- Perform basic maintenance: filter changes and lubrication.

- Schedule yearly maintenance by a professional.

- Identify and know how to use emergency shutoffs for electricity, gas, oil, etc.

Thermostat

The thermostat provides automatic control for heating and cooling systems. You set it to the temperature you want to maintain. The thermostat, located in the conditioned (heated and/or cooled) space, senses room temperature, and when the

room temperature varies from your setpoint, the thermostat activates the heating or cooling system. **See Figure 3-3**.

A dual heating/cooling thermostat will have switches that let you change the system from heating to cooling and operate the fan separately. Some thermostats also allow you to turn off the heating and cooling systems. **See Figure 3-4**.

All heating and cooling thermostats operate with similar buttons and controls. The basic and common controls are as follows:

HEAT – OFF – COOL

This switch will put the system in the heating mode (HEAT), turn the system off (OFF), or switch the system to cooling (COOL), if there is an air conditioning system. Once the system is set to HEAT or COOL the thermostat temperature setting controls the system based on the room temperature.

FAN – ON – AUTO

This switch allows operation of the fan manually (ON), independent of the heating and cooling system. This allows you to circulate air in your home without operating the heating or cooling system. In the automatic (AUTO) setting the fan will cycle on and off as needed by the heating or cooling system. AUTO is the setting normally used.

Heating Only Thermostat

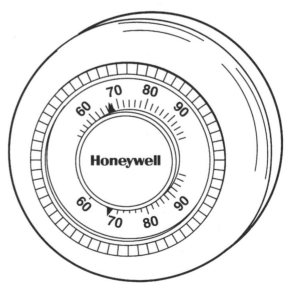

Figure 3-3.

**Figure 3-4. Heat-Cool Thermostat
with Top Removed**

The typical home system is either fully on or fully off; it doesn't provide variable heating/cooling. When the thermostat calls for heat, the furnace reacts at 100 percent capacity until the room temperature reaches the setpoint; then the furnace shuts off. Turning the thermostat up higher will not heat the room any faster. When you switch the system to cooling, turning the thermostat lower will not cool the room any faster. (A few homes do have complicated systems in which the furnace is capable of variable heating/cooling, but these are the exception.)

Electronic (or digital) thermostats can be programmed for automatic adjustment of the setpoint temperature based on time of day and day of week. **See Figure 3-5**. These help conserve energy; they can lower the temperature during sleeping hours or when your home is not occupied.

Thermostats should be installed and maintained by professionals. Special anticipator settings on the thermostat match its operation with the operation of the furnace. If you replace a thermostat, make sure that this anticipator setting is done properly.

Thermostats are very sensitive. Your thermostat should be level, out of direct sunlight, and away from direct heat sources. If a thermostat develops a major problem, the usual recommendation is replacement rather than repair, because much better electronic thermostats with modern setback capabilities are readily available at reasonable prices.

To obtain detailed information on thermostats, see the References section; many manufacturers will send instructions for a specific thermostat.

Warm Air Furnace

The most common type of warm air (forced air) furnace provides heat by burning a fossil fuel to warm air and then distributing the warm air inside your home. **See Figure 3-6**. The heat source is confined within a heat exchanger inside the furnace housing. For gas, propane, and oil systems, the fuel is burned inside or below a heat exchanger. The hot products of combustion flow through the heat exchanger and up a chimney or are drawn out through a vent pipe.

The hot products of combustion warm the metal of the heat exchanger. After a minute or so, when the heat exchanger's metal is warm, the circulating

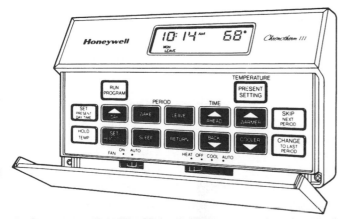

Figure 3-5. Digital Thermostat

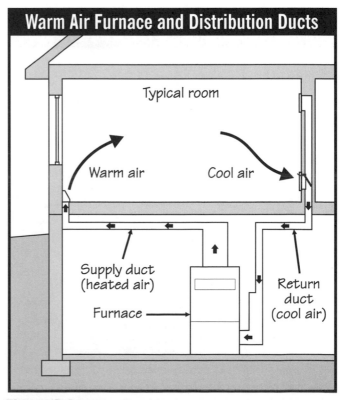

Figure 3-6.

(furnace) fan starts. This fan circulates air across the hot metal on the outside of the heat exchanger. The heated air warms your home.

For homes without basements or crawl spaces, warm air furnaces can be located in attics or closet spaces. The typical warm air furnace located in an attic or crawl space uses the same components as a basement (upflow type) furnace but the furnace is often designed to operate horizontally to save space. **See Figure 3-7**.

Furnaces for homes built on a concrete slab are located in the attic or in a closet. For the closet installations, a downflow warm air furnace may be used. **See Figure 3-8**. These furnaces are similar to the upflow furnace but the components are reversed. The heat supply ducts are in the in the floor slab. Homes on slabs can also have a warm air furnace in a closet the is a typical upflow furnace – the supply ducts will be in the attic and the return will be through the halls or in the floor slab.

The efficiency of gas furnaces has improved dramatically in recent years. You will find 80% efficiency furnaces that use a draft fan to force the products of combustion up the chimney. **See Figure 3-9**. You will find 90%+ efficiency furnaces that vent with

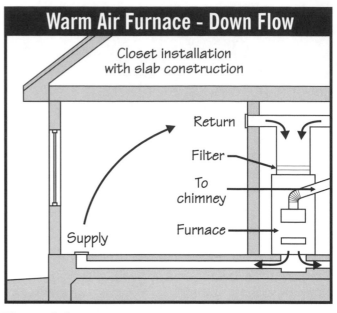

Figure 3-8.

plastic PVC pipe. These higher efficiency furnaces squeeze so much energy out of the products of combustion that they need special fans to help remove the products of combustion; the combustion gas is not hot enough to naturally draft up the chimney. **See Figure 3-10**.

In an electric warm air furnace, air circulates directly over an electrical resistance-heating element.

A propane gas furnace is similar to a natural gas furnace but uses a different burner and control system designed for propane.

Oil warm air furnaces, **(See Figure 3-17 later in this chapter)** have a special oil burner and combustion chamber. The burner pressurizes the oil and sprays it through a small nozzle, forming a mist. The burner also provides an air supply and a high-voltage spark. This results in a very hot flame that is contained in a ceramic combustion chamber. From the combustion chamber, the hot combustion gas flows up through the heat exchanger, just as in a gas furnace.

A warm air furnace recirculates air in your home. It does not draw in outside air unless there are special provisions for an outside air supply (which is not common). The fan circulates the air, which is drawn from the return grills and ducts inside your home and discharged through the supply grills. There will be a furnace air filter located near the fan; you must maintain this filter.

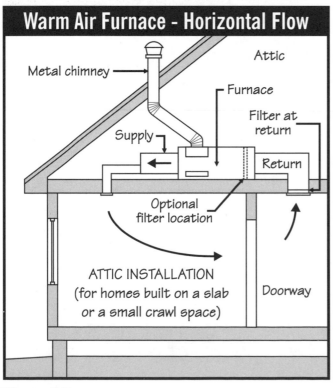

Figure 3-7.

Mid Efficiency Warm Air Furnace

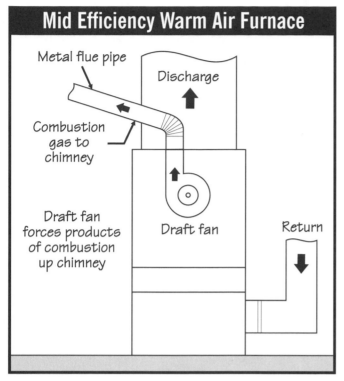

Metal flue pipe

Discharge

Combustion gas to chimney

Draft fan forces products of combustion up chimney

Draft fan

Return

Figure 3-9.

Systems for air supply and ducting have changed through the years. The early "gravity" warm air furnace system (commonly called an octopus) did not use a circulating fan. The air was said to move by "gravity"—that is, warm air simply rose up into the rooms. This type of system often has warm supply grills in the center of the home and the cold returns along outside walls.

When furnaces were improved with circulating fans (the forced air/warm air furnace), heating ducts made a transition to the upper portion of the center wall; return ducts were still located along the outer walls. In an older home, you may find a strange combination of supply and return grills, since they were added as heating systems were upgraded or replaced.

Warm air or forced air furnaces have a circulating fan or blower located near the heat exchanger **See Figure 3-11**. This fan circulates the house air over the warm metal of the heat exchanger inside the furnace. The fan may be powered directly by a fan motor mounted inside the fan housing. A motor through a belt and pulley arrangement may also power the fan.

High Efficiency Warm Air Furnace

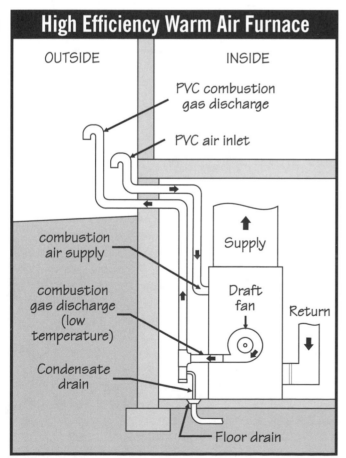

OUTSIDE

INSIDE

PVC combustion gas discharge

PVC air inlet

combustion air supply

combustion gas discharge (low temperature)

Condensate drain

Supply

Draft fan

Return

Floor drain

Figure 3-10.

Warm Air Furnace Fan and Motor: Two Basic Types

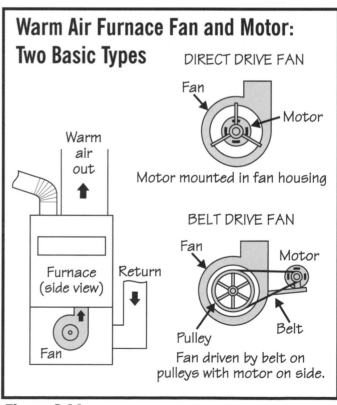

DIRECT DRIVE FAN

Fan

Motor

Motor mounted in fan housing

Warm air out

Furnace (side view)

Return

Fan

BELT DRIVE FAN

Fan

Motor

Pulley

Belt

Fan driven by belt on pulleys with motor on side.

Figure 3-11.

For a belt drive fan, **See Figure 3-12**. you need to maintain the belt and belt alignment. Turn the power off the unit before you open the fan chamber. The belt should not be cracked or frayed. If the belt is very hard and shiny on the driving "v" sides, it is old and needs to be replaced. The pulleys should align so the belt runs straight between each pulley.

Proper tension on the belt is required to transmit power. With moderate hand pressure applied on the belt one-half way between the pulleys, the belt should deflect about $1/2$ to $3/4$ inch. The motor mounting brackets are often adjustable to change the belt tension.

Warm Air Furnace Belt Drive Maintenance

(Disconnect power before inspecting fan!)

With unit off, belt should deflect 1/2" to 1" at center with moderate hand pressure

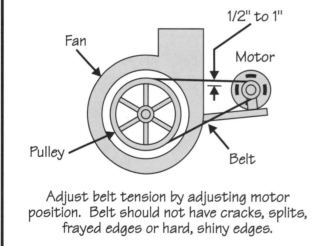

Adjust belt tension by adjusting motor position. Belt should not have cracks, splits, frayed edges or hard, shiny edges.

Figure 3-12.

Many older furnaces require lubrication of the bearings on the fan and fan motor **See Figure 3-13**. On newer furnaces, bearings may be lubricated for life and not need additional lubrication. Check your owner manual or with a heating contractor for the specific requirements for your furnace. You can also look at the ends of the fan and the motor. If you see little (1/4-inch) caps over little tubes, these are ports to add oil for lubrication. Generally these bearings should be lubricated with a few drops of light oil every few months.

Warm Air Furnace: Lubrication for Furnace Motor and Fan

(Disconnect power before inspecting fan and motor! Not all furnaces need lubrication.)

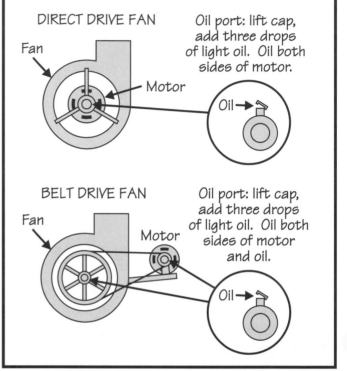

Figure 3-13.

Newer furnaces will also have a safety switch built into the fan access door **See Figure 3-14**. When the fan chamber door is removed, this switch shuts the furnace off. This is a safety device that prevents accidental injury from the moving part of the fan system. If you ever have a situation with no heat or no air conditioning, you should check this access door and safety switch. A loose fan access door can inadvertently shut the system down.

An older home may also have a supply grill without a return grill. This is common in the second story of Cape Cod style houses. Often this works well for heating but not for proper air conditioning.

With modern systems, heat ducts are located on the floor or ceiling near the outside walls, windows and doors. Returns are placed on interior walls. If the furnace is in the basement or crawl space, supply grills will be near the floor; if the furnace or supply ducting is in the attic, supply grills will be in the ceiling. This modern arrangement provides for good air distribution and greater comfort. Most modern systems have a return grill in every room except the bathrooms.

Warm Air Furnace Fan Door Safety Switch

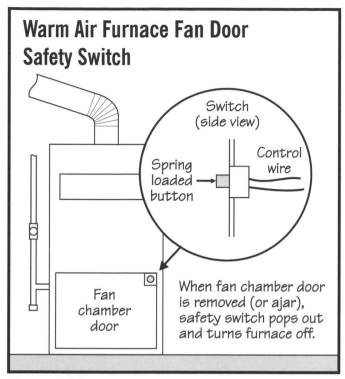

Switch (side view)

Spring loaded button

Control wire

Fan chamber door

When fan chamber door is removed (or ajar), safety switch pops out and turns furnace off.

Figure 3-14.

Air Filters

For the location of filters and different types of furnaces. **See Figures 3-2, 3-7, 3-8, 3-15.**

Air filters are provided on all forced air furnaces to remove dirt and lint from heated air. **See Figure 3-15**. This keeps the fan, heat exchanger and air conditioning coil clean. It also helps clean the air of your home as air circulates through the system **(Note the direction of the air flow)**.

Media Filters

ONE-INCH-THICK FIBERGLASS

The standard filter on most furnaces is a nominal 1"-thick media filter. **See Figure 3-16**. Usually, this filter is made of fiberglass. The filter should be changed when it is visibly dirty—usually every month or two, depending on the quality of the filter and the amount of dirt in your home's air. Children, pets, plants, and activity tend to produce more dirt that finds it way into the heating system.

Be careful about the direction of the airflow through the filter. Filters are designed to be installed with one particular side facing the air stream. Most filters

Filter Maintenance - Warm Air Furnace
(upflow type)

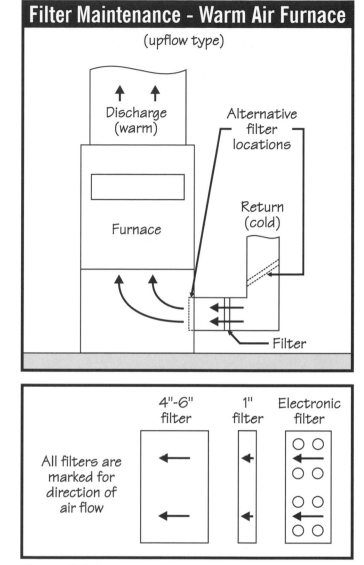

Discharge (warm)

Alternative filter locations

Furnace

Return (cold)

Filter

Figure 3-15.

All filters are marked for direction of air flow

4"-6" filter	1" filter	Electronic filter

Figure 3-15.

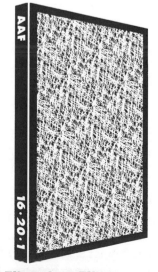

Figure 3-16. Fiberglass Filter

Must Know / Must Do

Routinely Maintain the Furnace Filter

Maintenance is based on the type of filter, how often the unit is running (heating and cooling), and how you use your home. The three basic types of filters are media, electronic, and electrostatic.

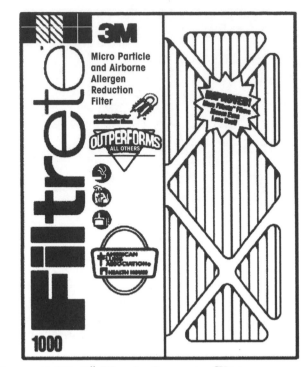

Figure 3-17. 1″ Pleated paper filter

have directions or an arrow telling you which side should be installed toward the furnace. The arrow is the direction of the airflow and should be toward the base or the fan of the furnace.

Remember: the furnace filter is also used when you operate the fan and/or central air conditioning, so you should check on the filter during the summer, too.

PAPER

I recommend that you try one of the pleated paper filters. These catch more dirt than inexpensive fiberglass filters. **See Figure 3-17**. Some even have a static charge to attract dirt. Others have a carbon filter content. Paper filters cost between $3 and $15 and can be found in most hardware stores. You will need to change this type of filter more often because it collects more dirt.

WASHABLE

Washable filters can be made of foam or woven synthetic fiber. They are about as effective as inexpensive fiberglass filters. You can improve the efficiency of a foam filter by spraying it with a special filter coating; this oily/waxy spray helps the filter hold dirt better.

PLEATED, 4- TO 6-INCH THICK

A big improvement over the standard 1″-thick filter is a pleated fiberglass or paper filter.

Often, the pleated paper filter is housed in a 6″-thick frame. The paper filter is very fine, and it catches smaller particles of dirt and dust. This type of filter is normally changed once per year, and you replace only the paper element. **See Figure 3-18**.

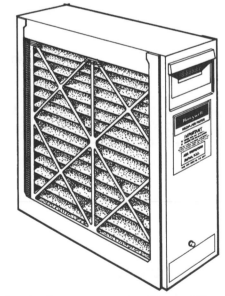

Figure 3-18. Pleated paper filter (6″)

A pleated fiberglass filter often is mounted in a throwaway paper frame. The entire unit is replaced about once a year.

Electronic Filters

Electronic filters use electrically charged metal plates and wires that attract dirt. **See Figure 3-19**. These filters can remove very small particles

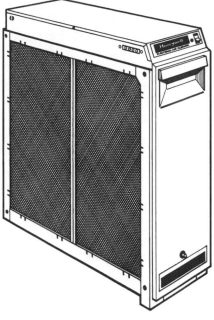

Figure 3-19.

from smoke and pollen which aren't caught by standard filters. If you have respiratory problems or are sensitive to dust or pollen, you may want to use this type of filter.

Electronic filters cost more than $600 to install. Maintenance involves washing the interior frame and metal plates and wires with detergent or running them through a dishwasher. Most electronic filters have a metal pre-filter that also must be washed. For more specific cleaning instructions, contact a heating contractor or the filter manufacturer. The References section includes contact information.

Electrostatic and Electronic Filters

Many types of washable filters have multiple layers of filtering material; vendors claim these layers contain an electrostatic charge that attracts and traps dirt more effectively than a standard media filter.

Several companies also make a 1"-thick electrostatic/electronic filter as a direct replacement for throwaway filters. This filter may have an electronic power supply and may require particular maintence procedures.

For more information on filters, look up manufacturers in the References section.

Warm Air Furnace— Maintenance Requirements

All heating equipment should be routinely checked by a qualified service technician. Most furnace manufacturers recommend yearly maintenance.

ROUTINE MAINTENANCE A HOMEOWNER SHOULD PERFORM

Note: Turn off power to the unit before inspection or maintenance.

- Maintain records. Have a professional service the unit yearly. Proper maintenance keeps equipment operating efficiently and ensures safety. Contact the manufacturer of your furnace for specific maintenance requirements. See the References section for contact information.

- Change the filter as required—often every other month.

- Switch high/low returns at the start and end of the heating season. For complete instructions, check the section on "Heating and Cooling Distribution" later in this chapter.

- Check all flue pipes and vents for rust, water leaks, and loose connections.

- Lubricate the fan motor and fan bearing with a few drops of oil twice per year. (This is only required on certain units.)

- Check the belt to make sure it's not cracked or loose. (This is only required with belt-driven fans.)

- Listen to the furnace operate. Follow up on any strange sounds.

- Check drain lines to make sure they are clear and draining properly.

- Look for water leaks or changes in the system.

ROUTINE MAINTENANCE A PROFESSIONAL SHOULD PERFORM

During a routine service call, the service technician should perform the following general maintenance measures. The technician may perform other checks, too, depending on the type of furnace.

- Check and clean burner.

- Check flue pipes, draft diverter, heat exchanger, and chimney.

- Remove burners to clean burners and heat exchanger if necessary.

- Check electrical wiring and connections.

- Check and clean circulating fan. Lubricate fan and motor if necessary.

- For belt drive fans: check for tension, wear and alignment.

- Check supply and returns ducts for air leakage, water stains, rust.

- Check and maintain filter.

- Perform an operational check of furnace and safety controls.

- Test for carbon monoxide in the flue gas and in the air around the furnace.

- Check for gas leaks.

- Check, clean, and adjust pilot light if necessary.

For a high-efficiency furnace, the technician should also:

- Check for water leaks (condensation from combustion).

- Check flue pipes and connections.

- Check for condensation on metal pipes and parts.

- Check for a clean condensate drain line.

- Check operation and condition of draft fan.

Duplicates of the above lists appear in the Service Checklists chapter. You may want to make a photocopy of the professional's list and send it to the service company when you arrange service and/or review the list with the technician at the beginning of the service call.

Hydronic (Hot Water) Heat

Hot water or hydronic systems provide heat by warming water and circulating it through piping to heating devices: radiators, baseboard convectors,

radiant pipes in the floors or walls, or even coils with a fan. Older system typically use cast iron radiators; newer systems typically use baseboard convectors (finned tubes). **See Figure 3-20**.

Hydronic systems usually burn oil, gas, or propane below a cast iron container or coil that holds water. The warmed water is then distributed to the radiators through a network of supply and return piping. Older systems use gravity to move the water—warm water rises, cool water falls. Newer systems use a small circulation pump to move the water.

The distribution system is sealed and should not leak, but water expands as it warms, so there will be an expansion tank to hold the increased volume. Most systems have an automated fill valve and backflow prevention.

The system automatically responds to a thermostat located in the heated space. When the thermostat calls for heat, the boiler and the pump start. Warm

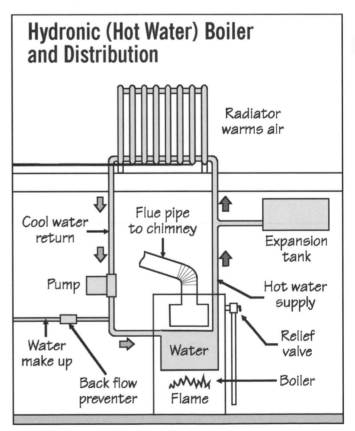

Hydronic (Hot Water) Boiler and Distribution

Radiator warms air

Cool water return

Flue pipe to chimney

Pump

Water make up

Back flow preventer

Water

Flame

Expansion tank

Hot water supply

Relief valve

Boiler

Figure 3-20.

water is delivered to the radiators. When the thermostat is satisfied, the boiler is turned off.

There are many variations to hydronic systems: multiple zones provided by thermostat and zone control valves or multiple pumps…boiler temperature water resets based on outside temperature….many control options…and variations in piping systems, to name a few. If you have a complicated system, ask a service technician to explain it to you.

Hydronic Heating— Maintenance Requirements

All heating equipment should be routinely checked by a qualified service technician. Most hydronic boiler manufacturers recommend yearly maintenance to keep equipment operating efficiently and to ensure safety.

Contact the manufacturer of your furnace for specific maintenance requirements. See the References section for contacts.

ROUTINE MAINTENANCE A HOMEOWNER SHOULD PERFORM

Note: Turn off power to the unit before inspection or maintenance.

- Maintain records, and have a professional service the unit yearly.

- Check all flue pipes and vents for rust, water leaks, loose connections.

- Listen to the boiler operate. Follow up on any strange noises.

- Check drain lines to make sure they are clear and draining properly. (This is required only for high efficiency condensing units.)

- Look for water leaks or changes in the system.

- Oil the circulating pump twice per year. (Use just a few drops).

- Check that the temperature/pressure gauge is in the operating range identified by a professional service technician. Mark the proper range on the gauge.

ROUTINE MAINTENANCE A PROFESSIONAL SHOULD PERFORM

A service technician should perform the following general maintenance measures. The service technician may also perform additional checks, depending on the type of furnace.

- Check and clean burner.

- Vent the system at the high points as necessary.

- Check all flue pipes, draft diverter, boiler housing, and chimney.

- Remove burners to clean burners and heat exchanger if necessary.

- Check electrical wiring and connections.

- Check and lubricate circulating pump(s).

- Check for water leaks.

- Check temperature and pressure relief valve.

- Check water supply system and backflow preventer.

- Add backflow preventer if none is present.

- Check expansion tank for proper water level.

- Perform an operational check of controls for temperature, pressure, and safety.

- Test for carbon monoxide in the flue gas and in the air around the furnace.

- Check for gas leaks.

- Check, clean, and (if necessary) adjust pilot light.

Additional checks for a high-efficiency boiler with a draft fan:

- Check draft fan for condensation and rust.

- Check flue pipe for condensation.

- Check condensate drain lines.

Duplicates of the above lists appear in the Service Checklists chapter. You may want to make a photocopy of the professional's list and send it to the service company when you arrange service and/or review the list with the technician at the beginning of the service call.

Steam Heating

A steam heating system is similar to a hydronic boiler system except that it produces steam at low pressure. Because they require more maintenance than hydronic systems, steam systems are rarely installed in newer homes, and older steam systems often are converted to hydronic systems. **See Figure 3-21**.

Steam systems can use oil, natural gas or propane as an energy source. The burning fuel heats water in the boiler, turning it to steam. The steam, under pressure, rises through the system to the radiators. Vents in the radiators release heated air. The steam condenses back into water as it releases energy in the radiator, and the water flows back to the boiler to be reheated.

While there are variations in the piping systems, almost all residential systems are "one-pipe" systems as described above. You can identify a one-pipe system because it will have only one pipe connected to the radiators.

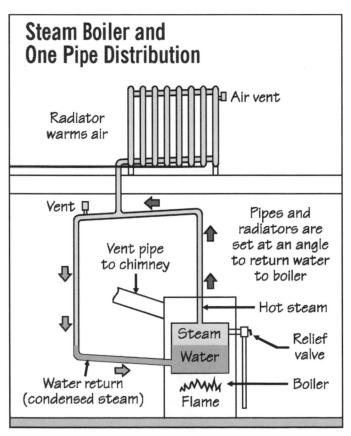

Figure 3-21.

Steam systems should have professional maintenance at least once per year, perhaps more often. Much of the maintenance required by a steam system is too complicated for most homeowners to perform.

ROUTINE MAINTENANCE A HOMEOWNER SHOULD PERFORM

- Maintain records.

- Check all flue pipes and vents for leaks, rust, and loose connections.

- Check the system for any leaks.

- Check the steam gauge. Have your contractor mark the normal range.

- Check the water level every month. The normal range should be marked on a sight glass.

- Make the sure the radiators slope slightly toward the steam inlet pipe. This will help keep the pipe from knocking or pounding.

- Make sure the vents on the radiators are operating; otherwise, radiators may be cold.

ROUTINE MAINTENANCE A PROFESSIONAL SHOULD PERFORM

A service technician should perform the following general maintenance measures. The service technician may also perform additional checks, depending on the type of boiler. (For a gas-fired system, see the information on oil burners, which require additional checks.)

- Check and clean the burner.

- Check all vents on radiators and piping.

- Check all flue pipes, draft diverter, boiler housing and chimney.

- Remove burners to clean them and the heat exchanger if necessary.

- Check electrical wiring and connections.

- Check for water or steam leaks.

- Check the temperature and pressure relief valve.

- Add a backflow preventer if none is present.

- Perform an operational check of controls for temperature, pressure and safety.

- Test for carbon monoxide in the flue gas and the air around the boiler.

- Check for gas leaks.

- Check, clean and if necessary adjust the pilot light.

Duplicates of the above lists appear in the Service Checklists chapter. You may want to make a photocopy of the professional's list and send it to the service company when you arrange service and/or review the list with the technician at the beginning of the service call.

Oil Burner

An oil burner can be used just like a gas burner in warm air furnaces, hydronic systems or even water heaters. All oil burners are essentially the same except for some very old style vaporizing or pot-type burners. Here we will only cover modern pressure burners or gun-type burners.

A modern oil burner pressurizes oil and sprays it through a small nozzle, forming a mist. At the same time, the burner provides an air supply and a high-voltage spark. **See Figure 3-23**. This results in a very hot flame that is contained in a ceramic combustion chamber. From the combustion chamber,

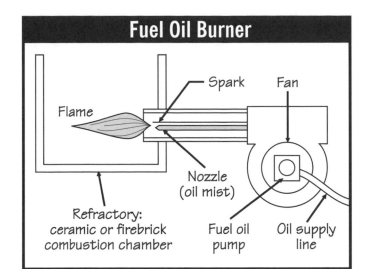

Figure 3-23.

the hot combustion gas flows up through the heat exchanger, just as in a gas-fired appliance. **See Figure 3-22**.

Oil Heat—Maintenance Requirements

Oil burners can be quite efficient, comparable to gas units. Oil burners require yearly maintenance. Also, never let your oil system run out of fuel. This can cause major problems with the burner, requiring a service call.

Most homeowners find it convenient to arrange for an oil delivery and burner service company to provide automatic oil tank filling and yearly service. This is the best way to ensure that the system is operating properly. You will also be placed at the top of the service call list if you are an established customer.

ROUTINE MAINTENANCE A
HOMEOWNER SHOULD PERFORM

Note: Turn off power to the unit before attempting inspection or maintenance.

- Follow the maintenance requirements listed above for warm air or hydronic boiler systems.

- Schedule routine maintenance yearly.

- Lubricate the burner motor if it has oil ports (ask your service technician).

- Make sure the system never, never runs out of fuel oil.

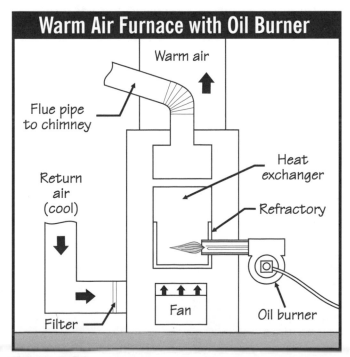

Figure 3-22.

ROUTINE MAINTENANCE A
PROFESSIONAL SHOULD PERFORM

A service technician should perform the following general maintenance measures. The service technician may also perform additional checks, depending on the type of furnace.

- Follow applicable maintenance requirements listed above for a hydronic boiler or warm air furnace.

- Remove and clean burner, clean blower blades, replace or clean filter and/or strainer, replace the nozzle, clean flame and heat sensors, check and clean or replace electrodes.

- Lubricate the burner motor.

- Check flue and barometric damper.

- Check for oil leaks.

- Check and clean oil pump.

- Clean and test stack control.

- Check and adjust draft regulator.

- Test for efficiency and make proper adjustments.

Duplicates of the above lists appear in the Service Checklists chapter. You may want to make a photocopy of the professional's list and send it to the service company when you arrange service and/or review the list with the technician at the beginning of the service call.

Central Air Conditioning

Central air conditioning uses a warm air furnace system to cool air and distribute it throughout the home. **See Figure 3-24**. The air conditioning system uses the fan, filter, thermostat and ducts; the heating portion of the system remains turned off.

When a home has hydronic heat, central air conditioning may be provided by a separate system. In this case, there is no heating equipment in the standard furnace housing; it has only a fan and cooling coil.

A central air system includes an interior coil (in the furnace housing) that removes heat from the interior air and an exterior coil that rejects heat into air outside the house.

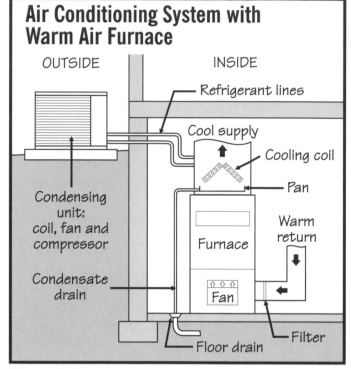

Air Conditioning System with Warm Air Furnace

OUTSIDE   INSIDE

Refrigerant lines

Cool supply

Cooling coil

Pan

Condensing unit: coil, fan and compressor

Warm return

Furnace

Condensate drain

Fan

Floor drain

Filter

Figure 3-24.

When the thermostat signals for cooling, this starts up the exterior refrigeration compressor, exterior fan and furnace fan. The exterior compressor moves refrigerant through the closed system of coils and valves to produce a cool coil inside. The furnace fan moves air across this coil. The air cools, and moisture condenses on the coil's surface. This moisture is caught in a pan below the coil and drains away through a hose.

It is not necessary to cover the exterior unit during the winter, since these units are designed to withstand the weather. If you do cover the unit for some reason (for instance, if the unit is located where debris might accumulate on it), it's best to cover only the top of the unit. If you were to securely wrap the sides, moisture could condense in the unit. Also, a wrapped unit provides a perfect winter home for animals that may chew wiring and cause other problems.

When it's time for the winter shutdown, turn off power to the unit to prevent accidental operation. The power disconnect could be the breaker or fuse at the main panel. Or the disconnect may be at the exterior unit, usually as a switch or a fuse block or plug that you pull out to disconnect the power.

Central air conditioning systems should never be operated in cold weather. This can cause serious damage.

Don't start the central air conditioner unless the outdoor temperature has been above 60 degrees for at least 24 hours. Remember to uncover the unit if you added a cover for the winter.

At the start of the cooling season, when you're about to turn on power to the unit, make sure that the thermostat is switched off, and leave the thermostat off for 24 hours before operating the unit. If the unit has a crankcase heater, this procedure allows the heater to warm the unit.

Central Air Conditioning Maintenance Requirements

Proper maintenance will keep the unit operating properly and save you energy costs. **See Figure 3-25**. Have your air conditioning system checked yearly by a professional service contractor.

You should also perform basic maintenance. Contact the manufacturer of your furnace/AC unit for specific maintenance requirements; see the References section for contact information.

ROUTINE MAINTENANCE A HOMEOWNER SHOULD PERFORM

Note: Turn off all power and disconnect switches before performing inspections/maintenance.

- Maintain records, and have a professional service the unit yearly.

- Change the filter as often as required (in some cases, every month).

- Switch high/low returns (and adjust ductwork if necessary) at the start and end of the cooling season. For complete instructions, check the section on "Heating and Cooling Distribution" later in this chapter.

- Listen to the air conditioner operate. Follow up on any strange noises.

- Check drain lines from the furnace to make sure they are clear and draining properly.

- Look for water leaks or changes in the system.

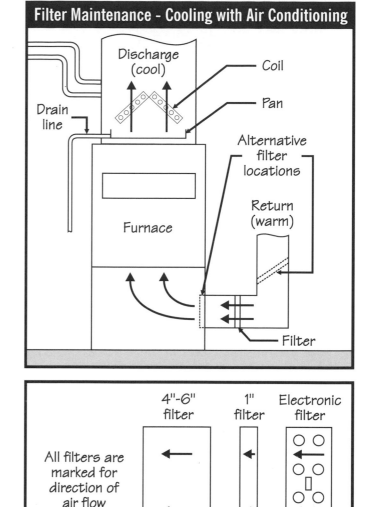

Figure 3-25

- Keep plants and obstructions away from the exterior coil and fan. Allow 3 feet of clearance at the air discharge and 1 foot all around the unit.

- Keep the exterior coil clean.

- Keep the exterior unit level and away from soil or landscape materials.

- Make sure that supply and return registers inside your home are not blocked.

FALL MAINTENANCE

1. Disconnect power to the unit to prevent accidental use.

2. (Optional)—Cover the top of the unit.

SPRING MAINTENANCE

1. Uncover the unit.

2. Turn the power on 24 hours before operation. Keep the thermostat off.

3. Perform the maintenance listed above and arrange for professional service.

ROUTINE MAINTENANCE A PROFESSIONAL SHOULD PERFORM

A service technician should perform the following procedures during a routine service call. The technician may perform additional checks, depending on the type of air conditioner you have.

- Check filter and replace as needed.

- Check exterior unit for level conditions, a clean coil, clearances, and adequate air flow.

- Check interior temperature drop across the cooling coil (15 to 22 degrees F).

- Check the condensate drain pan and line.

- Check secondary pan and line if unit is located in an attic.

- Look for signs of water leaks or excessive air leaks.

- Lubricate the fan motor and check the belt if required.

- Inspect electrical connections.

- Inspect refrigerant lines for signs of leaks.

- If performance problems exist, the technician may check for amp draw, clean the coils, check the refrigerant charge, and/or complete general performance tests.

Duplicates of the above lists appear in the Service Checklists chapter. You may want to make a photocopy of the professional's list and send it to the service company when you arrange service and/or review the list with the technician at the beginning of the service call.

Heat Pumps

A heat pump provides heating and cooling. Simply put, a heat pump is a central air conditioner that can cycle in reverse to provide heating. **See Figure 3-26**.

Local conditions will dictate whether a heat pump is an efficient alternative for heating your home.

A heat pump transfers heat from an exterior coil to an interior coil in the warm air heating system. A heat pump provides efficient heating in areas where exterior temperatures are moderate. In cold winter weather, though, a heat pump is no more efficient than electrical resistance heating, which costs more to operate than a natural gas or oil furnace.

Before you use your heat pump, have a professional explain its operation. Unfortunately, it's easy to accidentally operate the system with emergency electrical heat; in this mode, the heat pump is turned off and electrical resistance heating coils turn on. This method works fine, and you may not observe any problems—until you get your electric bill.

The emergency (electrical resistance) system should only be used when (1) the heat pump is not working, or (2) the outside temperature is so cold (about 30 degrees or lower) that the heat pump would be less efficient than electric resistance heating. When the outside temperature gets this low, emergency resistance heating turns on automatically. You do not need to adjust the controls.

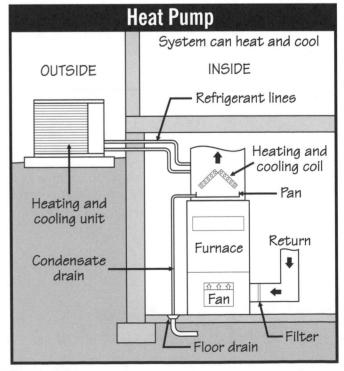

Figure 3-26

Heat Pump—Maintenance Requirements

Maintenance for a heat pump is similar to that for central air conditioning systems, but because a heat pump is operated winter and summer, it will require more maintenance.

ROUTINE MAINTENANCE A HOMEOWNER SHOULD PERFORM

Note: Turn off all power and disconnect switches before performing inspections/maintenance.

- Schedule professional service yearly.

- Watch for ice forming on the exterior unit. This is a serious problem indicating that the unit needs service.

- Follow all the maintenance recommendations for central air conditioning.

ROUTINE MAINTENANCE A PROFESSIONAL SHOULD PERFORM

A service technician should perform the following procedures during a routine service call. The technician may perform additional checks, depending on the type of air conditioner you have.

- Follow all maintenance requirements for central air conditioning.

- Follow specific recommendations by the heat pump manufacturer.

- Check filter and replace as needed.

- Check exterior unit for level conditions, a clean coil, clearances, and adequate air flow.

- Check interior temperature drop across the cool ing coil (15 to 22 degrees F).

- Check the condensate drain pan and line.

- Check secondary pan and line if unit is located in an attic.

- Look for signs of water leaks or excessive air leaks.

- Lubricate the fan motor and check the belt if required.

- Inspect electrical connections.

- Inspect refrigerant lines for signs of leaks.

- If performance problems exist, the technician may check for amp draw, clean the coils, check the refrigerant charge, and/or complete general performance tests.

- Follow any specific recommendations by the heat pump manufacturer.

Duplicates of the above lists appear in the Service Checklists chapter. You may want to make a photocopy of the professional's list and send it to the service company when you arrange service and/or review the list with the technician at the beginning of the service call.

Heating and Cooling Distribution: Ducts and Dampers

Warm air heating (and central air conditioning) is distributed throughout your home by a system of ducts, dampers and grills. Supply grills provide con-ditioned air, and return grills provide a route for the air to return to the central heating/cooling unit. The central fan circulates air through these ducts and grills. **See Figure 3-27**.

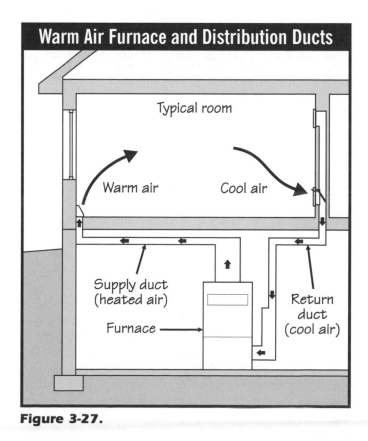

Warm Air Furnace and Distribution Ducts

Typical room

Warm air   Cool air

Supply duct (heated air)

Furnace

Return duct (cool air)

Figure 3-27.

These ducts may be metal, fiberglass or even flexible plastic. When there is a basement or crawl space, the ducts are often located just below the first floor. When the furnace is in the attic, distribution is routed through the attic. **See Figure 3-28**. Often, framing in joist or stud spaces forms return ducts. For homes with slab foundations, the ducts may be buried in the foundation slab. **See Figure 3-29**.

This distribution system often has adjustable dampers that control the air flow to certain points in your home. Frequently, these dampers are adjusted during installation and are never re-adjusted later. At times, though, dampers should be adjusted when switching from heating to cooling or to accommodate a central humidifier that is turned on in winter and off in the summer.

For a two-story home, you may need to make air flow adjustments for winter and summer. In the winter, warm air rises to the second floor, and you don't need as much heating up there. In the summer, warm air still rises, and the hot attic adds more heat, so you'll need more cooling (air flow) to the second floor than the first.

Dampers are located inside the ducting system. Often, you'll find dampers where round supply ducts connect to the main rectangular ducts. All you

Must Know / Must Do
Ductwork and Dampers

- Never allow openings or holes in ductwork. This wastes energy and makes living spaces uncomfortable.

- You may need to adjust ductwork dampers when switching from heating to cooling or vice versa.

- If your furnace has a damper on the humidifier, you may need to adjust it. Turn it off during summer.

- Ask your service technician if your warm air furnace has a damper for a winter/summer switch.

- Ductwork in attics and crawl spaces should be well insulated to prevent loss of energy.

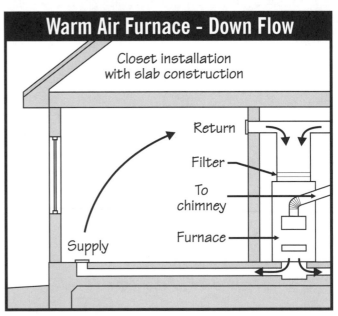

Figure 3-29.

will see of a damper is a small lever and lock nut or a small shaft and a wing nut. You can determine the position of the damper by checking the direction of the lever or the screwdriver slot in the end of the shaft. If the lever or slot is **parallel** to the duct, this means the damper is open. If the lever/slot is **perpendicular** (at a right angle) to the duct, the

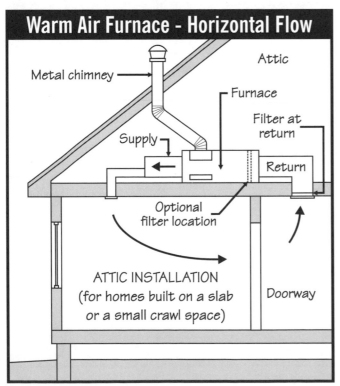

Figure 3-28.

damper is closed. Some systems have levers indicating the direction of the damper. Some rectangular ducts have dampers and levers. **See Figure 3-30.**

You can adjust these dampers to close off rooms you don't want to heat/cool or to provide more heating or cooling to specific rooms.

At the start of hot summer weather, you may need to direct more cool air to the second story. Start by fully opening all second-floor dampers. Next, partially close dampers to first floor rooms that are cold and receiving lots of air. The dampers often fit loosely in the ducts, so you may find that closing the damper 50% (turning the shaft 45 degrees) will only partially slow the air flow. Sometimes air will flow through a fully closed damper.

However, don't close off more than one-quarter of all the dampers; operation can be hindered if too little air flows through the system. If you need to make major changes to the system, consult a professional.

Once you've found a desirable balance, mark the damper settings for winter and summer.

High and Low Returns

Some distribution systems have "high" and "low" return grills on interior walls. These grills are located one above the other. They aid in air distribution and comfort. **See Figure 3-31.**

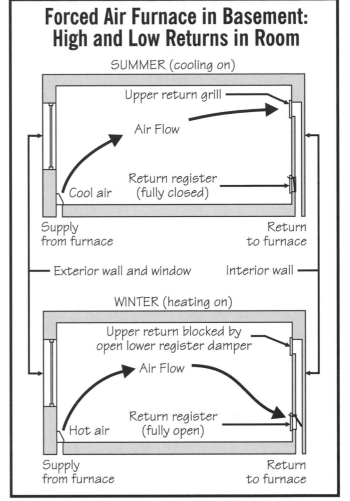

Figure 3-31.

High returns should be opened for cooling. Remember that warm air rises, and you want to return the warm air to the air conditioning coil in the furnace.

During the heating season, the low returns should be open to return cold air at floor level to the furnace.

Humidifier Controls and Settings

In northern heating climates, homes can become very dry in the winter. As warm air leaks out of our homes, it is replaced with cold, dry air. This is less severe if we have tightened up our homes for energy conservation, but it still can be a problem. Excessive dryness can damage furniture and harm your physical well-being.

The simple way to add moisture to the air of your home is with a central humidifier on your warm air furnace. A modern system is easy to maintain

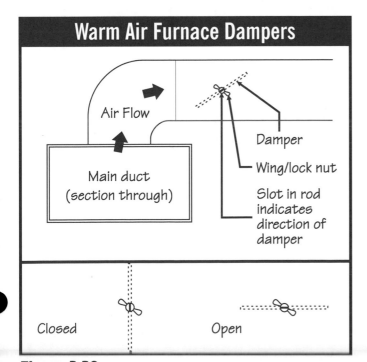

Figure 3-30.

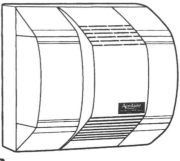

Figure 3-32.

Must Know / Must Do
Central Humidifier

- Routinely check for leaks in the humidifier. Leaks will ruin the furnace.

- Routinely clean and service the unit to prevent bacteria that endanger the health of those in your home.

- Check that the drain line is clear and draining.

- Turn off the unit and its water supply in the summer.

- Adjust the duct damper on the unit if necessary: off for summer, on for winter.

- If condensation forms on your windows in the winter, lower the humidity setting.

- Newer, tighter homes rarely need a humidifier.

You must also adjust the humidistat to compensate for the outside air temperature. **See Figure 3-33**. The humidistat looks like a thermostat and is located next to the thermostat or on the ductwork of the furnace. The colder the outside temperature, the lower the interior humidity level should be. Your windows provide a great humidity indicator. If moisture condenses on the windows, the interior humidity level is too high.

and should not leak. Modern systems have automatic controls that sense humidity level and operate automatically.

Older systems are not the best, but some are serviceable. Do not use the type that employs a water pan with an automatic fill valve. These are hard to maintain, may harbor disease-causing bacteria, and can leak water and ruin a furnace by rusting it out.

The type with a water panel and drain (Aprilaire is a common brand) works well if you maintain it. **See Figure 3-32**. This system slowly flushes water across a perforated metal panel, where the air picks up moisture. Excessive water drains through a pan and hose. In general, maintenance requires changing the water panel yearly and cleaning the pan and drain lines. Routinely check for water leaks, and keep the drain line clear.

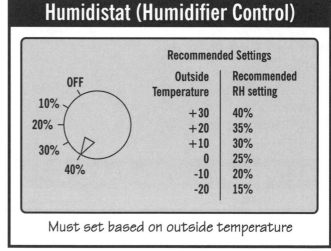

Humidistat (Humidifier Control)

	Recommended Settings	
	Outside Temperature	Recommended RH setting
OFF	+30	40%
10%	+20	35%
20%	+10	30%
30%	0	25%
40%	-10	20%
	-20	15%

Must set based on outside temperature

Figure 3-33.

Aprilaire offers a humidistat that automatically compensates for outside air temperature.

For more specific information, see the contacts listed in the References section.

Utility Systems—Electrical

The electrical supply to your home begins outside, where you will see either an overhead feed and piping down the side of your home or (if you have underground service) a metal box near the ground. **See Figure 4-1**.

The overhead service wire should be clear of trees and other wires. It should be at least 10 feet above any surface you can walk on.

With underground service, you will see a meter mounted on the metal box. This box hides the entrance of the service wire into your home.

The main electrical panel will be located in the basement or utility room. From this panel, electricity is divided into circuits through individual breakers or fuses and is fed through the wiring system, outlets and cords to various electrical devices.

Most modern homes have 220-volt systems with a minimum of 100 amps of power. Older houses may have fuses and can have 60-amp systems. Very old houses can have 110-volt, 30-amp systems, but these are rare.

Main Panel

Take a tour of your main electrical panel. Do this with a professional or an experienced friend if you are confused or if you have particular questions or concerns.

During this tour, identify the main disconnects so you can turn off power in an emergency. Also, determine how to reset a breaker and/or replace a fuse.

To begin, locate the main panel and open the door. Do not remove the metal cover beneath, since that would expose bare wires.

You will find fuses or breakers but not bare wires or exposed connectors. Breakers look like switches that can be moved from "on" to "off." Fuses will be either a round screw-in type or the larger cartridge type mounted in a fuse block that can be pulled from the main panel.

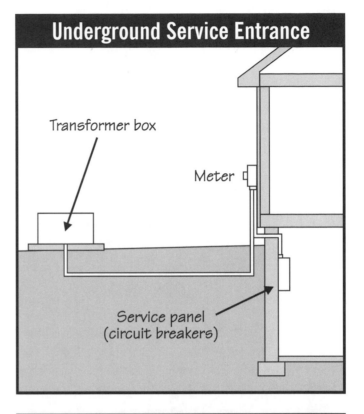

Underground Service Entrance

Transformer box

Meter

Service panel
(circuit breakers)

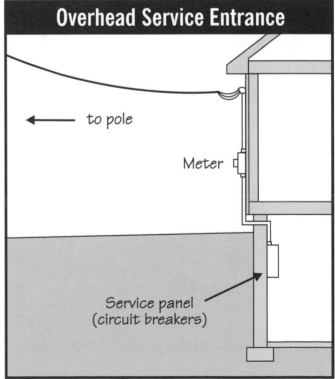

Overhead Service Entrance

to pole

Meter

Service panel
(circuit breakers)

Figure 4-1.

Must Know / Must Do—Electrical

Properly installed electrical systems are very safe and efficient. To prevent safety problems, though, you should understand the basics.

- Know where the main electrical disconnect is located and how to use it.

- To prevent shocks, any outlets near water (such as next to a sink) and all exterior outlets should have GFCI protection installed. (These outlets are explained below.)

- Know which outlets are GFCI protected. Test GFCI outlets and breakers monthly.

- Avoid using extension cords.

- Never attempt an electrical repair unless you know exactly what you are doing.

- Never perform wiring or re-wiring work. Use a professional.

- Identify which breakers/fuses control which outlets.

- If you replace a fuse, always use the same size—20 amp for 20 amp, 15 amp for 15 amp. Have a few spare fuses on hand.

- Know how to reset a breaker. The usual procedure is to turn it off, then on. Some systems use red indicators or an "off" indicator to show that a breaker has been tripped.

- Never cut or modify electrical plugs or outlets.

Other configuration are possible. There may be a combination of fuse panels and breaker panels. There may be "sub-panels" located next to the main panel.

Breaker Panel—Main Switch

On most panels, you will find one breaker marked "main." This breaker will be near the top of the box and will be 100, 150 or 200 amp. If you

switch this breaker off, all power in your home will be disconnected, and you will be in the dark. I don't suggest turning off the power. **See Figure 4-2**.

An older breaker panel may have several breakers marked as main disconnects. Some may be marked "lighting" or "air conditioning." There may also be a fused main with breakers for distribution circuits.

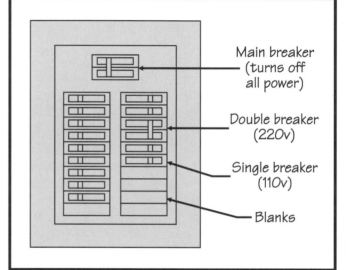

Electrical Main Circuit Breaker Panel

Main breaker (turns off all power)

Double breaker (220v)

Single breaker (110v)

Blanks

Figure 4-2.

Breaker Panel – Reset a Breaker

Modern circuit breaker panels are convenient because you can "reset" a breaker if it trips and you don't need to search for a replacement fuse. You do need to use common sense and caution when resetting a breaker. If a breaker trips, there may be an overload on the circuit. Before you switch a breaker back on, check for devices that may be causing the overload – hair dryers, electrical resistance heaters, power tools or other devices that use a lot of power. Remove the device before you reset the breaker. If the breaker trips a second time – consult a professional.

There are several types of breakers and methods to reset breakers **See Figure 4-3**. Most breakers flip to an "off" position when an overload occurs. For these breakers, you flip the switch back to the "on" position. Some breakers also have a little window that shows a red "flag" when the breaker is tripped.

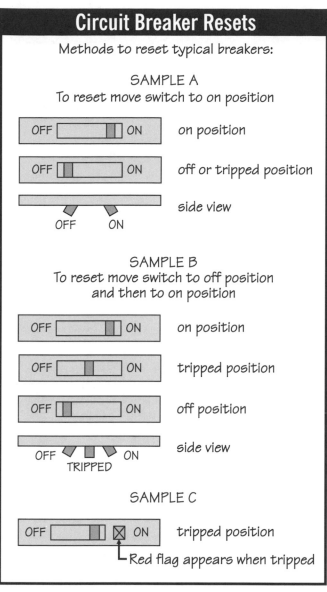

Figure 4-3.

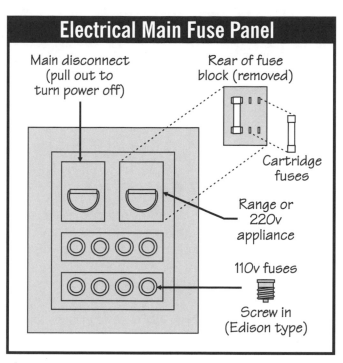

Figure 4-4.

Other breakers flip to a center position when tripped. The handle will be halfway between "on" and "off". You will need to look carefully to find this type of tripped breaker. This type of breaker often requires you to move the breaker handle to the "off" position and then back to the "on" position to reset the breaker.

Fuse Panel—Main Switch

You will see a main fuse block, about 4" x 3", with a small handle. Turning off ("pulling") this main turns off all power to your home. **See Figure 4-4**.

Some older systems have multiple main disconnects—instead of pulling one main, you must pull multiple fuse blocks to turn off all power. Main disconnects should be clearly identified at the fuse blocks or on the cover of the panel. They may be marked "lighting main," "range," "dryer," "air conditioner," and so on. Usually, each 220-volt appliance has its own main.

If this sounds confusing, review the sketches I've provided. If you still don't understand your system, or if it's not well-marked, go over the panel with a professional and rewrite the markings.

Fuses and Replacement

Typical screw-in type fuses are called Edison Base fuses. They fit into a threaded socket just like a light bulb. **See Figure 4-5**. If a fuse "blows", it will appear dark or burned in the cover window. To replace a fuse you unscrew the old fuse and screw in a new fuse of a matching amperage rating. The "blown" fuse is discarded. You should always match the amperage rating and never put a larger fuse in the socket. For example, a 15-amp fuse must be replaced with a 15-amp fuse NOT a 20-amp fuse.

You can improve the safety of your fuse system by adding S-Type fuse bases. **See Figure 4-5**. This base is a special socket that is threaded into the standard size, Edison socket. Once in place, they will only accept the correct size fuse. Each S-Type fuse has a unique threaded base. Safety is provided because a 20-amp fuse will not fit in a 15-amp S-Type fuse socket.

Wiring, Flow of Electricity

Distribution wiring is what routes electrical power to lights, outlets and appliances. Most of this wiring is buried in walls and attics, but some will be visible near the main panel and in basements and crawl spaces. Since the 1970s, plastic shielded wiring (Romex is a common brand) has been used in residential construction. Older homes may have cloth-shielded wiring, BX or flexible metal-shielded wiring, or even conduit (metal pipe). There are many variations and exceptions. **See Figure 4-6**.

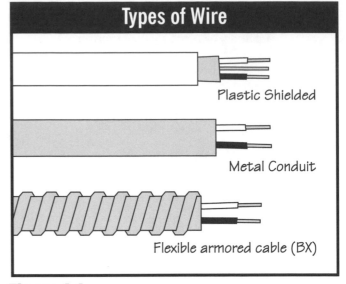

Types of Wire

Plastic Shielded

Metal Conduit

Flexible armored cable (BX)

Figure 4-6.

Homes built around 1910 may have "knob and tube" wiring that consists of two strands of wire run parallel. This wiring is strung on knobs, around corners, and through tubes in framing. It should only be modified by a professional. If your home has this type of wiring, plan for an upgrade.

Electricity flows like water, so it requires at least two wires: it pushes through the live wire and returns through the neutral wire. This is why all electrical devices have plugs with at least two prongs. Modern systems add a third (ground) wire for safety.

Devices like electric ranges run on 220 volts and require two power wires (110v plus 110v) plus the neutral wire. Some 220-volt appliances have four wires: two power, one neutral, and one ground.

Sound complicated? It is. Don't modify or tamper with the system. Consult a professional when repairs are needed. Experience and knowledge are necessary when working with electricity. Electricians spend at least six years in school and training just to learn the basics of their trade.

Outlets, Cords, 110 vs. 220

220 volt—what?? Is that 110, 220, 240 or 90210? Terminology used with electrical systems is confusing, but you really don't need to sweat it. In

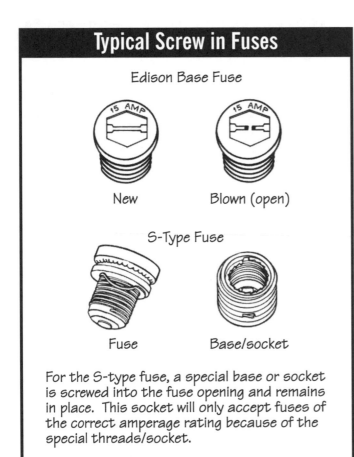

Typical Screw in Fuses

Edison Base Fuse

New   Blown (open)

S-Type Fuse

Fuse   Base/socket

For the S-type fuse, a special base or socket is screwed into the fuse opening and remains in place. This socket will only accept fuses of the correct amperage rating because of the special threads/socket.

Figure 4-5.

fact, electric utility companies don't provide an exact voltage. Just remember this:

Electricity is provided to your home with a nominal (approximate) voltage of 110 to 120 volts per wire. When you connect between the two live wire feeds, you double the voltage to about 220 or 240 volts. So you can call it 110 or 120 volts for smaller appliances and 220 or 240 volts for large appliances.

How can you tell the difference? 110 volt is provided to all convenience outlets, light switches, and lighting fixtures in your home. The standard electrical outlet is 110 volt. **See Figure 4-7**.

Large appliances like stoves and electric clothes dryers use 220/240-volt outlets. These are the big clunky outlets. Electric water heaters, central air conditioners, and heat pumps are directly connected to 220/240-volt power without a plug. Some large electric appliances may also be directly wired.

Just to confuse you, you may find a funny looking small outlet and plug that is the same size but a different shape than a standard 110-volt outlet. These are 20 amp, 220/240-volt outlets. These are not common but they may be found for large window air conditioners, woodworking equipment, and shop air compressors. A standard plug will not fit into a 220/240-volt outlet.

Service Disconnects

Electrical equipment is often connected to the electrical system with a plug or service disconnect as a safety measure. All equipment must have a readily available means of disconnection from the electrical system in case the unit needs servicing. **See Figure 4-8**.

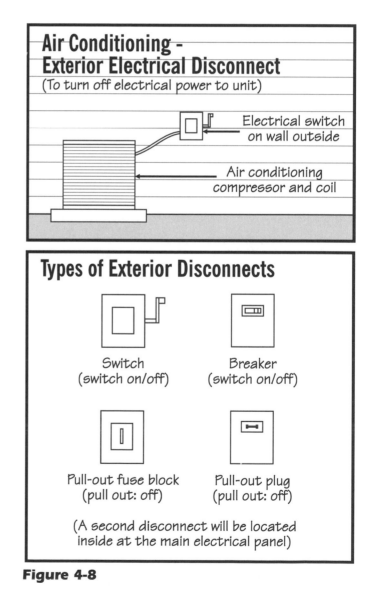

Figure 4-8

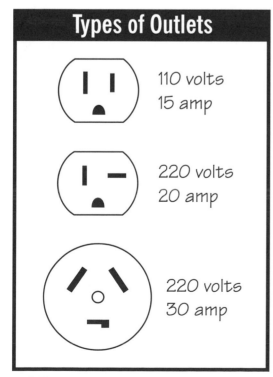

Figure 4-7.

Common service disconnects:

- Furnace—"light switch" on the side of the unit

- Central air conditioner—switch or pull-out in a box next to the exterior unit

- Dishwasher—"light switch" above the kitchen counter.

Know where the service disconnects are located and how to use them.

Electrical Polarity

Polarity is an important concept. For safety's sake, you need to understand the basics.

Electricity circulates through wires just like water moves through a hose. In the case of a lamp, for instance, electricity pushes through the "hot" wire, lights the bulb, and returns through the neutral wire. Got it?

Plugs on modern lamps and other devices have one wide blade and one narrow blade so that they can be plugged into an outlet, **see Figure 4-9**, in the correct position only—unlike plugs on old lamps, which could be reversed. Electrical devices with three-prong plugs have a ground wire; these,

too, can only be plugged into an outlet in one position. **See Figure 4-10**.

You may find a modern electrical tool with a plug that has two narrow blades that can be inserted in either direction. These are special "double insulated" tools with plastic housings that isolate the electrical components from contact with your skin.

What happens if you power a device with "reversed polarity"—that is, with the plug reversed? Stereo equipment may buzz; electrical and computer equipment may be damaged. Lights and lamps pose a serious hazard. When turning off the switch, you would be turning off the neutral (return) wire, not the live (hot) wire. This means that even when the lamp is off, the ring around the base of the bulb is still live, and if you touch the ring you can get a serious shock. **See Figure 4-11**.

What does all this mean to you? Never change a plug or outlet unless you understand polarity and know exactly what you are doing.

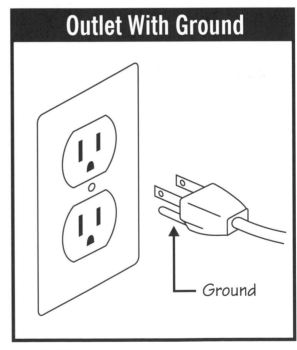

Figure 4-10.

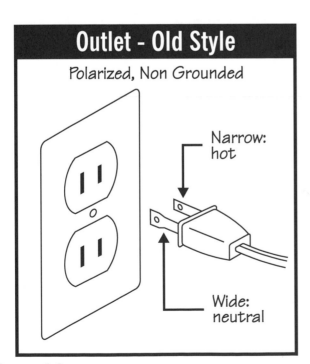

Figure 4-9.

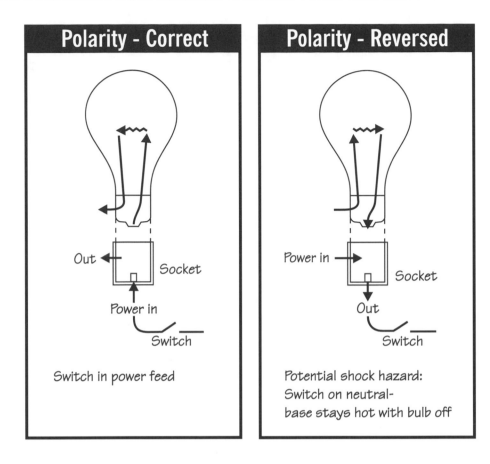

Figure 4-11.

Electrical Grounding

Electrical devices with metal housings—stoves, dryers, tools—often have a grounded plug. A grounded plug has a third, round connector. Grounded plugs provide an extra level of safety by grounding the metal housing of the device. Never remove the grounding device from a grounded plug. Never use adapters that convert a grounding plug to a standard two-prong plug. If your electrical device has a grounded plug, it should only be used with a grounded outlet. If there's no grounded outlet where you need it, have one installed.

Ground Fault Circuit Interrupters

A ground fault circuit interrupter (GFCI), **See Figure 4-12**, is a valuable safety device that should be installed in bathrooms, kitchens, sink locations, the garage, and exterior outlets. GFCIs have been required in new construction and

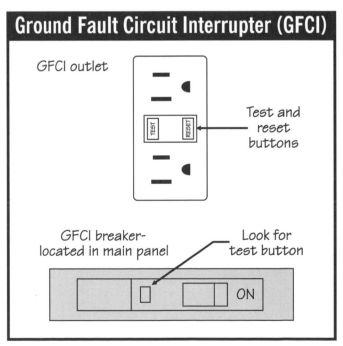

Figure 4-12.

remodeling since the mid-'70s. If you are remodeling, add GFCI outlets in the bathroom and any other damp or wet location. Have an electrician perform this work.

GFCI outlets or circuit breakers provide a high level of safety for very little cost. The GFCI outlet costs less than $10 and can be installed in a few minutes in most locations.

A tiny imbalance in the power and neutral lines will trip the GFCI. The imbalance indicates potential current leakage that could deliver a shock.

Don't confuse a GFCI with the fuse or circuit breaker in the basement. The fuse or breaker protects the wire from overloads, overheating and burning. A fuse will allow 15 or 20 amps to flow through the circuit before it trips. This is more than enough power to electrocute you.

Once the GFCI is installed, test it monthly with the test/reset button on the face of the breaker or outlet. Testing is simple and essential. Push the test button, and the GFCI will trip. Reset the GFCI outlet by pressing the reset button on the face of the outlet. Reset a GFCI breaker (at the main panel) by moving the switch from the center "tripped position" to fully "off" and then to the "on" position. **See Figure 4-13.**

Unfortunately, most outlets are not tested. I provide home inspection services, and I find that 5% to 10% of existing GFCI outlets are not working properly.

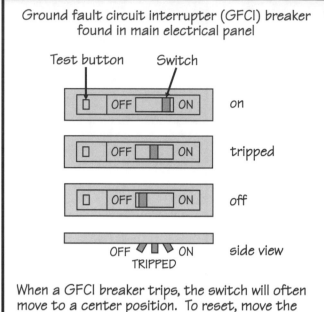

Figure 4-13.

Water Service—Municipal

Most homes in urban areas receive water from municipal water systems. The original water source may be a lake, a river, or large, deep wells and storage facilities. Municipalities are required to test water for safety and purity. Often they filter the water and treat it with chemicals. If you have questions about the quality of your water supply, contact your local water utility.

In a municipal system, water is distributed through piping mains beneath the streets. It enters your home under the basement slab or at the first floor slab. In cold climates, piping is buried below the frost line. **See Figure 5-1**.

Inside the house, there is usually a shutoff valve, a meter, and then a second shutoff valve. You can use either of these valves to turn off the water, but the second valve is used more often. Sometimes the valve on the street side of the meter can only be operated with a wrench.

Water is distributed through the house by steel, plastic or copper piping. Check your system, identify valves, and look for any potential problems. Locate

> ### Must Know / Must Do
> ### Municipal Water Supply
>
> - Make sure that all adults in your home know how to turn off the main water shutoff valve.
>
> - If the valve is old, rusted or leaking, have it serviced by a plumber so it will function when needed.

the main that feeds the water heater, and check for a shutoff valve before the water heater in case you need to turn off all hot water in your home.

Water Service—Your Own Well

Well, well, well...OK, that's pretty corny; but if your home has a sick water delivery system, you can lose your water supply and spend hundreds of dollars on repairs.

Most damage to private wells comes from lack of basic homeowner knowledge. As one service company representative told me, "Waterlogged pressure tanks sell more replacement pumps than any marketing I could possible do."

Do you know the symptoms of a waterlogged tank? Can you correct simple well problems? Do you know how to turn off your well water system?

Let's walk through the basics of a residential well water system and discuss how you can recognize common problems and correct them. We will discuss the most common systems in residential use. If you are presently on a municipal water system, fine—you still may enjoy the information or save it for your brother up north. You should also know that most municipal water systems are just larger versions of residential systems.

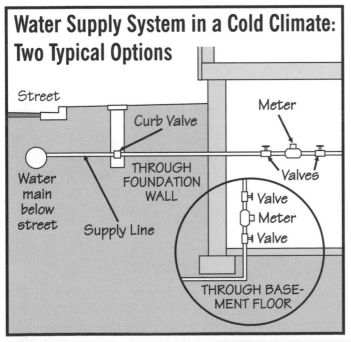

Water Supply System in a Cold Climate: Two Typical Options

Street

Curb Valve

Meter

Water main below street

THROUGH FOUNDATION WALL

Supply Line

Valves

Valve
Meter
Valve

THROUGH BASEMENT FLOOR

Figure 5-1

The Basic System 60

Most wells have a 6" steel casing that is drilled into the ground to reach a clean water supply. **See Figure 5-2**. The well casing may extend several hundred feet to reach a clean and adequate water supply. Water rises to a static level of equilibrium inside the steel casing and surrounds smaller internal piping. This internal piping is connected to a pump that lifts the water from the well and delivers it under pressure to your home plumbing system.

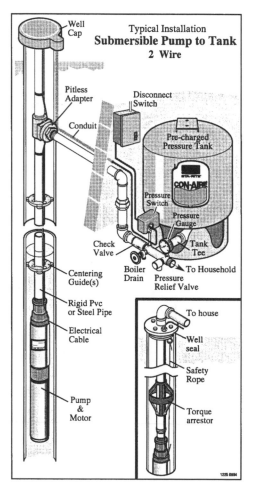

Figure 5-2.

The top of the well casing is covered with a cap and should be 12" above the surrounding soil to prevent contamination from surface water and other sources. The cap should be securely fastened to prohibit tampering. Recently, problems with insects have prompted many people to replace older caps with modern vermin-proof caps.

From the well casing, piping extends underground into your home, entering the basement near a pressure tank. The piping may be steel, copper, or plastic and is installed at least 6 feet below the surface to prevent freezing.

The Pump

For shallow wells and older systems, a jet-type centrifugal pump lifts water out of the well and delivers it to your home's piping. This type of pump is surface mounted in a pit near the well head or the pressure tank in the basement. The pump is driven by an electrical motor and is connected to the piping.

Deeper wells and newer systems use submersible pumps that are placed under the water's surface inside the well casing. This kind of pump is long and slender—normally only 4" in diameter—and hangs from the supply piping. This type of pump pushes water up and out of the well.

When you "pull" a pump, you physically remove the cap of the well casing and pull the submersible pump out of the hole by the supply pipe.

Working Under Pressure

A pressure tank, normally located in the basement, stores water and prevents the pump from turning on and off every time you use water. There is a compressed air cushion above the water in the tank; it expands and compresses with changes in pressure. As you use water in your home, the air cushion in the tank expands to maintain pressure and force water into your piping. **See Figure 5-3**.

The cushion of air generally varies in pressure within a normal operating range of about 40 to 60 pounds per square inch (psi). As water is used, the pressure decreases; when it reaches 40 psi, an automatic pressure sensing switch turns on the electricity to the pump. With the pump running, water is forced into the tank, raising the pressure of the air and water. As the tank is fully recharged with water, the pressure approaches 60 psi, and the pressure switch turns the pump off.

This pumping cycle repeats automatically as you use water from the tank. If you use a small amount of water, the pump will not need to start. You may notice a slight variation in pressure in your home as the system cycles slowly between 40 and 60 psi.

Modern Well Storage Tank - Water in Expandable Bladder

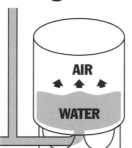

Separator is completely empty:

A new cycle is ready to begin. Positive action produces maximum drawdown on every cycle.

Water begins to enter the tank:

Air is compressed above the separator as it fills with water,

Pump-up cycle completed:

Air is now compressed to the cut-off setting of pressure switch.

Water is being drawn from the tank:

Compressed air in the tank forces water out of the separator.

Sequence of Operation

Figure 5-3.

When the system operates properly, the slow pressure changes are barely noticeable. A larger tank will draw more water per cycle, and there will be less pressure variation.

Tank Types Make a Difference

There are three basic types of pressure tanks. The conventional or galvanized "air over water" tank, generally found on systems over 30 years old, holds water in direct contact with the air cushion. This tank loses its air cushion as air is absorbed in the water, so you will need to service it several times per year to maintain the air cushion. You will recognize this type as a large, upright, galvanized steel tank. **See Figure 5-4**.

An improved galvanized tank separates the air from the water with a floating disc. This tank will not lose air to the water as quickly, but it still requires routine maintenance.

Modern tanks are a big improvement over the older tanks. They are smaller and usually are made of painted steel. Inside the tank, the elements are separated by a sealed diaphragm or bladder which holds either the air or the water. Since there is no direct air/water contact, this tank system maintains the air cushion indefinitely.

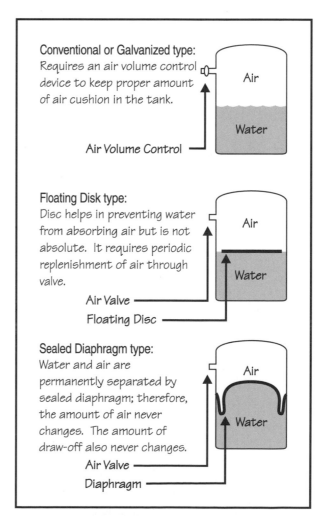

Conventional or Galvanized type:
Requires an air volume control device to keep proper amount of air cushion in the tank.

Air Volume Control

Floating Disk type:
Disc helps in preventing water from absorbing air but is not absolute. It requires periodic replenishment of air through valve.

Air Valve
Floating Disc

Sealed Diaphragm type:
Water and air are permanently separated by sealed diaphragm; therefore, the amount of air never changes. The amount of draw-off also never changes.

Air Valve
Diaphragm

Figure 5-4. Well Tanks

Steps to Well Wellness

The best route to a trouble-free well is to become familiar with the system's important parts and know how it is supposed to look and sound when running properly. Take the time to identify the components of your system and to watch it operate. Read any instructions and information available for your system. Look for the pressure tank, pressure switch, and gauges. Find the circuit breaker or switch that turns off the power to the pump.

Turn on a faucet and watch the pressure gauge to see the system's pressure vary. As it approaches 40 psi, you will hear a click when the pressure switch turns the pump on. With a submersible pump, you may hear a hum while the pump runs. When the pump is on, water flow into the tank will gradually increase the pressure to about 60 psi; then the pump will click off. It should take a minute or two for the pressure to increase from 40 to 60 psi.

If your system operates as described, now you know how a properly operating system responds when water is used.

The Helpful Turn-Off

It's important to know how to turn off the system completely. To stop the water flow to your home, you must turn off both the house service valve and the electrical supply to the pump. At least two people in your household should know how to do this.

Trace your home's piping back toward the pressure tank. The large valve in the line between the tank and the house piping is your house service valve.

If you turn off only the power to the pump, all the water under pressure in the tank will still flow into the piping system. If you turn off only the valve, the pump and electrical system can still malfunction.

Spotting a Waterlogged Tank

The most common and damaging problem in this system is a waterlogged pressure tank. A tank is waterlogged (full of water) when there is no air cushion in the tank. Without an air cushion, there is no air pressure to push water out of the tank into the home's piping. The pressure will vary quickly whenever a small amount of water is used.

This quick change in pressure causes the pump to start and stop almost every time you use water. As soon at the pump starts, the pressure will go up very quickly. For instance, if you are running a yard sprinkler, the pump will constantly turn on and off, and you will notice the pressure change at the spray of the sprinkler. If the pump is allowed to continue turning on and off (short cycling), eventually it will be ruined.

You can identify a waterlogged tank by quick changes in pressure and the way the pump switches on almost every time water is used. You must correct this situation to prevent damage to the pump.

Correcting a Waterlogged Tank

If you need to correct a waterlogged tank but don't fully understand your well system's operation, call a service company. Watch their repair person service the tank. Ask lots of questions, and take notes so you can do it yourself next time.

The bladder-type tank should not lose its air cushion unless there is a bladder failure or a valve stem leak. If there is an air leak, you will need to recharge this bladder-type tank.

When an air-over-water tank requires replacement of the air cushion, follow these steps:

1. Turn off the electrical power to the pump.

2. Turn off the house service valve.

3. Open the drain valve at the bottom of the tank and drain off all the water under pressure Normally, a hose is connected to this valve, and water is routed to a drain.

4. Using an air compressor or bicycle pump, add compressed air to the tank through its tire-stem-type fill valve.

5. Continue adding air until all the water is out of the tank and air flows from the drain valve.

6. Close the drain valve.

7. Pressurize the tank to about 5 psi below the normal operating range of the system. (In our example of a pump with a range of 40 to 60 psi, this would mean a pressure of 35 psi.)

8. Turn the electrical power to the pump back on and watch the pressure increase to the normal range as the pump fills the tank with water.

9. Open the drain valve again to drain away any debris that may have loosened inside the pipes and tank when they were under low pressure. Close the valve.

10. Slowly open the house service valve.

If your tank frequently becomes waterlogged, an air leak in the tank is probably the culprit. To check for this, make sure the tank has a full charge of air; then sponge a strong solution of soapy water on the tank and its parts. Check the air fill valve, fittings, and weld joints. Bubbles will indicate an air leak. Fittings and valves can be replaced or sealed to eliminate leaks. However, if the tank welds are leaking, you may wish to replace the unit with a modern bladder-type tank.

Other Problems

Many other problems can occur with well systems. Jet pumps can lose their prime. Pressure switches can fail. Fuses can blow. Pipes can freeze. Excessive air can be pumped into the system. As with any home system, the list of potential problems goes on and on, and most of the more serious problems should be solved by a professional.

However, a properly maintained system will work smoothly and provide years of trouble-free service. Ironically, that may eventually lead to trouble, for we take the system for granted and forget to watch for symptoms of problems. We may fail to perform simple maintenance or notice quick changes in pressure.

What, Me Worry?

Even so...don't worry, be happy. Modern pumps and systems are almost trouble-free. Do your homework and understand your system. Consult a professional if you have any concerns or problems you don't understand. Watch for that waterlogged tank—it can cost you a new pump. Consider replacing an old tank with a modern bladder-type tank if you don't like routinely replacing the air cushion.

Watch for any changes in the water; changes in water clarity, color, and odor can all indicate problems. You should also have your water tested for bacteria at least semi-annually. Some wells require routine chlorination.

Must Know / Must Do
Your Own Well

- Make sure that all adults in your home know how to turn off the main water valve and the electrical power to the well pump.

- If water pressure varies as you draw a small amount of water, this indicates a pressure tank problem: the pump is "short cycling." Add air to the pressure tank, or call for service.

- Have your water tested routinely—perhaps once per year.

For detailed informational brochures on wells, water, and water treatment, contact your local municipal health department or plumbing inspector or your state's department of natural resources. You can also obtain operational information from the companies that manufactured your well pump, tank, and pressure switch. Well service companies are another good source of information.

Water Heaters

A water heater is simply that—a device to heat water. **See Figure 5-5**. It consists of a storage tank with a gas, electric or oil heat source. If your home has an oil-fired hydronic boiler, there may be a coil in the boiler that heats water. Sometimes hot water is referred to as domestic hot water or potable water.

Water heaters work year after year with very little maintenance, so it is easy to ignore them. Yet routine maintenance checks should be performed on electric, gas and oil water heaters.

The water heater has a temperature dial. Keep it at a low or middle setting, and check your water temperature at the faucet. It should be about 120 degrees to prevent scalding. **See Figure 5-6**.

The temperature dial controls a thermostat in the water tank. **See Figures 5-7 and 5-8**. When the water cools, the burner or electrical heating element is switched on. When the water reaches the specified temperature, the heating unit shuts off.

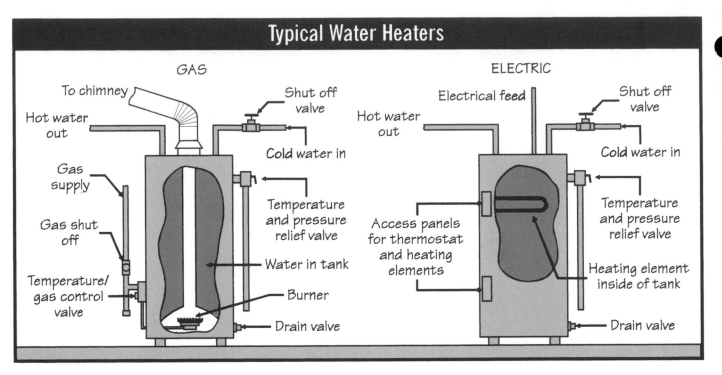

Figure 5-5.

Water Scalding Chart	
Set water heater to 120 degrees or less for safety!	
TEMPERATURE	TIME TO PRODUCE SERIOUS BURN
120 degrees (hot)	More than 5 minutes
130 degrees	About 30 seconds
140 degrees	Less than 5 seconds
150 degrees	About 1 1/2 seconds
160 degrees (very hot)	About 1/2 second

Figure 5-6.

The water heater's tank stores hot water, giving you a reservoir to draw from.

Routinely check your water heater for leaks. A leak is a sign of an impending failure, and you should replace the unit as soon as possible.

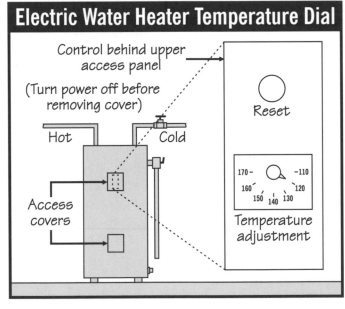

Figure 5-7.

Also, routinely check the temperature and pressure (T and P) relief valve. **See Figure 5-9**. This valve, which has a small lever, will be located on the top or side of the heater tank; the relief pipe should extend from the valve to within 6" of the floor. If water leaks from the relief valve, the valve should be replaced, because a leak may plug the valve with scale and debris. A plugged valve may fail to open if the tank overheats—a dangerous situation.

Gas Water Temperature Dial

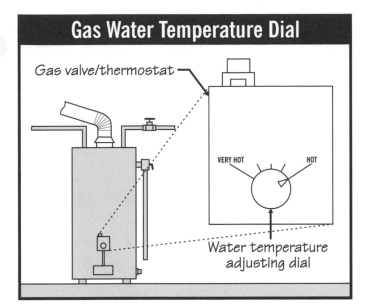

Gas valve/thermostat

VERY HOT   HOT

Water temperature adjusting dial

Figure 5-8.

Typical Water Temperature and Pressure (T&P) Relief Valve

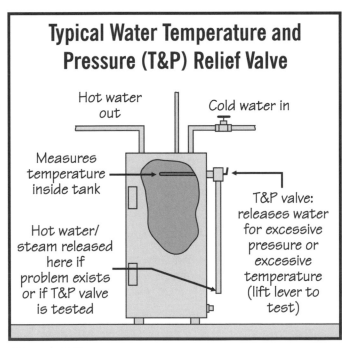

Hot water out

Cold water in

Measures temperature inside tank

Hot water/ steam released here if problem exists or if T&P valve is tested

T&P valve: releases water for excessive pressure or excessive temperature (lift lever to test)

Figure 5-9.

Manufacturers of T and P valves recommend testing the valve periodically by lifting the lever and allowing water to flow from the valve. They recommend this as a safety measure so you will know whether the valve will work if needed. But there's a risk that the valve won't close properly and will keep leaking, and then it will need to be replaced. When you do test the relief valve, do it when you can buy a replacement or get quick service from a plumber.

Manufacturers also recommend that you periodically drain water from the valve at the base of the water heater. This is a good procedure to follow if there is sediment in your water supply—but, again, few people follow this procedure, because their water systems have little sediment. If you do drain the tank, use a hose to direct water to a drain. Be careful—the water will be hot. If you haven't used the drain valve in several years, it probably won't close properly because of sediment buildup. If the valve leaks, you must replace it or cap it with a hose cap.

For a gas water heater, routinely inspect the metal flue pipe to the chimney. It should be free of rust, and it must be securely fastened to the water heater and the chimney. Also, have a contractor routinely inspect and clean the burner. A burner covered with rust indicates that the unit is not drafting well; the internal flue pipe is rusty, and the unit could be producing carbon monoxide. Every time you have your gas furnace tested and tuned, ask the service technician to test the gas water heater and check the flue gas for carbon monoxide.

For an oil-fired water heater, follow maintenance procedures (including yearly service by a professional) recommended in the section on the oil burner furnace.

The following problems should be corrected by a professional: difficulties with the T and P valve; lack of hot water; failed electrical elements; and problems with the anode, dip tube, thermocouple, or pilot light.

Piping and Valves

Operating your home also requires a basic understanding of plumbing valves and piping. You may need to turn off the water in an emergency. You may need to shut off water to one sink or tub while it's being serviced.

Pipes route water from the main feed to individual fixtures. Piping can be galvanized steel, copper or plastic. Each type of piping has elbows, tees, couplings and reducers to connect lengths of pipe and route them through walls and framing. Take a look at your system. You will notice that it starts with 3/4" or 1" pipes and reduces to pipes of smaller diameters as fewer fixtures are served.

Valves control the flow of water and enable you to disconnect parts of the system. You will find a combination of valves. Take a good look at your plumbing system to identify valves, determine what they control, and learn how they operate. It is a great idea to place a small tag on each valve identifying what it controls.

Ball Valve

Ball valves are used where full flow is required. This valve is unique in that it turns fully on and fully off with a 90-degree turn of a short lever. When the lever is parallel to the pipe, the water is on; when the lever is perpendicular, the water is off. Ball valves are often used at the main feed line and the water heater. **See Figure 5-10**.

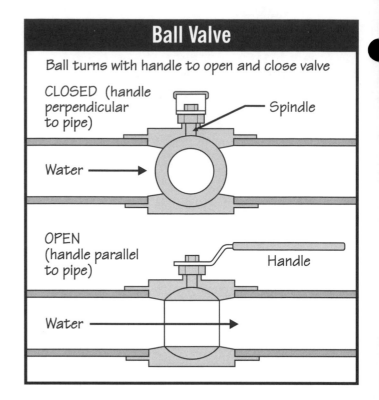

Figure 5-10.

Gate Valve

As you turn the handle, a "gate" inside the valve closes, controlling water flow. A gate valve is designed to be completely open or closed. It is often used at the main feed line. **See Figure 5-11**.

Globe Valve

A globe valve uses a washer and a set. It can be throttled to control water volume, but generally it is not used in the main shutoff. **See Figure 5-12**.

Saddle Valve

This is a small valve mounted on the side of a pipe like a saddle mounts on a horse. Saddle valves are frequently found on the water supply line for icemakers and humidifiers. They provide only a low flow of water and are prone to leaks. **See Figure 5-13**.

Hose Bib

A hose bib is an exterior hose connection valve. You may also find a hose bib at a utility sink. The hose bib has a threaded end to accept a garden

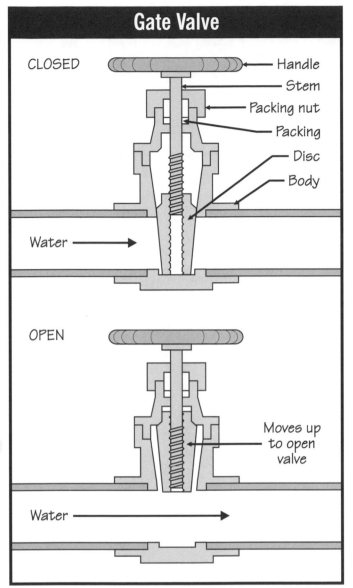

Gate Valve

CLOSED — Handle
— Stem
— Packing nut
— Packing
— Disc
— Body

Water →

OPEN

Moves up to open valve

Water →

Figure 5-11.

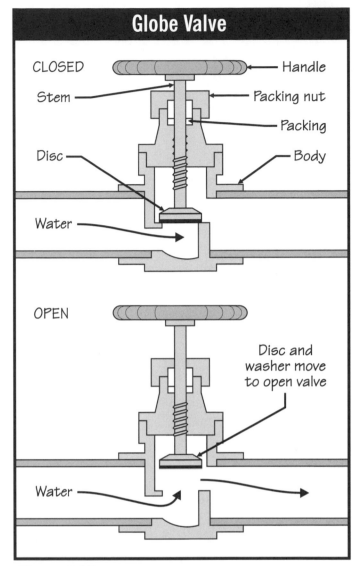

Globe Valve

CLOSED — Handle
Stem — Packing nut
— Packing
Disc — Body

Water →

OPEN

Disc and washer move to open valve

Water →

Figure 5-12.

hose. More information about hose bibs appears later in this chapter and in the section "Dripping Water Hoses" in the chapter on Plumbing Mysteries and Secret Solutions **See Figure 5-14**.

Water Softener

If your home has hard water (minerals in the water), you'll probably want to use a water softener. **See Figure 5–15**. Hard water can corrode piping and fixtures and cause a buildup of deposits. It leaves spots on dishes cleaned in the dishwasher, makes surfaces hard to clean, and interferes with detergents in the clothes washer and shampoos you use on your hair.

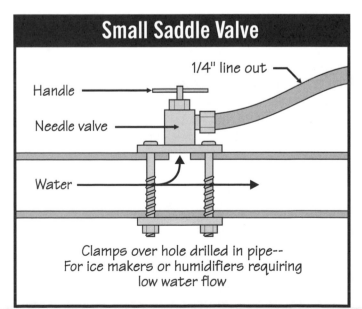

Small Saddle Valve

Handle — 1/4" line out

Needle valve —

Water →

Clamps over hole drilled in pipe--
For ice makers or humidifiers requiring low water flow

Figure 5-13.

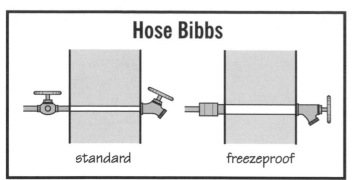

Figure 5-14.

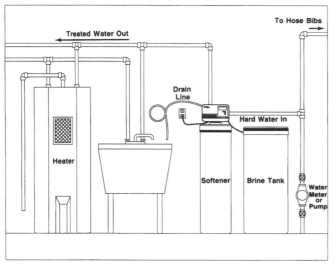

Figure 5-15. Water Softner Installation

A water softener removes the offending minerals, calcium and magnesium and adds a small amount of sodium. A softener can also remove small concentrations of iron.

The softener is often located near the water main. Normally, it is connected to hot water and bathroom fixtures. It is not routinely connected to tap water in the kitchen because of the slight amount of sodium being added to the water. Also, the softener is not routinely connected to exterior hose piping because there is no need to soften exterior water.

A professional should test water for hardness and estimate the amount of water usage, then set up the softener. Some of the better models of softener will base their cycle on the amount of water used. Others cycle on a timer device.

To maintain a water softener, you must keep a supply of salt in the salt brine tank. Use salt that has been processed into pellets, or whatever salt is rec-

Must Know / Must Do
Water Softener

- Use the proper salt, and keep some salt in the brine tank at all times.

- Watch for leaks.

- If spots appear on dishes and the water doesn't feel "slippery," your softener is not working. Check the salt supply first.

- If the unit cycles on a timer, make sure it's set properly for the number of people in your home. Review the manufacturer's instructions.

ommended by the manufacturer. Do not use plain rock salt; it contains small amounts of impurities that will ruin the system over time.

Water treatment systems are almost always installed with a method to "by-pass" the system for maintenance and repairs. **See Figure 5-16**. The by-pass involves three valves that are opened or closed to route the water through the system or to by-pass the system.

Other Water Treatment Options

If your home has water problems beyond basic hard water, consult a professional. Treatments for problem water include special iron filters, sediment filters, and reverse osmosis.

Garbage Disposal

A garbage disposal is a simple device that grinds food and washes it down the sewer system. **See Figure 5-17**. I suggest that you use the disposal sparingly, placing larger quantities of food waste in the garbage or in a compost pile. Remember that any waste you put down the sewer system must be treated in a municipal sewage treatment facility or in your own private septic system.

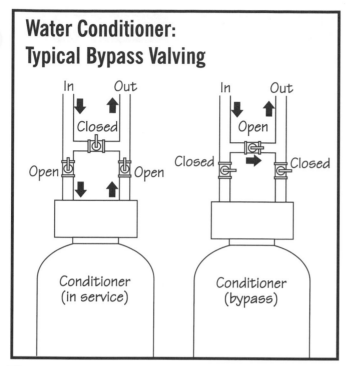

Water Conditioner: Typical Bypass Valving

In   Out

Closed

Open   Open

Conditioner (in service)

In   Out

Open

Closed   Closed

Conditioner (bypass)

Figure 5-16.

cause premature failure of the system. If you do use a garbage disposal, have the system pumped more often.

The key to using a disposal is to run the water before you add waste. Run a strong flow of cold water, turn on the unit, then slowly feed waste into it. Keep running water for several seconds after grinding stops to make sure all waste is flushed away. Never fill the unit and then turn it on—you will have a big, big mess of clogged pipes.

When a loud noise comes from the unit while operating, it usually means that a metal object like a spoon is caught in it. Turn the unit off and remove the object with tongs. Never put your hand in the disposal.

If you switch the disposal on and nothing happens (not even a hum), the thermal overload may have tripped. Under the sink, check the body of the unit for a small red or black button that may be marked "reset" or "overload." **See Figure 5-18**. Turn off power to the disposal by flicking the "light switch"

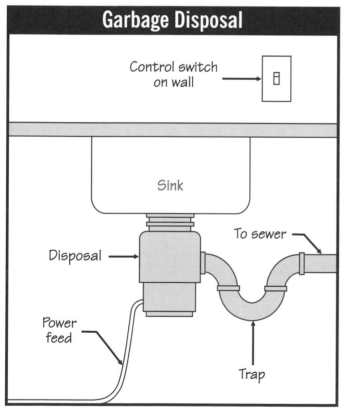

Garbage Disposal

Control switch on wall

Sink

Disposal

To sewer

Power feed

Trap

Figure 5-17. **Garbage Disposal**

Most experts suggest that you do not install a garbage disposal if you have your own septic or mound system. Introducing excess food waste can

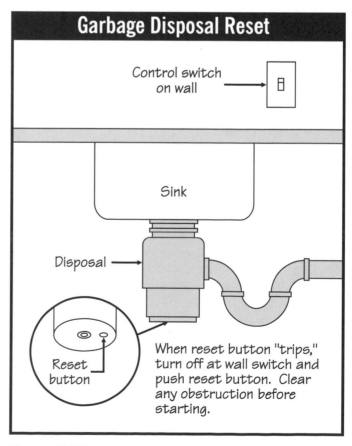

Garbage Disposal Reset

Control switch on wall

Sink

Disposal

Reset button

When reset button "trips," turn off at wall switch and push reset button. Clear any obstruction before starting.

Figure 5-18.

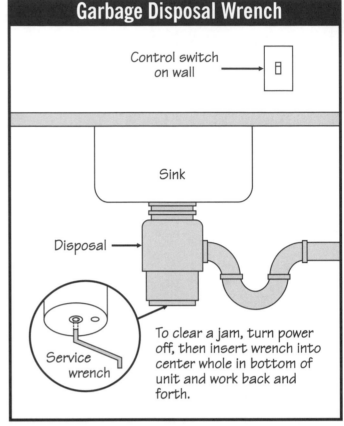

Garbage Disposal Wrench

Control switch on wall

Sink

Disposal

Service wrench

To clear a jam, turn power off, then insert wrench into center whole in bottom of unit and work back and forth.

Figure 5-19.

above the kitchen counter and then push in this button. Now try the unit again. If it just hums without running, it is stuck and needs to be cleared.

To clear the unit, turn off the power again. Look inside the unit for foreign objects, and if you see any, remove them with tongs. Next, look under the sink for a small six-sided wrench (usually stored in a plastic pouch near the disposal). **See Figure 5-19.** Insert the bent end of this tool into a recessed hole at the center bottom of the disposal. Turn the wrench several revolutions in both directions until the shaft spins freely. Remove the wrench, turn the power back on, and try the unit again.

Hose Bibs
(Exterior Hose Faucets)

A hose bib is an exterior faucet. There are several types.

In a cold climate, the hose bib valve may extend up to 12" into the house. When you turn off this type of hose bib, you are actually turning off a valve inside your home...but (and this is important), it may not drain properly and could freeze during cold weather if there is a hose connected to it. To prevent this problem, some older installations provide an additional shutoff valve in the basement. Properly turning off water in the winter requires that you (1) turn off the inside valve, (2) open the outside valve, and (3) open the small drain knob (if there is one) on the inside valve to drain off the pipe. **See Figure 5-20.**

A newer home may have a backflow preventer on the outside hose bib. This could trap water in the pipe and cause a freeze-up. To release water from

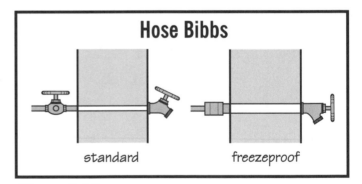

Hose Bibs

standard   freezeproof

Figure 5-20.

the pipe, you must either push the little button in the center of the backflow preventer to release the pressure, or open the small knurled knob at the inside shutoff valve to drain water from the pipe.

Every hose bib should have a backflow preventer or an anti-siphon device to keep contaminated water from the hose out of your drinking water system. To find out if such a device is required in your area, check with your water utility, plumbing inspector, or health department.

Water Hammer Arresters

Modern plumbing systems have water hammer arresters (anti-water-hammer devices) that prevent water pipes from pounding when water is quickly turned off. Basically, these are air chambers that can be compressed by moving water.

When halted quickly—for example, by an electrically-operated valve in a washing machine—water has lots of energy to dissipate. If the water can bounce against an air cushion, pipes won't pound . (For you electrical/electronic designers: this is equivalent to a capacitor in an electrical circuit.)

In older homes, anti-hammer devices are located near the main valve. In newer homes they are located near the washing machine, dishwasher, laundry tubs, and perhaps near the water main. They look like a short length of piping with a cap on the end. **See Figure 5-22**. In a newer home, an anti-hammer device may be a small, specially designed chamber about 1" around and 4" long. **See Figure 5-21**.

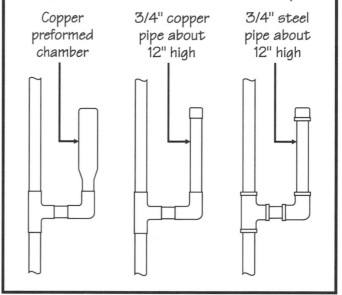

Water Hammer Arresters

Old style - air chamber made with standard parts

Copper preformed chamber   3/4" copper pipe about 12" high   3/4" steel pipe about 12" high

Figure 5-22.

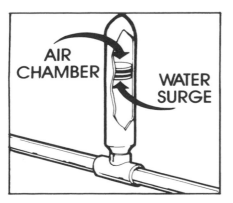

AIR CHAMBER   WATER SURGE

Figure 5-21.

If your pipes pound or bang when the water shuts off, add water hammer arresters or check any existing arresters. Old-style arresters may have filled with water and need to be drained. Before you try this, though, be sure the main valve is in good working order. If it leaks, is hard to turn, or has excessive corrosion, call a plumber. Also, be aware that in older homes with steel piping, turning off the water may loosen sediment inside the pipes; you may see rust and debris in the water. And since this technique introduces air into the system, an air/water mix may shoot out of the faucets when you turn them on again.

To drain the system and restore air to the arresters, turn off the water main, shutting off all water to your home. Then open all faucets and allow all water to drain from them. Next, slowly open the main valve part way and close the faucets one by one as the water runs steadily. After all faucets are closed, fully open the main valve.

Drainage, Waste and Vent System

After water is used in your home, it exits through a drainage, waste and vent (DWV) system. **See Figure 5-23**. Large pipes allow wastewater to flow by gravity from your home to a municipal sewer or private septic system. A series of traps and vents allow wastewater to flow freely while preventing sewer gas from entering your home.

Older systems are constructed of cast iron and galvanized steel piping. Newer systems are made of plastic. Copper was used for some systems built about 1970.

The sketch shows common components of a DWV system, which uses pipes that are larger than those in the water-supply plumbing system. The pipes range from $1\frac{1}{2}"$ to 4", with the larger pipes installed where the system exits your home. Horizontal pipes are angled to allow for proper waste flow.

The vent portion of the system starts with the vent pipe or stack routed through the roof. This open pipe allows air to enter the system so all pipes can drain properly. Think of the drainage system as

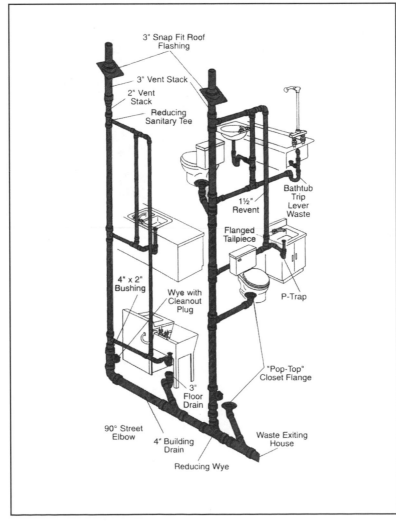

Figure 5-23. Drainage. Waste and Vent

a big straw. If you fill a straw with water, cover the top end with your finger and pick it up, water will not drain from the straw. When you release your finger and allow air to "vent" the straw, water drains quickly.

All piping and fixtures must be vented. If problems occur with the venting system, drains will "glug-glug" and empty slowly.

Each fixture has a trap—a P-shaped device below a sink (or built into the base of a toilet) that remains full of water. **See Figure 5-24**. "Trapping" water creates a seal that prevents sewer gas from entering through the drain. If a trap dries up, you will notice a sewage smell.

Traps are designed to be dismantled to remove blockages or retrieve lost objects. Drain piping has covers ("clean-outs") that can be removed to help

Must Know / Must Do
Drainage, Waste and Vent System

- If you notice a sewage smell, check for a dry trap.

- If a sink or other fixture backs up, there's a blockage in the trap.

- If your whole system backs up or wastewater backs up out of the lowest fixture, this indicates a problem with the main drainage line. Call a plumber.

- Any leaks from the waste system are potentially dangerous and should be repaired as soon as possible.

clean out clogged pipes. The main system cleanout will be located in the basement floor or where the main pipe exits your home. **See Figure 5-25**.

If you have a septic system, this cleanout will be outside, about 4 feet below the soil.

Sewer and Septic Systems

After wastewater leaves your home, it must be treated and cleaned before it is released into the environment. In a municipal sewage system, wastewater is routed to a treatment facility. If you live in the country, your home will have its own private treatment system—a septic or mound system.

Sewer System

Municipal sewer systems collect sanitary waste (sewer water) through pipes below the street. **See Figure 5-26**. Wastewater flows through a series of pipes that increase in size as they approach the treatment facility. Pipes can be 6 feet or more in diameter.

In many systems, all sewage flows by gravity until pumping stations "lift" (pump) it into the treatment facility. Once treated, the water is released to rivers and streams.

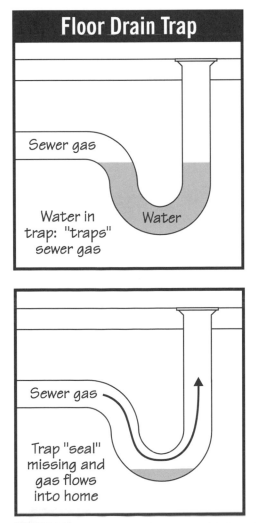

Floor Drain Trap

Sewer gas

Water in trap: "traps" sewer gas   Water

Sewer gas

Trap "seal" missing and gas flows into home

Figure 5-24.

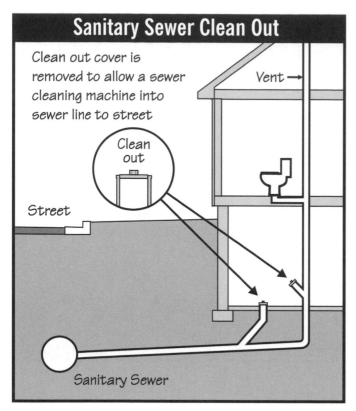

Sanitary Sewer Clean Out

Clean out cover is removed to allow a sewer cleaning machine into sewer line to street

Vent →

Clean out

Street

Sanitary Sewer

Figure 5-25.

Septic System

In rural areas without a municipal sewage treatment facility, residential sewage is treated in a septic system—a large underground tank and absorption field. Bacteria in the tank break down sewage solids. This treated sewage becomes sludge that settles at the bottom of the tank. Grease, fat and soap scum rise to the top of the tank, where they are trapped by baffles. **See Figure 5-27**.

As wastewater enters the tank, processed water is released to a drain field or absorption field consisting of a series of perforated pipes that release the water into soil. The soil then filters the wastewater; soil microorganisms decompose many contaminants in the wastewater. **See Figure 5-28**.

Although the septic system works automatically through the actions of bacteria, microorganisms, tank and piping, you must arrange for a professional to pump and inspect the tank.

Generally, a family of four should have the tank pumped and inspected every 2 years, but this varies

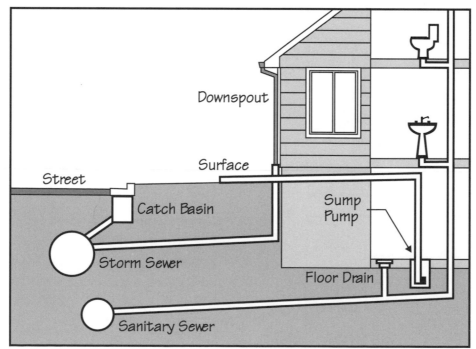

Downspout

Surface

Street

Catch Basin

Sump Pump

Storm Sewer

Floor Drain

Sanitary Sewer

Figure 5-26. Sewer Connections

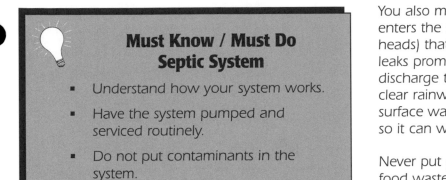

Must Know / Must Do
Septic System

- Understand how your system works.
- Have the system pumped and serviced routinely.
- Do not put contaminants in the system.
- Learn ways to conserve water.

You also must limit the amount of water that enters the system. Use fixtures (toilets, showerheads) that limit water use. Repair all plumbing leaks promptly. Don't connect the sump pump discharge to the septic system—the sump handles clear rainwater that doesn't need treatment. Divert surface water away from the septic drainage field so it can work properly.

Never put grease, fat, coffee grounds, paper towels, food waste, sanitary napkins, or disposable diapers down the drains—they will clog the system. Also, do not put toxic substances like solvents, oils, paints, disinfectants, or pesticides down the drains.

Most experts agree that "sweeteners" or septic system "starters" are not useful.

For more information, consult local health officials, the local plumbing inspector, or your nearest department of natural resources.

Mound System

Mound systems are installed in rural areas where the soil can't accept water from a standard septic system. **See Figure 5-29.** A mound system usually has a second holding tank/pump tank. After sewage is processed in the septic tank, water flows into the pump tank, which lifts the water to the top of the mound.

The mound is specially constructed of gravel and soil that's mounded above the surrounding surface. The mound functions the same as the absorption field in a conventional septic system, and the requirements for maintenance are the same as those described above for a septic system.

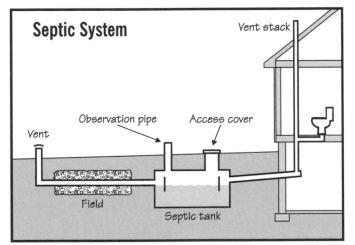

Figure 5-27.

with the type and size of the system and with local conditions. A professional septic service company can determine when your system should be pumped. Pumping the tank involves removing the sludge and scum before an excess builds up.

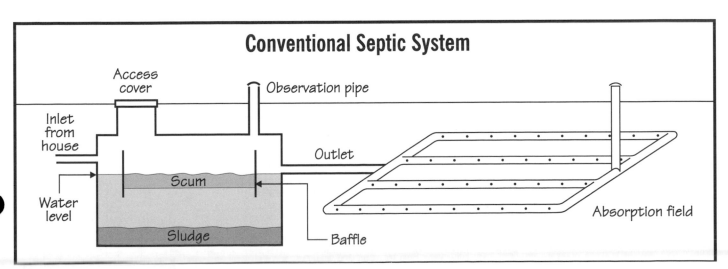

Figure 5-28.

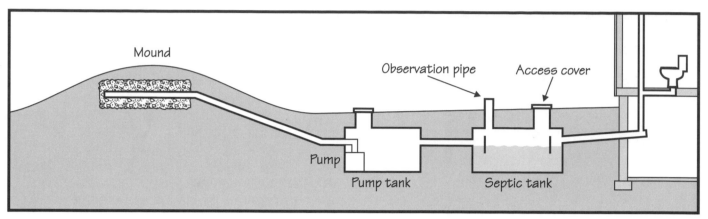

Figure 5-29. Mound System

You should understand the operation of the pump/second holding tank. Also, there may be an alarm that goes off if the pump is not working. If the alarm sounds, contact professional help.

Sewage Ejector

In most homes with basements and septic systems, sanitary system drainage will exit the basement 4 feet below the exterior soil depth, or about halfway up the basement wall. Sewage flows by gravity through the drainage pipe. But if there is a laundry tub, sink, bathroom, or floor drain in the basement, their wastewater must be pumped up to the main waste line. In this case, a sewage ejector or wastewater pump lifts the sewage water. **See Figure 5-30**.

You can tell if your home has a sewage ejector by looking for a sealed crock with piping that leads to the septic system. Modern systems are sealed and vented. An older system may consist of an open crock if it just services a laundry tub or floor drain.

These pumps and crocks require little maintenance, but if the pump fails or water leaks from the crock, stop using water in the lower level, and call a plumber.

Sometimes a home that's on a municipal sewage system will have a sewage ejection pump. This depends on the height of the main sewer line in the street and the height of the connection to the home.

Storm Sewer—Municipal or None?

Modern municipalities have two distinct sets of piping beneath roads and streets: sanitary sewers and storm sewers. **See Figure 5-31**. The sanitary

(municipal) sewer system routes all toilet, sink and drain water to a sewage treatment plant for processing, after which the clean water is released to rivers, lakes and streams.

Cities, and some subdivisions, also have a separate system—the storm sewer system—that handles rainwater. This system directly discharges untreated rainwater/runoff into rivers and streams. Your sump pump and rain gutters may be connected to this system through an underground pipe. The storm sewer line in your basement may look just like the sanitary sewer line except that it's not connected to toilets and sinks and doesn't have a vent on the roof.

If your sump pump is routed to the **sanitary** sewer system instead, you are sending clean rainwater to the sewage treatment plant. That overloads the plant and creates an unnecessary treatment expense. So don't connect your sump pump to the laundry tubs, because this water is routed to the sanitary sewer.

In rural areas, storm water may be routed into an open ditch beside the road. In densely populated areas, storm sewer piping below the street handles rainstorm runoff from hard surfaces like roofs, driveways, and parking lots. Such runoff is too great to be absorbed by the limited area of exposed soil in the city. Whenever you see sewer grates in the street, you are looking at parts of an underground storm sewer system.

Palmer valve

In some metropolitan areas, homes built between the 1920s and the 1950s had a "palmer valve" that routed clear storm water into the sani-

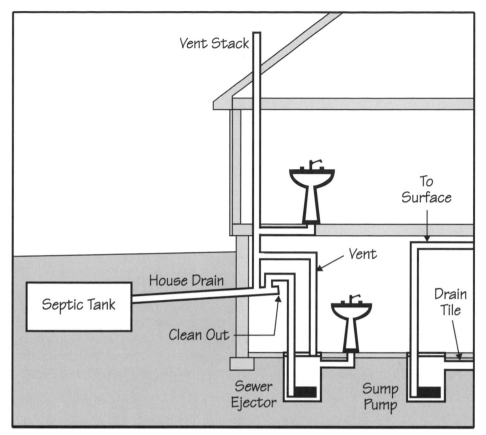

Figure 5-30. Sewer Ejector / Septic System

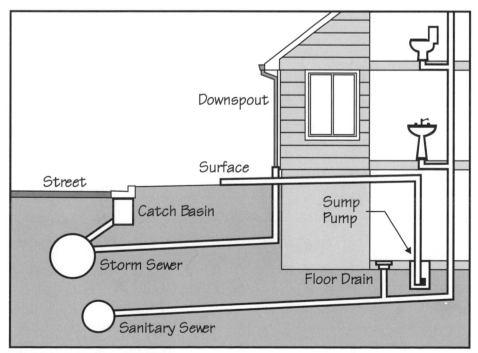

Figure 5-31. Sanitary and Storm Sewers

tary sewer lines. **See Figure 5-32**. This practice is no longer permitted in new home construction. We cannot afford to treat clear water in the sewer treatment plants. We also can't size sanitary sewer systems to accept large quantities of storm water during heavy rains.

If your house doesn't have a sump pump, it probably has a palmer valve— and if so, you should maintain it. **See Figure 5-33**. In the basement, remove the cover from the floor drain and shine a bright flashlight down into it. The palmer valve is a round brass disc at the side of the vertical pipe, just above the water in the trap.

Hook the lower edge of the palmer valve brass disc with a stiff wire or tool to make sure it moves freely—the brass disc should swing easily from the hinge at its top. If this disc is stuck closed (and most of them are), water that collects in the basement drain tile system cannot be drain away. You may end up with water rising in your basement.

To loosen a stuck palmer valve, spray it with lubricating oil a few times over several days, and bang it with a stick or tool. Try to hook the bottom and lift it up. You could also grab it with your hand if you are a brave soul. Or hire a plumber to free the valve.

Natural Gas and Propane

Natural gas and propane are commonly used in central heating systems and may also be used for cooking, drying clothes, and operating fireplaces. Know the basics of the distribution system in your home and how to turn off the system in an emergency.

Natural Gas

Natural gas is provided by a public utility in many areas. Underground piping distributes the gas, and a small line brings it to the house through a metering/control system outside or in the basement. Gas enters your home at very low pressure.

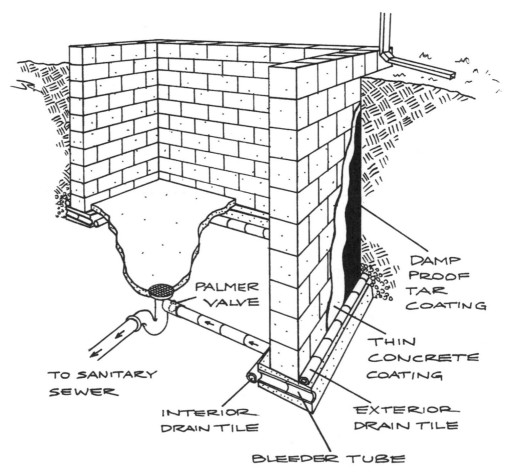

OLDER CONSTRUCTION

DAMP PROOF TAR COATING

THIN CONCRETE COATING

EXTERIOR DRAIN TILE

INTERIOR DRAIN TILE

BLEEDER TUBE

PALMER VALVE

TO SANITARY SEWER

Figure 5-32.

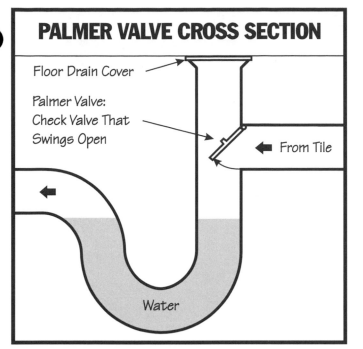

Figure 5-33.

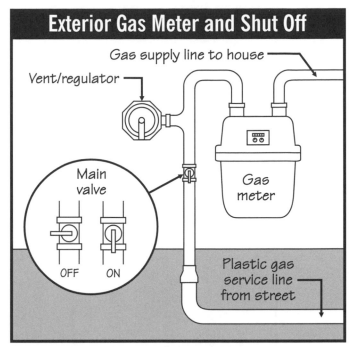

Figure 5-34. Gas Meter & Shut Off

There is a main shutoff valve near the meter, and the system has a relief valve and vent piping for safety. **See Figure 5-34**.

Inside your home, natural gas may be distributed by "black iron" steel-screwed pipes. It can also be distributed by brass or copper pipes, depending on local requirements.

Natural gas piping should be well-supported and protected from damage. There should be a shutoff valve at each appliance connection to the piping. Most fixed gas appliances like the furnace or water heater will be directly connected to the gas piping without a flexible connector. Most connections will include a "drip leg," a small vertical pipe below the appliance connection that catches any contamination before it reaches the gas control valves.

All flexible connectors should be the modern type that extend directly from the gas piping and shutoff valve to the appliance. Normally, flexible connectors are used only with appliances like stoves or dryers that can be moved for maintenance, but areas prone to earthquakes may allow or require flexible connectors at furnaces and water heaters.

The Consumer Product Safety Commission advises that older flexible gas connectors made of uncoated brass can leak. Your connectors should be made of

plastic-coated brass or stainless steel. The CPSC advises that any uncoated brass connector should be immediately replaced by a professional. You will recognize uncoated brass by its coppery color, even if it's old. Older connectors made of flexible aluminum or aluminum piping also should be replaced. See the References section to find out how to contact the CPSC for more information.

If a gas appliance is removed from the system, have a professional turn off the gas valve, cap the line beyond the valve, and check for leaks.

Gas valves turn off with a quarter-turn. When the valve handle is parallel to the piping, the valve is on. When the handle is perpendicular to the piping, the valve is off. Many valves must be turned with an adjustable wrench or pliers. **See Figure 5-35**.

Propane

Propane is a gas that's similar to natural gas, except that propane is provided in a storage tank on your property. Distribution piping is similar to that for natural gas except that there is no meter; you pay for the gas when it's placed in the tank. **See Figure 5-36**.

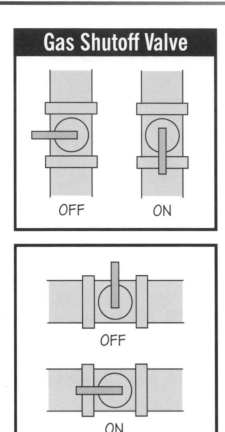

Figure 5-35.

The main shutoff often is at the top of the tank. It may be a valve that requires several turns to shut off the gas. Review the valve and the rest of the system with your supplier. Follow all precautions noted above for natural gas.

Must Know / Must Do
Natural Gas and Propane

- Identify the main shutoff valve and know how it operates.

- Identify the shutoff for every gas appliance.

- Inspect all flexible gas connectors per CPSC standards (noted above).

- If you smell gas, leave the house. Don't light a match, and don't turn on a light. Use a neighbor's phone to call the gas supplier.

It's wise to sign up with a supplier who automatically fills the tank as needed. Often, the supplier can also service your heating equipment.

Heating Oil

Oil can be used in a heating system and may also be used to heat water. An oil system consists of a storage tank, valve, filter, and distribution piping. **See Figure 5-37**. A fill and vent line will extend to the exterior of the house.

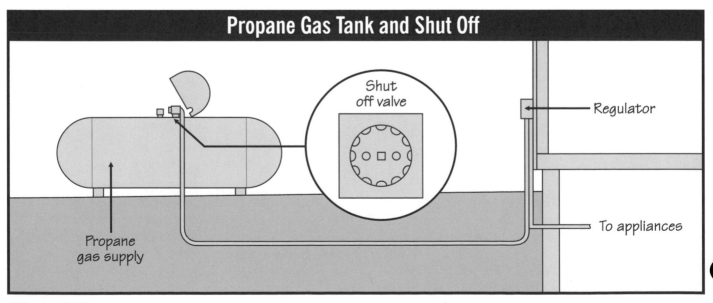

Figure 5-36.

Typical Fuel Oil Tank in Basement

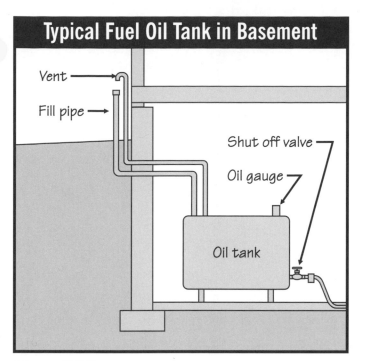

Vent

Fill pipe

Shut off valve

Oil gauge

Oil tank

Figure 5-37.

The oil storage tank often is located in the basement, but it may also be underground in your yard. If your tank is underground, contact the oil supplier or your municipality or state to check maintenance requirements and code regulations. Usually, underground storage tanks are tightly regulated because of the potential for a spill that could contaminate the environment.

Must Know / Must Do
Heating Oil

- Identify the shutoff valve and know how to operate it.

- Never allow the system to run out of oil.

- The system should not smell or leak. Fix all leaks promptly.

- For underground tanks: contact municipal or state agency for registration and maintenance requirements.

Arrange to have a supplier automatically fill the tank and maintain the oil burner. Never, never, never let the system run out of oil—this can lead to a very expensive service call.

Foundation Basics

A foundation provides a stable, rigid base to support a home. The foundation supports the frame and structure and protects it from moisture and contact with the soil. The foundation must rest on firm soil and be protected from water entry or excessive dampness. **See Figure 6-1**.

Foundation types vary with local weather conditions and accepted local practices. In northern climates, the foundation must be deep enough to extend below the frost line. This can be 4 feet or more, so full basements are common. (Frost causes soil to expand, and the foundation must be below the frost line so it won't move with this expansion.) In warmer climates that have little or no frost, the foundation may be a crawl space or concrete slab poured "on grade" or directly on the soil. In a coastal region, the foundation may be piers or posts that raise the house above potential high water levels. In some areas, foundations are made of pressure-treated wood.

The majority of homes, however, are built on foundations that form a crawl space or full basement. The basement rests on a footing that supports the home's weight. Foundation walls are constructed of brick, concrete block, poured concrete, clay tile, stone, or similar materials. The basement floor usually consists of poured concrete. Crawl spaces often have a dirt floor.

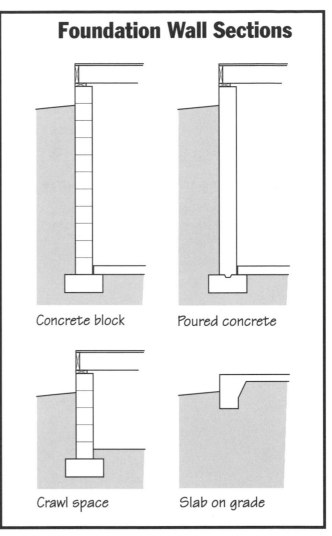

Foundation Wall Sections

Concrete block   Poured concrete

Crawl space   Slab on grade

Figure 6-1.

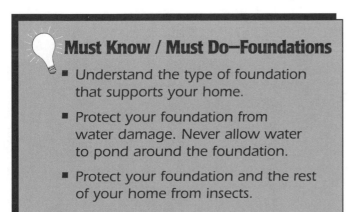

Must Know / Must Do—Foundations

- Understand the type of foundation that supports your home.

- Protect your foundation from water damage. Never allow water to pond around the foundation.

- Protect your foundation and the rest of your home from insects.

Full-depth basements are the most complicated type of foundation because of potential water problems and the pressure of soil outside the basement walls. While full-depth basements require the most maintenance, crawl spaces and slab foundations must also be protected from excessive moisture.

I will focus on the construction and maintenance of full-depth foundations. The necessary maintenance of crawl spaces is similar. For slabs on grade, follow the recommendations for protecting the foundation from water.

Protecting Your Basement

Basements require simple, routine maintenance to prevent damage that requires costly repairs. Since most damage to basements occurs slowly, over many years, if you ignore routine maintenance you may not notice a problem until there is a water leak or a major crack and wall movement. So take some time to inspect your basement and its environment. A little common sense and simple maintenance will prevent potentially serious problems and extend the trouble-free performance of your basement.

Basement/Foundation Works—Course #101

A foundation serves two basic functions: it supports your home, and it holds water and dirt out of the hole in the ground we call a basement. Supporting the home is easy. Block or concrete walls are very strong and rarely have structural load problems. A typical foundation wall can support many times the weight of your home. The tough job for a basement foundation is to resist water, soil and frost pushing against the walls year after year.

To help resist the water and soil pressures, basements use drainage systems and water diversion. **See Figure 6-2**. Water is the major problem. Water soaks soil, making it heavy and potentially fluid. The combination of water, soil and freezing temperatures can product extreme pressure from frozen ground. Keep water away from your walls and you will prevent problems.

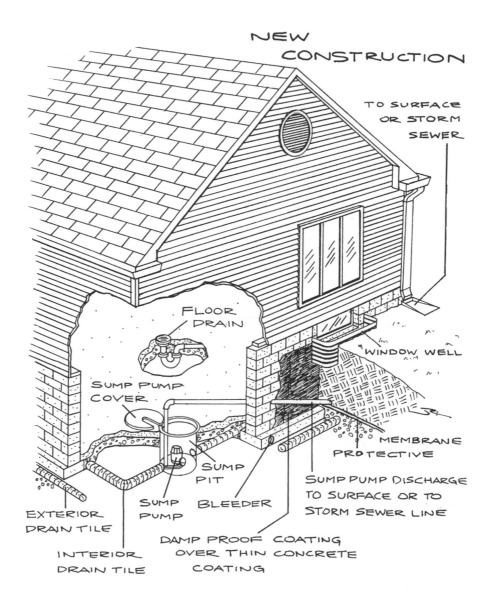

NEW CONSTRUCTION

TO SURFACE OR STORM SEWER

FLOOR DRAIN

WINDOW WELL

SUMP PUMP COVER

MEMBRANE PROTECTIVE

SUMP PIT

SUMP PUMP DISCHARGE TO SURFACE OR TO STORM SEWER LINE

EXTERIOR DRAIN TILE

SUMP PUMP

BLEEDER

INTERIOR DRAIN TILE

DAMP PROOF COATING OVER THIN CONCRETE COATING

Figure 6-2.

Over the years, your home's original water diversion systems require maintenance and repair. They simply can't be ignored. Let's walk through the basics of maintaining your hole in the ground.

Grading to Protect the Foundation

Proper grading around the house is your best protection against seepage into the basement that may cause expensive damage. **See Figure 6-3**. When a home is built, workers dig the excavation several feet larger than the basement walls to allow for construction clearances. At the base of the hole, near the footing, they install a drain tile system and cover it with a small amount of gravel. After they apply a damp-proof coating to the wall, the hole is filled.

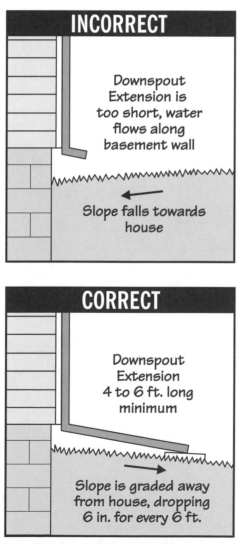

Figure 6-3. Grading, Downspout

Most of the hole around your basement is filled with soil from the site. This may contain gravel, rock, wood, paper, and unfortunately almost anything no longer useful for home construction. For the next 20 years, this soil and "stuff" settles around your basement walls. It settles quickly for the first few years and more slowly after that.

To divert surface water, the soil should pitch away from your home with a 1" pitch per linear foot for about 6 feet beyond the foundation. That is a 6" drop in 6 feet. You can measure this with a level and a straightedge held on top of the soil next to the foundation. At a minimum, the pitch should always have some slope for 6 feet beyond the foundation.

The soil should also be 6" below siding and wood trim to prevent water and insect damage. If wood siding touches the ground, water will wick up and rot the siding and framing. Also, the top course of block is less resistant to soil moisture because it probably lacks the moisture-proof coating applied to lower levels of the foundation wall.

To improve the grade, you have several options, depending on the landscape materials near your home.

Bushes near the foundation, planted above the original foundation hole, often settle. If there is bare soil under the bushes, just add more soil. However, adding more than a few inches of soil can damage bushes by eliminating air from the roots. Check with a professional landscaper on the potential damage to your type of bushes. You may need to raise the bushes and fill under them.

If the area around the foundation has a planting bed or bushes with a ground cover, the soil **under** the ground cover must pitch away from the foundation. **See Figure 6-4**. Dig through the ground cover in several areas to check the grade of the soil. To improve this situation, remove the ground cover and fill with soil. Then replace the ground cover.

You may wish to use a fabric weed barrier or black plastic over the soil. The weed barrier will stop weeds while allowing air and water movement— good for plants but not ideal for the basement.

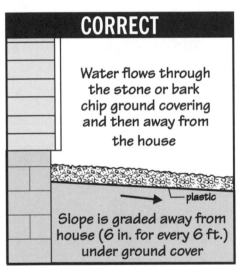

Figure 6-4. Surface Grade

When grading, don't use a light moss-type soil; it will settle too much and hold moisture. In areas where you will not be planting, you can use clay. In planting beds use a blended or brown planting soil, or garden soil. This heavier mixture will not wash away into the yard.

Don't forget to grade areas under decks. You can use black plastic over the properly graded soil to deflect water and stop weeds. A thin cover of gravel or stone will hold down the plastic and make the area more attractive.

All hard surfaces such as walks and driveways should also be pitched away from your foundation. The good news is that only a slight grade, as little as 1/4" per foot, is adequate for hard surfaces. **See Figure 6-5**.

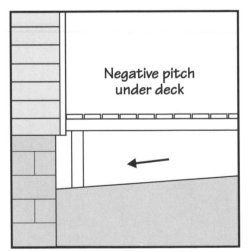

Figure 6-5. Poor Surface Grade

Black plastic does the best job of deflecting water and protecting your basement, but it can be hard on plants. If you use black plastic, cut large holes for plants to improve access to moisture and air.

If there is sod next to the foundation, cut it with a sod cutter and fold it away from the foundation. Add soil, then lay the sod back in place. You could add soil directly over the sod, but that would require re-seeding, and the area will settle as the buried sod decomposes. Cover the sod only if it is in very poor condition or if you need a dramatic change in grade.

For flower beds and bare soil, just add topsoil fill.

Check Gutters and Downspouts

Gutters collect tremendous quantities of water from the roof and must deliver that water away from the foundation. Keep your downspouts extended at least 6 to 8 feet away from the foundation to a spot where the natural grade of the soil continues moving the water away. **See Figure 6-6**.

If your area has underground storm sewers, make sure all downspouts are properly connected to the visible pipe fittings and that water flows into the storm sewer pipe during rainstorms. If this pipe backs up during a storm, it indicates that the storm sewer line is plugged or broken. Test the line by running a hose into the gutter. You can have this line cleaned by a sewer cleaner. **See Figure 6-7**.

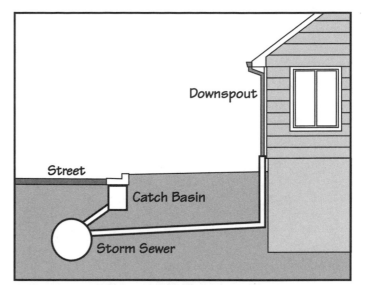

Figure 6-7. Storm Sewer Connection

If dampness and seepage appear on basement walls near an underground storm sewer connection, a broken storm sewer line may be the cause. You can run water into the gutter during a dry spell; if moisture seeps into the basement, it indicates that the underground line is damaged. A sewer cleaner can evaluate and repair the line.

Keep gutters clean to prevent plugging and overflowing of downspouts and storm sewer lines.

Inspect Interior Drainage Systems

When soil conditions—for instance, clay soils—require additional drainage to protect the basement, both interior and exterior drain tile systems may be used. In areas with free-draining soils like gravel or sand, there may be no drain tile system. **See Figure 6-8.**

In some parts of the country, homes may have an exterior drain tile system and an exterior sump with no interior tile.

You can find out about the type of system used in your area by contacting a local home inspector, municipal building inspector or builder.

Any water that does reach your foundation walls will be removed by a properly functioning drain tile

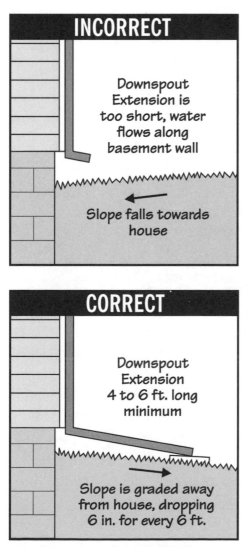

Figure 6-6. Downspout Extension

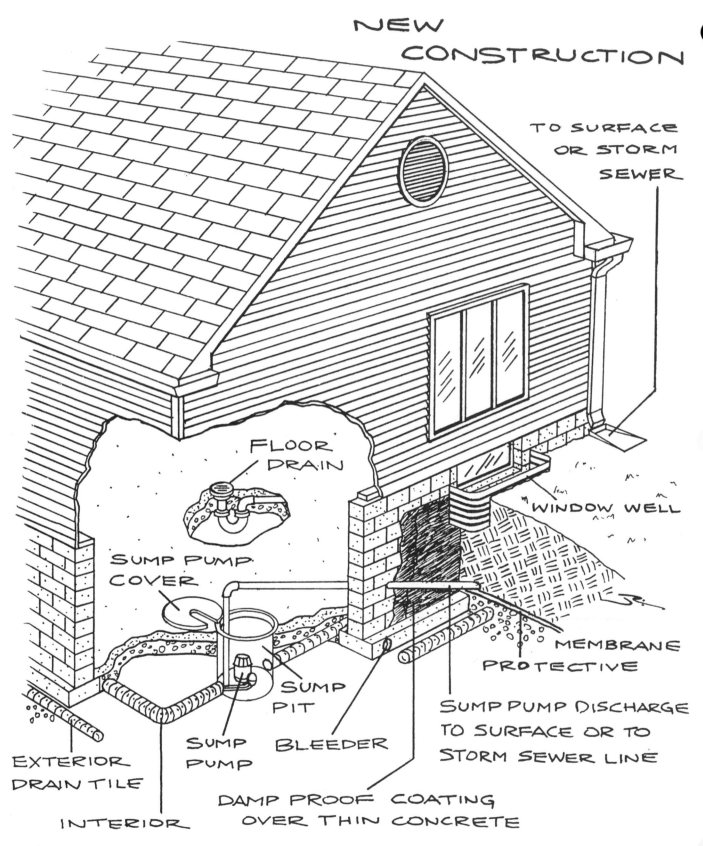

NEW CONSTRUCTION

TO SURFACE OR STORM SEWER

FLOOR DRAIN

WINDOW WELL

SUMP PUMP COVER

MEMBRANE PROTECTIVE

SUMP PIT

SUMP PUMP DISCHARGE TO SURFACE OR TO STORM SEWER LINE

EXTERIOR DRAIN TILE

SUMP PUMP

BLEEDER

INTERIOR

DAMP PROOF COATING OVER THIN CONCRETE

Figure 6-8.

system. There is an interior drain tile loop under the floor slab near the foundation walls. Bleeder tiles through the footings connect this interior loop to drain tiles circling the outside of the foundation.

Homes built around 1900 may not have a drainage system.

A city home built before 1950 will have a drainage system that leads to a valve in the basement floor drain. **See Figure 6-9**. (This valve is identified with various names; in the Midwest, it's called a palmer valve.) Water then flows by gravity down the sanitary sewer lines. Because it routes rainwater into the sanitary sewer, this type of connection is no longer used.

In newer homes, the drainage system leads to a sump pump that pumps the water up to the exterior grade or to a storm sewer line.

Maintain Drainage Systems

The sump pump removes water that collects in the drain tile system around the footing and basement walls and floor. Your basement is a hole in the ground, and nature tries to fill that hole with water, mud and soil. Removing groundwater with the sump pump protects the floor and walls from water pressure and helps keep the basement dry.

In a properly designed and installed system, the sump pump turns on when the water level is 8" to 12" below the bottom edge of the drain tile entering the crock. Periodically test the pump to be sure it is moving water out of the crock. To trigger the pump, lift the float or add water to the crock. Don't just listen for the pump to run—make sure water is removed. The pump should turn off when the sump crock is almost empty or just before the pump starts drawing air.

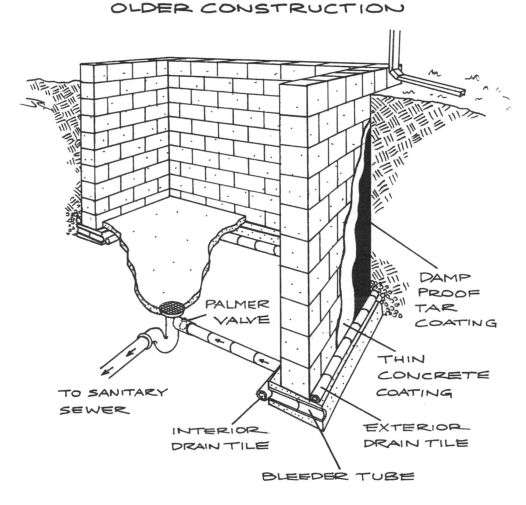

OLDER CONSTRUCTION

PALMER VALVE

TO SANITARY SEWER

INTERIOR DRAIN TILE

BLEEDER TUBE

EXTERIOR DRAIN TILE

THIN CONCRETE COATING

DAMP PROOF TAR COATING

Figure 6-9.

At most times the water level in the crock should be 8" to 12" below the floor slab and below the connecting interior drain tiles. The tiles leading into the sump pump crock should not be filled with water.

Ideally, you want the sump pump crock to hold a reservoir of water so the pump does not turn on and off frequently, removing only a small amount of water each time it runs. Often, the sump crock is shallow, so when the pump is set to turn on at 12" below the floor, it only removes a few inches of water before turning off. Correcting this problem may require extending the bottom of the crock or installing a deeper crock.

Outside, if the sump pump discharges on the soil around your foundation, extend this discharge pipe just as you may have extended the downspouts. You can also make an underground connection from the sump to a storm sewer line.

If your house doesn't have a sump, look in the basement floor drain for the palmer valve. **See Figure 6-10**. This is a round brass disc on the side of the vertical pipe, just above the water in the trap. This disc should always open freely to drain water from the tile system into the sewer line. If the palmer valve is stuck closed, water may back up into your basement near the base of the wall and the wall floor joint. Eventually, water backup will damage basement walls.

Hook the palmer valve flap with a stiff wire to check whether it moves freely. If the valve is stuck closed (which is usually the case), spray it with penetrating oil several times over a few days. Then break it loose with your hand, a pry bar or a stick. The valve must swing open easily to drain away water.

The 100-year-old homes without drainage systems were almost always built with the foundation only 4 or 5 feet "in the hole." This helps prevent excessive water and soil pressure. These homes may also have thicker basement walls. Maintenance of grading and gutters is key to these basements, and normally they perform without problems except for minor seepage during very wet weather.

Check Trees and Shrubs

Trees and large bushes can damage basement drainage tiles, sewer lines and even foundation walls. Now don't remove all your trees and bushes!

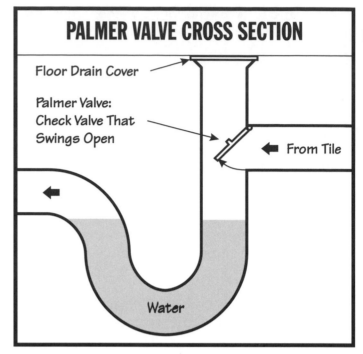

PALMER VALVE CROSS SECTION

Floor Drain Cover

Palmer Valve:
Check Valve That
Swings Open

← From Tile

Water

Figure 6-10.

Use common sense to determine whether there is a problem.

Roots of trees and bushes look for moisture. They can find moisture in basement drain tiles and sewer lines. If roots plug the drain lines, basement drainage can be slowed, and water-saturated soil outside the foundation can cause wall damage. Very large tree and bush roots can push in basement block walls. Trees can also break sewer lines, causing a backup into your basement.

Check for potential problems by following these tips.

- A tree's root area usually is bigger than its leaf area. If a tree rubs against or hangs over your home, its roots may cause problems in your basement.

- Willow, locust, cottonwood and Chinese elm trees are particularly troublesome in extending their roots into sewer and drain lines. Their roots extend much further than those of other treees.

- Inspect your sump pump crock and the drain lines at the crock. There should be no roots inside.

- Locate the main sewer line in the basement. Find the sewer cleanout—a large cap in the floor, normally near the water main/meter. Then look outside from the cleanout area to the streeet; no large trees should be growing over the sewer line. If you have storm sewers, also check the underground lines from the down spouts and the sump pump discharge to the storm lines under the street.

- Small trees and bushes growing in window wells or within 2 feet of the foundation may pose a problem.

Window Wells

Window wells hold soil away from foundation windows as the grade is raised. The window well should fit tightly against the foundation wall to prevent leaks. **See Figure 6-11**. The grade around the well should pitch away so water isn't directed into the well. If a window well fills with water, check the fit of the well and the grade around it.

Keep window wells clean and free of all plant material. Fill the bottom of the well with gravel to allow for good drainage and to stop any plant growth.

If the grade and fit around the window well are in good condition but the well still fills with water, dig out the bottom of the well about 18" and fill with washed stone. The stone will ensure proper drainage to the tile system. If you have a problem window well, dig down several feet inside it with a post hole digger; then fill the hole with washed stone. This channel helps drain the window well to

the basement tile. However, you should only dig this channel if you know the drain tile system is working. If it isn't, you will create a tube of frozen water that can push against the basement wall.

Basements—The Bottom Line

If you follow these simple inspection and maintenance tips, your basement will perform for many years without failure. All basements have some problem symptoms, but if you maintain your basement, minor problems will not become major crises. If you notice severe drainage problems, wall cracks or wall movement, contact a professional home inspector or basement consultant to evaluate your specific situation.

If a major problem is identified, don't feel threatened, and don't jump at the first evaluation or repair proposal. It often takes years for a basement problem to develop, and the situation will not require immediate repair. Take time to solicit several evaluations and repair proposals. Check each contractor's references, and make sure the contractor belongs to a professional builders' or remodelers' organization.

Structure, Frame and Siding

The structural frame of your home rests on the foundation or basement and holds up the floors, interior walls, and roof. **See Figure 6-12**. Most homes in the U.S. are framed with wood, but a few are built with a brick or block support structure. Once the frame and structure are properly designed and installed, little maintenance is needed except to protect the structure from water and insects.

Platform Framing

Most homes are built with platform framing. The framing starts with a "platform" of floor joists built over the foundation walls. **See Figure 6-13**. The joists suppport the deck. There is usually a beam down the center of the foundation that supports the center of the joists. Posts resting on footings and the foundation wall support the beam.

A variety of materials are used. Wood joists can be manufactured of plywood and wood products. Beams can be steel, wood or manufactured wood products. The platform decking can be wood,

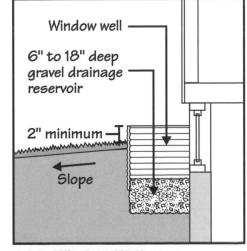

Figure 6-11. Window Well

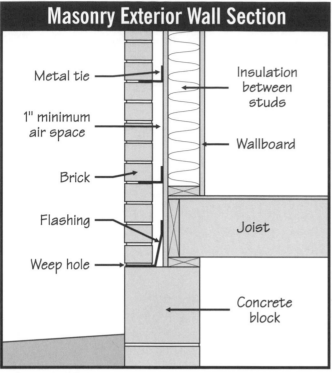

Figure 6-12.

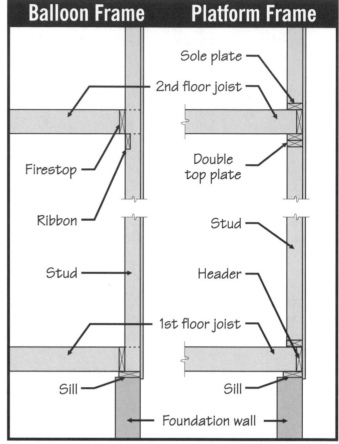

Figure 6-13.

plywood, oriented strand boards or other special products. Metal studs can be used in place of wood studs. Joists can be replaced with trusses.

The rest of the structure arises above this first platform. It is supported with 2 by 4 or 2 by 6 exterior walls and interior support walls. For a two-story home, a second platform is built above the first floor

walls, and then more walls are framed above this platform. Finally, a roof is framed above the wall framing.

The basic platform frame has many possible variations. An older home may have "balloon" framing in which exterior wall studs extend from the foundation to the roof without platforms. Some homes are built with post and beam framing like that used for barns. Some homes have brick or block exterior walls that support the structure.

Since your home's framing is completed, all you need to know (if it's performing well) is that you shouldn't modify the structure of your home without contacting a professional.

Exterior Walls

The exterior walls are framed to support the structure, allow for window and door openings, and protect the structure from the elements. Most exterior walls are framed with 2 by 4 studs spaced 16" on center. The studs are braced in the corners and doubled around window and door openings. Special "headers" are placed over openings to support the weight above the opening. **See Figure 6-14**.

Exterior wall framing allows space for electrical, cable, telephone and heat distribution components. The framing also supports exterior siding or cladding and includes space for insulation.

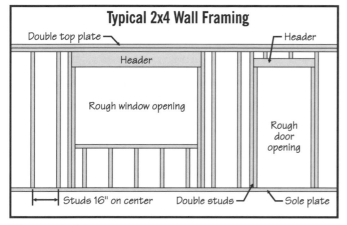

Figure 6-14.

Siding

Many options exist for siding homes: brick, stone, wood, aluminum, vinyl, cement, asbestos, logs, steel siding, wood products, stucco, and even steel panels. Identify the type of siding you have, and maintain the surface. This usually requires caulking and painting. Watch for excessive movement, water leaks and excessive paint damage.

Remember that homes built before 1978 may be painted with lead-based paints. Take special precautions if these finishes chip and flake or if you need to remove them. See the chapter on Environmental and Safety Concerns as well as the References section for more information on lead hazards.

Must Know / Must Do—Siding

- Maintain all painted surfaces.
- Maintain caulk and sealants.
- Be aware of potential lead hazards.

Brick

So you have an all-brick home, and it is beautiful, low-maintenance, cozy and warm. Brick homes are beautiful and valuable, but very few really have a brick structure; rather, they're brick veneer. Don't worry, you **want** a home that's brick veneer.

If your home was built before 1900, there is a chance that it actually has a brick structure. That means the exterior wall is solid brick, several layers thick, and the brick supports the home's framing and floors. Very few modern brick homes are built this way.

A typical modern brick home has a wood frame that supports the structure. The brick is applied as a veneer or siding over the outside. This method allows for better insulation of walls and a more user-friendly stucture that meets the needs of modern construction. **See Figure 6-15**.

With brick veneer, you do need to watch for cracking and movement, as well as deterioration of mortar joints. Most brick veneer performs well for years with little maintenance.

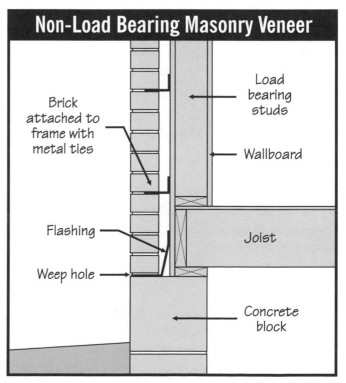

Figure 6-15.

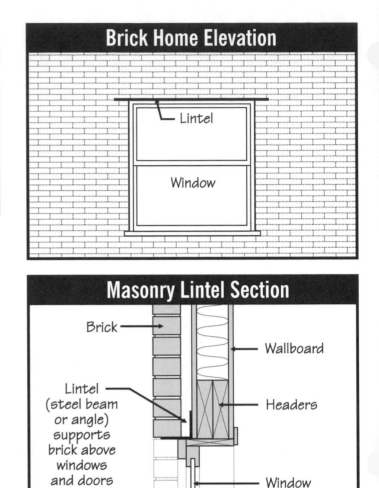

Brick Home Elevation

Lintel

Window

Masonry Lintel Section

Brick

Wallboard

Lintel
(steel beam
or angle)
supports
brick above
windows
and doors

Headers

Window

Figure 6-16.

Must Know / Must Do—Brick

- Maintain steel lintels.
- Watch for cracks or excessive movement.
- Maintain caulk and sealants at penetrations and windows/doors.

One important element of maintenance involves the steel lintels over window and door openings. A lintel is a steel angle iron or beam that supports the masonry above the opening. **See Figure 6-16.** Since window frames and door frames are not designed to support masonry, the lintel spans the opening and transfers the load to the masonry on either side. The exposed steel of the lintel must be painted with exterior metal paint to prevent rust. If the lintel rusts, the metal expands, creating cracks in the mortar joints at the top corners of the openings. If excessive rust builds up, the lintel will fail and must be replaced.

Look at any brick building and you'll probably see many rusted lintels causing mortar cracking and failure. You may also see that in some buildings, arches, cast concrete or large stones span the openings, eliminating the need for a metal lintel.

Windows and Doors

It would take an entire book to cover all types of windows and doors and their maintenance. I will cover basic types and provide important maintenance tips. For specific information on maintaining and repairing the windows and doors in your home, contact the manufacturer. The References section contains information on manufacturers and after-market repair parts.

Maintenance information and parts are readily available for windows and doors produced in the last 20 years. For older windows and doors, you will rarely find information and must rely on after-market products. Thousands of companies produced windows and doors through the years, and many are no longer in business.

Windows

Windows come in all shapes, sizes and types. Various types include double-hung, casement, sliders, hopper, fixed, garden, bow and bay. The list goes on and on.

Materials used for window frames include wood, steel, aluminum, vinyl, and combinations of these products. Higher-cost windows have wood framing on the inside for enhanced appearance and a metal coating on the outside for low maintenance.

There are also many glass options. In older homes you will find the basic single-pane glass, usually with a separate storm window. From there we have insulated glass consisting of two panes with a sealed air space between layers. Newer insulated glass is improved with an invisible "low E" coating on one side that lowers heat transmission. Glass can also be tripled-glazed, meaning there are three sealed panes. Other modern advances include a special inert gas that fills the space between panes; special coatings; and insulating spacers.

The keys to maintaining your window are to (1) keep exterior portions of the window weathertight, and (2) maintain painted and varnished surfaces.

On the outside, maintain all painted surfaces and the glazing compound that seals the window glass to the sash. Make sure that caulk which seals the window frame to the brick or siding is tight and secure. Investigate excessive mildew or peeling paint—these are signs of moisture problems.

The spacing between the primary (interior) window and the storm window on an older system can cause problems. Most storms have a small slot or hole on the lower edge, next to the wooden sill. This "weep hole," which is 1/4" or smaller, allows condensation and water to drain ("weep") to the outside, preventing rot and mildew that could cause serious damage. However, well-intentioned home-owners sometimes caulk weep holes shut, hoping to save energy. Weep holes should always be left open. **See Figure 6-17**.

Meticulously check and maintain the condition of painted wood-framed windows and doors. Pay special attention to south-facing surfaces because the sun accelerates deterioration of caulk, paint and glazing products. Check the corners and ends of wood framing; this is where wood rot starts, and it can cause serious problems.

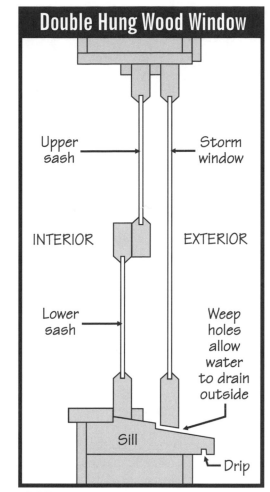

Figure 6-17.

If you are lucky enough to have casement windows—great. They seal tightly and work well. But when they stick, it is easy to damage the crank mechanism. If you are trying to open a sticky casement window, never force the crank. It will break. Remove the screen and then gently force the window open with your hand, not with the crank.

To open a sticky double-hung or slider window, try to jar the window closed by striking the frame with a closed fist. Be careful. Don't hit it so hard that you break the glass. If the window is painted shut, you must break away all the paint before you try to open it.

Garage Doors

Garage doors are made of hundreds of possible combinations of materials, rollers, tracks, operators, springs, locks, and other options. Your main responsibilities are to maintain finishes, tighten

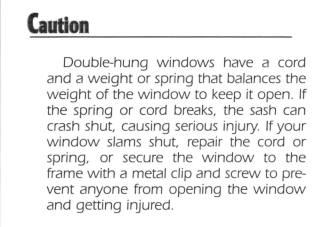

Caution

Double-hung windows have a cord and a weight or spring that balances the weight of the window to keep it open. If the spring or cord breaks, the sash can crash shut, causing serious injury. If your window slams shut, repair the cord or spring, or secure the window to the frame with a metal clip and screw to prevent anyone from opening the window and getting injured.

> ## Must Know / Must Do
> ## Windows
>
> - Maintain paint, putty, caulk and glazing compounds.
> - Check the "weep holes" of storm windows.
> - Repair broken sash cords and springs to prevent injury.
> - Peeling paint on older windows may be a lead hazard – **See Chapter 2**.

> ## Must Know / Must Do
> ## Garage Door
>
> - Maintain painted finishes on the door.
> - Tighten hardware twice a year.
> - Hire a professional for repair of springs, cables and rollers.
> - Check with the manufacturer of your door for specific maintenance information. **See References section**.

hardware, and test the safety of operation. **See Figure 6-18**.

Many garage doors are made of wood and wood products that require routine painting. When you paint a garage door, paint all six sides of each panel. Don't neglect the inside of the door panel, and don't neglect the edges.

Hardware—rollers, hinges and tracks—requires routine maintenance. Because the doors are open and closed so often, hardware and fasteners are always being jarred and bounced, which loosens bolts, screws and other fasteners and eventually affects the smooth operation of the door. Tighten all hardware on your garage door at least twice a year. Put the door in the closed position, make sure all hinges and rollers are aligned, and then tighten bolts and nuts. Inspect rollers to make sure that they line up with the tracks. Tracks should be parallel to the edges of the door. Replace any rollers that have damaged bearings. Lubricate rollers and hinges with a special garage door lubricant, silicone spray, or light oil.

If the door has damaged springs, pulleys or cables, have them repaired by a professional. These springs store tremendous amounts of force, and they can cause serious injury if not handled properly. Professional service is also a good option if the door is not properly aligned to the tracks and the frame opening.

Garage Door Openers

Many of us take our garage door openers for granted: push the button, and we drive into our

dry and lighted garage. These openers provide many years of trouble-free service, but they do require routine maintenance and safety tests. An improperly maintained garage door opener poses a safety hazard.

Contact the manufacturer of your opener for specific safety and maintenance requirements. See the References section.

Follow these safety precautions:

- Do not stand or walk under a moving door. Do not try to rush under a door as it closes.

- Keep the remote control units away from children.

- Explain to children that garage doors are not toys and that the door can hurt them.

- Mount the pushbutton control at least 5 feet from the floor to keep it out of reach of children. **See Figure 6-19**.

- When closing the door, observe it until it is fully closed.

- Check the safety reverse once monthly.

Every garage door should have a safety device that reverses the door if it meets resistance while closing. Very old units may not have a safety reverse; these should be replaced.

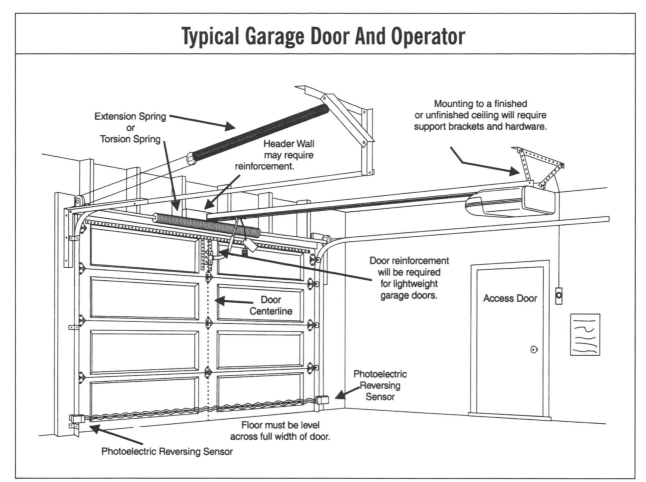

Typical Garage Door And Operator

Extension Spring
or
Torsion Spring

Header Wall
may require
reinforcement.

Mounting to a finished
or unfinished ceiling will require
support brackets and hardware.

Door reinforcement
will be required
for lightweight
garage doors.

Door
Centerline

Access Door

Photoelectric
Reversing
Sensor

Floor must be level
across full width of door.

Photoelectric Reversing Sensor

Figure 6-18.

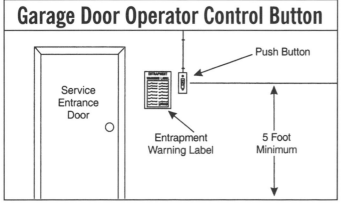

Garage Door Operator Control Button

Push Button

Service
Entrance
Door

Entrapment
Warning Label

5 Foot
Minimum

Figure 6-19.

Openers manufactured after April 1, 1982, must
have a safety reverse that activates after striking a 1"-
high object. Openers manufactured before that time
were required to reverse off a 2" object. If your door
does not reverse with the 1" test, replace it.

Must Know / Must Do
Garage Door Openers

- Follow all safety precautions.

- Perform monthly safety tests of the automatic reverse.

- Check the balance of the door once a year.

- Always consult a professional for repair of springs, pulleys and cables.

- Contact the manufacturer for specific safety and maintenance recommendations. See the References section for contact information.

Openers sold after 1993 also have a photocell. When anything blocks or crosses the photocell beam as the door is closing, the door reverses. If your garage door opener doesn't have this optical safety device, I suggest you replace it with one that does.

Here's the procedure for the monthly safety reverse test. (Check with the manufacturer of your operator for more specific details)

1. With the door open, place a 1"-thick block under the center of the door. Use an actual 1"-thick object, not a nominal 1" piece of wood that is actually ¾" thick. A 2 by 4 laid flat is often used for this test. **See Figure 6-20**.

2. Activate the opener to close the door.

3. When the door hits the piece of wood, it should reverse and reopen.

4. Activate the opener again. This time, as the door closes, hold up the bottom of the door with your hand. The door should reverse with a few pounds of pressure.

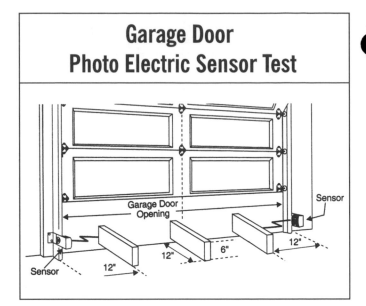

Garage Door
Photo Electric Sensor Test

Figure 6-21.

6. If the opener fails any of these tests, consult a qualified professional for adjustments and repair.

If the remote control fails to operate your garage door, first check for a weak or dead battery in the remote unit. A cold receiver unit with a weak battery could also cause this problem. If batteries are good, check the transmitter and receiver codes and the antenna on the receiver.

Your garage door opener is designed to open and close a balanced garage door. Strong springs provide lift that balances the weight of the door. If the operator unit sounds loud and works very hard to open or close the door, the door may be unbalanced or there may be a broken spring or damaged hardware.

Inspect the springs and hardware. If there is any damage, consult a professional.

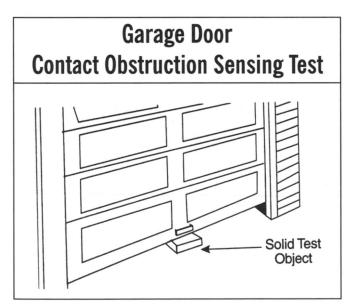

Garage Door
Contact Obstruction Sensing Test

Figure 6-20.

5. If your door has a photocell safety control, perform the test again by breaking the beam as the door closes. The door should reverse itself. **See Figure 6-21**. You can test the door with a 6 by 12 inch object placed progressively along the door opening. With the object in place, the door should stop and reverse to the full open position.

You can also test the balance of the door if the springs appear to be in good condition. Start with the door closed. If you start with the door open, it can crash shut, causing damage and possible injury. With the door closed, disconnect the release mechanism—a cord or lever where the operator arm attaches to the operator frame. **See Figure 6-22**. You should then be able to lift the door with little resistance; the door should "balance" around the center of its motion. If the door is hard to lift and

Garage Door Emergency Release

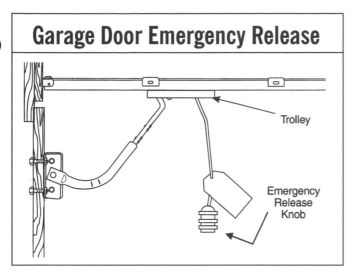

Trolley

Emergency
Release
Knob

Figure 6-22.

does not balance, consult a professional to adjust the spring mechanism. Don't attempt to adjust the springs yourself. They store a dangerous amount of energy and can easily injure you.

Insulation and Ventilation

All homes are insulated in some fashion to protect against heat loss and gain. Older homes may have little insulation; newer homes have insulation that meets government standards for energy efficiency.

Ventilation systems remove excessive moisture and protect insulation from moisture damage. Vapor retarders or barriers prevent moisture from flowing into insulation.

Insulation

Most newer homes are insulated with fiberglass, cellulose fiber, rigid plastic foam, or a combination of these products. Older homes may have vermiculite, wood shavings, paper products, and other types of insulation. Often, homeowners add insulation to walls and attics of older homes to increase energy efficiency.

Insulation is rated with an R-value, which simply indicates the resistance to heat flow. The higher the R-value, the higher the resistance. The key thing to remember is that when you double the R-value, you cut the heat loss in half; so the first several inches of insulation result in huge energy savings.

Most fiberglass is rated at about R-3 per inch of thickness. A 6"-thick section is fiberglass would be rated about R-19. **See Figure 6-23**. The R-value for rigid foam ranges from 5 to 7 per inch. Cellulose and mineral wool provide about R-3 per inch.

Typical Wall Section (2x6 Framed)

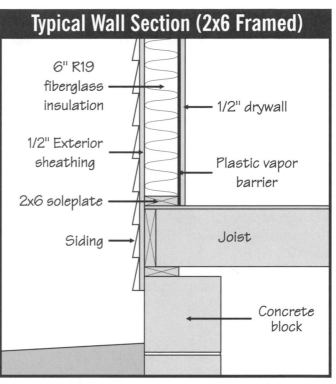

6" R19 fiberglass insulation

1/2" drywall

1/2" Exterior sheathing

Plastic vapor barrier

2x6 soleplate

Siding

Joist

Concrete block

Figure 6-23.

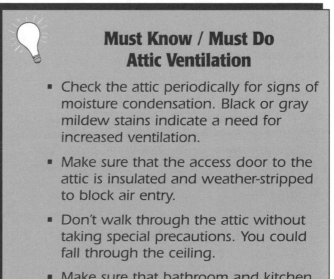

Must Know / Must Do
Attic Ventilation

- Check the attic periodically for signs of moisture condensation. Black or gray mildew stains indicate a need for increased ventilation.

- Make sure that the access door to the attic is insulated and weather-stripped to block air entry.

- Don't walk through the attic without taking special precautions. You could fall through the ceiling.

- Make sure that bathroom and kitchen exhaust fans aren't dumping moist air into the attic.

Insulation recommendations vary with climate conditions and state code requirements. In northern climates, attics are insulated to R-38 or more, and walls are insulated to R-19 or more. In southern zones, attics are insulated to about R-26 and walls to R-11.

Vapor Barriers

Vapor barriers or vapor retarders protect insulation and structural framing from moisture damage. Vapor barriers are usually made of polyethylene film. They can also be aluminum foil or kraft paper (brown paper coated with tar).

The vapor barrier, placed behind drywall, plaster or wood flooring and in front of insulation, prevents moisture from moving through the surface and penetrating the insulation. The barrier also prevents air movement through walls and floors; air movement carries tremendous amounts of water vapor.

If moisture were allowed to enter the insulation, it would condense on the cold wood framing of the exterior, causing water damage and potential rot.

In hot and humid climates, such as southern Florida, vapor barriers are not used because the relative humidity outdoors is greater than that in the home, and moisture tends to move into the house. If you have questions about requirements for vapor barriers in your area, consult the local building inspector.

Attic Ventilation

No matter how well a home is constructed, moisture will reach the attic; it's impossible to completely seal this area. So ventilation is necessary to remove moisture and excessive heat from the attic. This is achieved through various combinations of roof vents, soffit vents, gable end vents, ridge vents, and ventilation fans. **See Figure 6-24**.

For proper air flow, ventilation must be provided both high and low on the roof. Heat and wind help the vents move air through the attic. As an additional benefit, ventilation reduces the temperature inside the attic, lowering the cost of air conditioning and extending the life of an asphalt shingle roof.

Bathroom and kitchen exhaust fans are needed to remove excessive moisture, but they must be routed

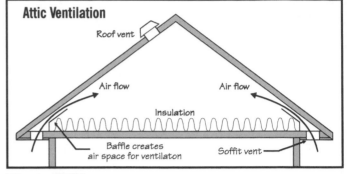

Figure 6-24.

to an exterior wall or through the roof. Make sure that the exhaust fans in your home aren't dumping moist air into the attic.

Vapor Barrier in Crawl Space

A crawl space or dirt floor in the basement can release significant amounts of moisture in your home. Even if the soil looks dry, moisture may evaporate from the surface. Cover any bare dirt with a thick (6-mil) poly vapor barrier. The barrier should provide a continuous cover with joints overlapped 12". Edges should lap up several inches on the foundation wall. Place stones or gravel atop the barrier to keep it in place.

Bathroom Ventilation

Ventilation for bathrooms has been required for many years. The minimum requirement is a window or an exhaust fan. Most of us would prefer, and our homes would like, a dedicated exhaust fan controlled by a switch in the bathroom. This allows us to effectively remove excessive moisture from showers and baths.

Confirm the discharge location of your fan. Make sure it discharges moisture through an exterior wall or through the roof. **See Figure 6-25**. These fans remove a tremendous amount of moisture, and you don't want that moisture in your attic.

Homes built prior to 1980 often have ventilation fans that exhaust into the attic space. These should be rerouted through the roof with a simple vent kit available at building supply centers. If there are adequate roof vents, you can route the exhaust duct into a roof vent.

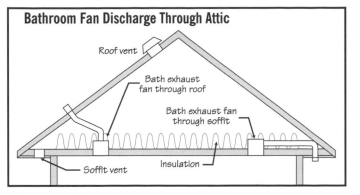

Bathroom Fan Discharge Through Attic

Roof vent

Bath exhaust
fan through roof

Bath exhaust fan
through soffit

Insulation

Soffit vent

Figure 6-25.

Often, bath exhaust fans can't keep up with the steam of a hot shower, and the bathroom remains full of moisture. This can cause excessive condensation, mildew, peeling paint, and damage to windows. A simple solution is to replace the ordinary fan switch with a timer switch—the type found on heat lamps. Use a timer that will operate for 1 or 2 hours, and run the fan for a timed period after you leave.

Roofs and Gutters

Roof framing and roofing materials contribute significantly to the look and style of your home. The roof also protects your home from the elements. While a roof is easy to ignore, its components do need routine maintenance.

Performing this maintenance requires access to the gutters and valleys and may involve walking on the roof. It's essential to follow all safety precautions for working at heights and climbing ladders. While some homeowners are comfortable with ladders and heights, others are not. If you are not completely comfortable with the idea of working on your roof, hire a professional.

Roof Styles and Framing

Many roof designs are dictated by the style of the home and the spans between exterior walls. Roofs are also designed to accommodate snow loads, winds, and other environmental factors.

All roofs have structural framing of joists or trusses that support a wood deck. The deck may be boards, plywood or oriented strand board. Roofing material is attached to the wood deck. **See Figure 6-26**.

In general, the two basic styles are sloped and low-slope (or flat) roofs.

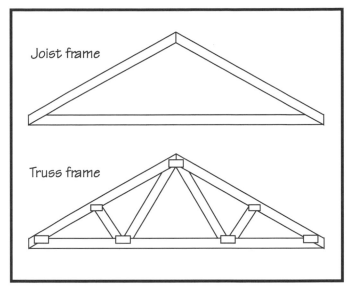

Joist frame

Truss frame

Figure 6-26.

Sloped roofs are those with a slope greater than "4 in 12" or $^4/_{12}$. This is equivalent to a $^1/_4$ slope (just convert the fraction), meaning that the roof drops 1 foot for every 4 feet of horizontal run. To determine the slope of your roof, level a 4-foot board and measure the drop at the outer edge. If the pitch drops 4 feet within this 4-foot length, the slope is 4 in 4—and, by extension, 12 in 12. This is often expressed as a $^{12}/_{12}$ roof. Styles of sloped roofs include gable, shed, hip, gambrel, mansard, and combinations of various types. **Figure 6-27**.

Low-slope or flat roofs have a slope that is less than 4 in 12. These require special waterproof or membrane materials because they do not shed water as well as roofs with a steeper slope. Most "flat" roofs do have a slight pitch to drain water to the edges or to roof drains.

Other components of a roof include valley and sidewall flashings, edge flashings, and flashings at all roof penetrations. The roof will have a ventilation system and may have a gutter and drainage system.

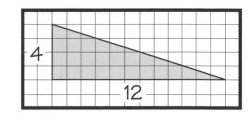

4

12

Figure 6-27.

Roofing Materials

Asphalt shingles are the material most commonly used on conventional pitched roofs (1 in 4 and greater). An organic or fiberglass "mat" that forms the body of the shingle is covered with granules to protect the mat from the sun and add color and visual variety. A typical asphalt shingle will last from 15 to 40 years, depending on the original quality and local weather conditions. Asphalt shingles come in many shapes and sizes. Some are designed to imitate wood or tile.

Other materials used for pitched roofs include wood shakes, wood shingles, cement asbestos, tile, slate, metal, and cement tile. All of these are more expensive than asphalt shingles, but they offer unique design qualities and potentially longer life. Tile, slate and cement often last 50 years or more and are highly resistant to sun damage, wind and fire. However, heavier roof materials require special structural designs. **See Figure 6-28**.

Low-slope or flat roofs require a special roofing material to seal against moisture. Since the slope is low, water does not easily run from the surface. Materials used include single-ply rubber, roll roof-ing, torch down (a modified bitumen), metal, and built-up roofing. Rubber roofing is quite common; technically, this material is ethylene propylene diene monomer, or EPDM. All of these materials require special installation and maintenance by experienced contractors.

A flat roof should have a slight slope to prevent ponding of water. Roof drains may be placed along the edges or in the center.

Gutters and Downspouts

When it rains, your roof sheds a tremendous quantity of water that must be moved away from the foundation to protect the basement or crawl spaces. Gutters, downspouts and downspout extensions serve this function.

Gutters may drain to the surface of your yard. They may be channeled underground to drain into a lower area of your yard. In urban areas, where storm systems collect rainwater, gutters may drain underground into the storm sewer system. For more information on storm sewers, see the section about basements. **See Figure 6-29**.

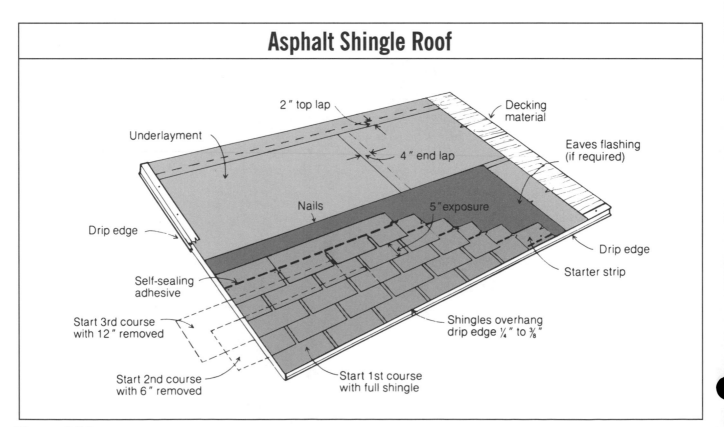

Asphalt Shingle Roof

2" top lap
Decking material
Underlayment
4" end lap
Eaves flashing (if required)
Nails
5" exposure
Drip edge
Drip edge
Starter strip
Self-sealing adhesive
Start 3rd course with 12" removed
Shingles overhang drip edge ¼" to ⅜"
Start 2nd course with 6" removed
Start 1st course with full shingle

Figure 6-28.

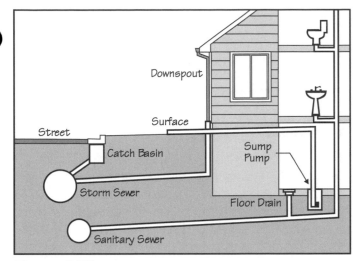

Figure 6-29.

Roofing material manufacturers provide excellent free information in printed materials and on their websites. See the References section for details on how to contact them.

Chimney, Flue and Vent

When you burn natural gas, oil, wood or any other fossil fuel, the toxic smoke and other products of combustion must be vented from your home through the chimney. Toxic gas rises up the chimney and flows outside because the gas is lighter than air. Various types of chimneys will accomplish this effect. You should understand chimney basics and know how to recognize problems.

Masonry Chimney

An older home may have a masonry or brick/stone chimney. **See Figure 6-30**. This type of chimney can vent a wood-burning fireplace as well as an appliance like a furnace or water heater. The clay tile liner of a masonry chimney provides a smooth, uninterrupted surface that eases the flow of combustion gas. The liner harnesses combustion products and protects the brick of the chimney from heat and moisture.

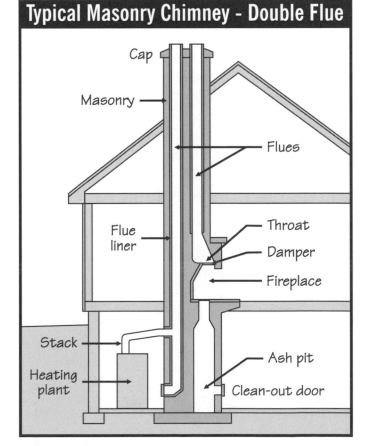

Figure 6-30.

You can view the tan or red tile liner by looking down into the chimney from the top or peering up the fireplace with a flashlight. It's common for a masonry chimney to have several flue liners. Gas and oil appliances often share a liner but cannot use the same flue as a wood-burning fireplace.

A home built before 1900 may have a masonry chimney with no clay tile liner; instead, the inside has exposed brick and some mortar coating. Never use this type of chimney without evaluation by a specialist. Also, be aware that this chimney can't be used to vent a gas appliance.

Must Know / Must Do
Chimneys and Vent Pipes

- Never modify a chimney or flue pipe. Hire a professional for repairs and maintenance.

- Frequently inspect the vent pipe and draft hood. It should not be corroded, loose or leaking.

- Vent pipes are hot. Provide adequate clearance—at least 6" away from any combustible material. Don't use vent pipes as storage shelves or as racks to dry rags.

- Schedule professional inspection and cleaning for wood-burning stoves and fireplaces. The frequency of the need for maintenance depends on how often you build fires. Annual inspections are the norm.

- Routinely check the condition of the chimney top. A masonry chimney must have tile, brick mortar, flashings and the concrete cap in excellent condition to prevent serious moisture problems. A metal chimney must have a cap in good condition. Chimney damage can create safety problems.

- Install a carbon monoxide alarm.

- Add a rain cap to your chimney to keep out rain and animals.

Metal Chimney

A newer home may have a metal chimney, which may be a simple round chimney pipe with a metal liner. A metal chimney might be built into a masonry or wood chimney structure. **See Figure 6-31**.

All Chimneys

Chimneys look simple, but they are actually complex devices, designed and installed with safety in mind. Chimney designs take into account the type of fuel burned, the heat of the fire, the size of the burner or fireplace, the height of the chimney, the horizontal distance to any appliance they vent, and other factors.

A flue pipe or smoke pipe connects gas- and oil-fired appliances to a chimney. **See Figure 6-32**. This pipe, specifically sized for the appliance, must be pitched upward into the chimney. The gas appliance also has a special draft hood or draft diverter that allows air to enter the flue pipe, helping to create a proper draft up the chimney. At the chimney, the flue pipes are connected to the flue liner by special metal connectors or mortar.

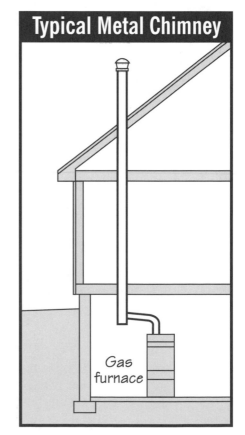

Typical Metal Chimney

Gas furnace

Figure 6-31.

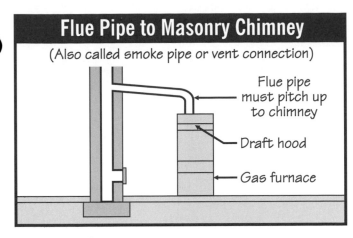

Flue Pipe to Masonry Chimney
(Also called smoke pipe or vent connection)

Flue pipe must pitch up to chimney

Draft hood

Gas furnace

Figure 6-32.

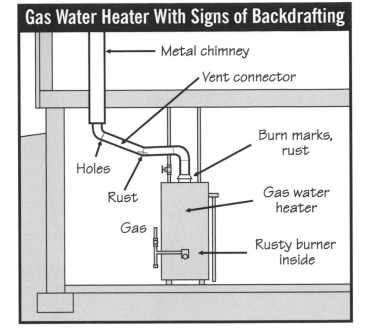

Gas Water Heater With Signs of Backdrafting

Metal chimney

Vent connector

Burn marks, rust

Holes

Rust

Gas

Gas water heater

Rusty burner inside

Figure 6-33.

Backdrafting

Proper operation of combustion appliances and chimneys requires a supply of combustion air and dilution air. A burning fire consumes oxygen from the air supply and draws additional air up the chimney. This additional (dilution) air is provided by the draft hood or opening in the flue pipe or above the burner in the housing of the appliance.

The air that's exhausted up the chimney must be replaced somehow. This may occur as air enters through small leaks in the structure of the house. If you've ever built a large fire in the fireplace and then opened the front door, you may have noticed that air rushes in to help replace air flowing up the chimney. This same exhaust process occurs with all combustion appliances.

As we build our homes tighter and tighter to aid energy conservation, we limit the number of air leaks and decrease the supply of combustible air. Exhaust fans in the bathroom and kitchen, clothes dryers, and downdraft cooktops also draw air out of the home. This can create problems with backdrafting and spillage of combustion products into the home. For instance, combustion gas from an appliance can be drawn back down the chimney, and if the appliance isn't operating properly, dangerous carbon monoxide can linger indoors.

What can you do to prevent this? Watch for signs of backdrafting. **See Figure 6-33**. Check flue pipes for rust or water stains, and look for rust or burn marks at draft diverters. If you notice these signs, contact a specialist. Have gas appliances serviced yearly, and ask the contractor to check all chimneys and flue connectors.

Also, install a carbon monoxide alarm. It's good insurance against a backdrafting problem that allows carbon monoxide into your home.

No Chimney for a Gas Appliance?

A modern gas furnace may have a sealed combustion system that doesn't require a chimney; the furnace is vented by plastic pipes to the exterior. Some gas water heaters also direct-vent through a side wall with plastic pipe or a special metal vent. Newer gas fireplaces can vent directly through a side wall, and some have their own combustion air supply.

With today's tighter homes, always consider using fuel-burning appliances that have a built-in combustion supply that draws in air from outside.

Some states allow the installation of gas fireplaces without any vent or chimney, but many states forbid this type of installation because of the potential for safety problems. If you have any questions about the requirements in your area, check with the local building inspector.

For more specific information, look up the Chimney Safety Institute of America in the References section.

Fireplaces and Wood Stoves

Before modern heating sources were available, fireplaces were a primary source of heating. Today a fireplace can't compete with a modern heating system. Fireplaces and wood stoves are great fun and provide a cozy, romantic amenity to our homes, but you do need to understand their basic components and how they operate.

Poor maintenance and improper operation can cause a fire inside your home. Fireplaces and wood stoves can produce dangerous products of combustion, such as carbon monoxide.

Basic Fireplace Types

There are three basic types of fireplaces: masonry, prefabricated metal and direct vent. Masonry fireplaces are designed to burn wood and can be adapted for a gas log set. **See Figure 7-1.** Prefabricated metal fireplaces can be designed to burn wood, wood and gas, or just gas. Direct vent fireplaces are sealed high-efficiency units that only burn gas. We will look at each type and learn what's involved in safe operation.

A wood stove or fireplace insert should not be operated until a professional has checked it and determined that it conforms to local building codes and requirements. If you have any concerns or specific questions about your fireplace or wood stove, contact a local member of the Chimney Safety Institute of America (CSIA). Local fireplace and wood stove dealers can also provide assistance. **For more information, see the References section.**

Masonry Fireplace

Masonry fireplaces have been the standard method of home heating for centuries. Since about 1900, when efficient central heating systems were developed, fireplaces have taken on the role of a desirable feature that adds value to our homes and provides a gathering place for family and friends.

A standard masonry fireplace is constructed of brick, firebrick, cement block and clay tile to contain the fire and products of combustion. The fireplace is

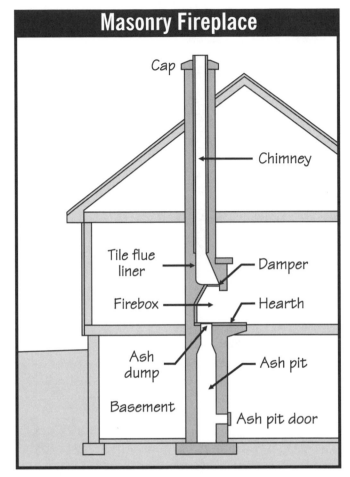

Masonry Fireplace

Cap

Chimney

Tile flue liner

Damper

Firebox

Hearth

Ash dump

Ash pit

Basement

Ash pit door

Figure 7-1.

custom built on-site by skilled masons. The design has changed little over the last 100 years, and masonry fireplaces aren't a very efficient source of heat. **See Figure 7-2.**

Before you build a fire, you should understand the components of your masonry fireplace. Start by examining the firebox (the area where the fire is built). You will notice that the box is built of smooth brick or firebrick. If the wall of the firebox is metal, you have a metal framed or metal fabricated fireplace.

Look inside the top of the firebox and you will see a metal damper (metal plate) and a handle that operates the damper. Most dampers are made of cast iron and are pushed open with a handle or pulled open with a chain. With the chain-operated units you will often see a pull marked "O" for open and

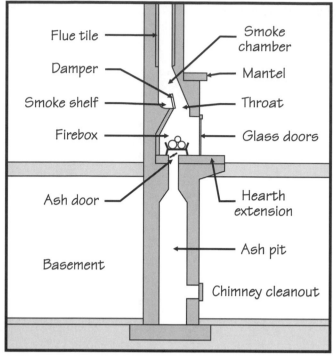

Figure 7-2.

"S" for shut. Pull the chain or push the lever to open the damper. Keep your face and body away from the damper as it opens, because soot may fall from the opening.

With the damper open, you should be able to peer up the clay tile flue and see part of the way up the chimney. You may notice some soot- and tan-colored fluff or deposit. This is creosote. If you see a heavy buildup that is ¹/₂" to ¹/₄" thick, have your chimney and fireplace cleaned before you build a fire.

When you build a fire, the hot gases of combustion flow past the damper and up the chimney flue. The firebrick and firebox contain the heat of the fire and radiate some heat back into the room.

A variation on a solid masonry fireplace uses a metal firebox placed inside a masonry fireplace frame. The metal firebox replaces the firebox constructed of firebrick. These units often were constructed with an air passage around the metal box and air duct connections to the room. The lower duct opening draws air from the room at the base of the fireplace. The metal firebox warms the air, which then flows upward through a duct above the fireplace and enters the room through a grill. This gives the fireplace some heating capacity, warming the air of the room.

You might also find a wood-burning metal stove insert fitted inside a masonry fireplace. These custom-designed units provide heat to a room. Often, such a unit has a partially sealed combustion chamber. It requires a special flue and custom installation. This kind of unit needs yearly maintenance; flue gases exit at a lower temperature, and the unit is prone to a buildup of deposits in the stove and chimney flue.

Metal-Framed Prefabricated Fireplace

Many fireplaces built since about 1970 consist of a metal fireplace and flue built in a factory, which is then installed in a wood frame inside the home. **See Figure 7-3**. These are called metal-framed, zero clearance, prefabricated, or factory-built fireplaces. They are designed and tested as a unit. Don't be confused by a solid brick or masonry front and mantle on such a fireplace; many metal fireplaces have a masonry front.

If yours is a factory-built fireplace, you will see a metal firebox with refractory panel liners, metal

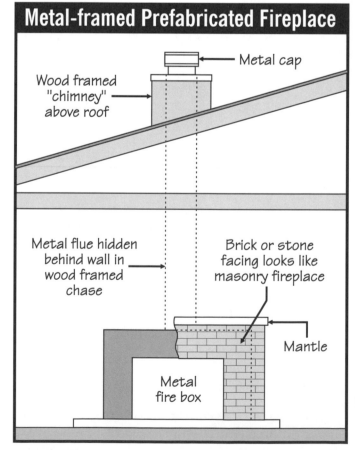

Figure 7-3.

damper and a metal flue. The refractory panels will look like brick cast into a flat panel on three sides of the firebox. The side of the firebox may show the manufacturer's data and nameplate. Outside the house, there will not be a brick chimney; instead, you will see a wood-framed chimney chase and a metal-capped flue pipe. The flue or discharge pipe at the top of the chimney will be metal. The chase can also be covered with masonry materials, but this is not common.

A prefabricated fireplace functions like a masonry fireplace but doesn't require the foundation and more expensive masonry construction. Glass doors are often included with the firebox, and the fireplace may have an outside air supply that provides combustion air for the fire. The reduces the need for inside air for combustion and makes the fireplace more efficient.

Many prefabricated fireplaces are equipped with a fan to circulate room air around the firebox so that the fire provides some heat in the room. The grills for air circulation are often placed directly above and below the glass doors.

Direct Vent Fireplace

Around 1985, fireplaces were greatly improved as heating appliances when "direct vent" and "sealed combustion" fireplaces started to become popular. These are natural gas or propane burning fireplaces that vent combustion gases directly through a side-wall or up a special metal chimney. They use an outside air supply for combustion. The front glass is totally sealed. **See Figure 7-4**.

This fireplace may have a pilot light or ignition device, just like a gas furnace. With a good set of gas logs, it provides an attractive flame and is an efficient source of heat. Some of these units are rated heating appliances, just like a warm air furnace, and can be connected to a thermostat for automatic control. The fireplace will have a fan to circulate heated air into the room. Many units are almost as efficient at heating the room as a good warm-air furnace.

Gas Fireplace Logs

A "gas" fireplace generally refers to a set of ceramic logs, a gas burner, and related equipment that allows the feel and look of a real fire while burning natural

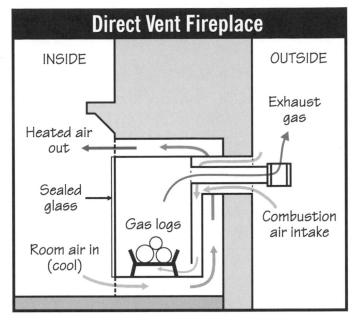

Figure 7-4.

gas or propane. The advantages of a gas fireplace are that it requires no fuss and creates no mess. You can have an instant fire, and when you turn it off, you know the fire is out. There is no wood to haul in and no ash to clean up.

Gas fireplace logs are often adapted to a wood-burning masonry fireplace or to a metal-framed fireplace that is designed to burn wood.

Since each system is a little different, refer to the manufacturer's instructions for your unit. Some will have a pilot light or an automatic ignition device. Some use a wall switch or even a remote control.

With most manually operated gas fireplace logs, the first step is to open the damper in the flue above the logs. Then you place a match or flame in the log set. Use a long fireplace match or a lighter with a long handle. Carefully and slowly open the gas valve after there is a flame in the log set.

If you smell gas near the gas fireplace, do not attempt to light the unit. Turn off the gas valve located in the floor or in the firebox near the log set. Call for service. There should also be another safety valve in the basement or near the fireplace.

If you intend to burn real wood in a gas fireplace, consult a specialist first. Some metal-framed fireplaces are rated for gas only and won't burn wood. If your unit has a gas log set and gas piping, it would be very dangerous to burn real wood without converting the unit.

How to Build a Real Wood Fire

Masonry fireplaces and wood burning metal-framed fireplaces are safe and easy to use if you follow a few simple steps.

First, get everything ready:

1. Assemble a simple set of tools for maintaining the fire. At a minimum, you need some type of poker to move logs as needed when the fire is hot.

2. Always use a grate in the fireplace. The grate raises the wood off the base of the firebox to allow for air circulation, which aids complete combustion. Place the grate to the rear of the firebox.

3. Use dry or seasoned hardwood. This wood will burn hotter and prevent excessive smoke and soot from building up in the chimney flue. Dry or seasoned wood will have been cut and stored out of the weather for about 12 months. It will feel dry and will have cracks and splits in the end grain.

4. Never burn treated wood, Christmas trees, plastic, or trash in a fireplace. Never use a flammable liquid.

5. Remove ashes as they build up below the grate. There must be room for air circulation below the grate. If yours is a real masonry fireplace, you can put cold ashes down the ash pit door. Leave a base layer of about one inch of ash in the fireplace.

Now, to build the fire:

1. Open the damper. Take a look up the flue with a flashlight to make sure the damper is open. (Once you have mastered the operation of the damper, you can stop checking with the flashlight.)

2. If your home is very "tight," you may need to open a window to allow for combustion air to reach the fire. You will learn about this as you use the fireplace; if there is a poor draft, or if smoke builds inside your home, try opening a window.

3. Start loading the fireplace with small pieces of scrap wood (kindling) on the grate. Using small pieces of dry wood for kindling is the key. Woodworking scraps are ideal. These will light quickly, spreading the fire easily to the logs.

4. Add three or four small logs in the grate atop the kindling. Arrange the logs so there is space for air and fire circulation between them.

5. Place wadded newspaper below the grate.

6. You may need to help start the draft with a torch made from rolled newspaper. Light the paper and hold it up near the damper until there is a strong draft. The flame will warm the air in the flue and start a draft (a draw) up the chimney. After you have burned a few fires, you will know whether you can skip this step.

7. Once there is a draft up the chimney, light the crumpled paper below the grate.

8. Keep the screen closed while you are burning a fire.

9. Add and move the logs if needed. Don't build a huge fire.

10. Monitor the fire as it burns. Allow it to burn out before you leave the room. If your fireplace has glass doors, close them when you leave the fire.

11. Don't close the damper until the next day, and make sure the grate and remnants of logs are totally cold. A wood fire can smolder for a long time, and if you close the damper when the fire is still burning, you will trap smoke and dangerous products of combustion inside your home.

Fireplace Draft Problems

One problem with fireplaces in newer, more airtight homes is that they lack combustion air unless a window is open. This was not a problem with older homes, which had so many air leaks around windows, doors and framing that there was plenty of air for combustion. **See Figure 7-5**.

This condition can be dangerous: as a fire is starting or burning out, it may lack draft, and it can back up dangerous carbon monoxide into your home.

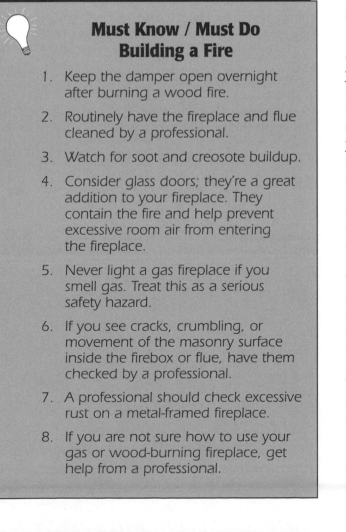

Masonry Fireplace - Outside Air Supply

Flue tile

Smoke chamber

Damper

Mantel

Smoke shelf

Throat

Air Supply

Firebox

Ash door

Hearth extension

Ash pit

Basement

Chimney cleanout

Figure 7-5.

A fire with a strong draft can cause gas-fired appliances such as a water heater or furnace to back-draft combustion fumes into your home. Any gas-burning appliance vented by gravity up a chimney could be affected. The draft of a fire can overcome the natural venting of these gas appliances.

An air supply directed into the firebox would be a good solution. Consult a qualified brickmason, fireplace contractor or chimney sweep for the installation. This is definitely not a do-it-yourself project. The vent must penetrate an outside wall and the side or front of the fireplace. The vent may also need to be combined with fireplace doors.

Remember that when most natural fireplaces are operated in cold weather, most of the heat goes up the chimney.

There is one situation when a fireplace works well: if the home has excessive moisture levels in the winter, the fireplace will draw lots of air into your home for ventilation (provided that a window is open!)

Fireplace Cleaning

The ideal schedule for cleaning your fireplace and chimney depends on many factors. How often do you use your fireplace? What type of wood do you burn? Is the wood always dry hardwood? Is your home in a wooded area? Is there a cap on the chimney? Have you had problems in the past? Do you close the glass doors? Is there always a good draft? Is the chimney in the center of the home or on an outside wall?

If you live in a wooded area, you may wish to have the chimney checked every year just to make sure that no animals or their nests have blocked the flue.

You should inspect your fireplace, damper and flue every year. Operate the damper to see that it opens fully and latches open. The damper should also close tightly. Peer up the flue while shining a bright flashlight on it. You should not see any buildup of creosote or soot on the sides of the firebox or liner. The shelf behind the damper should not be full of debris. Proper inspection also includes looking at the top of the chimney, inspecting the cap, and peering down the flue with a bright light.

Creosote buildup creates a fire hazard. Creosote, a black or brown deposit, can be crusty and flaky,

Must Know / Must Do Building a Fire

1. Keep the damper open overnight after burning a wood fire.

2. Routinely have the fireplace and flue cleaned by a professional.

3. Watch for soot and creosote buildup.

4. Consider glass doors; they're a great addition to your fireplace. They contain the fire and help prevent excessive room air from entering the fireplace.

5. Never light a gas fireplace if you smell gas. Treat this as a serious safety hazard.

6. If you see cracks, crumbling, or movement of the masonry surface inside the firebox or flue, have them checked by a professional.

7. A professional should check excessive rust on a metal-framed fireplace.

8. If you are not sure how to use your gas or wood-burning fireplace, get help from a professional.

tar-like, or shiny and hardened. You might see different types of buildup on one fireplace. If creosote builds up in sufficient quantities, it can burn, destroying the chimney and even burning down your home.

Wet wood, restricted air for combustion, and cool chimney temperatures all increase the buildup of creosote, so no general rule of thumb can be safely determine when a fireplace needs to be cleaned.

Have your fireplace cleaned, and ask the chimney sweep for recommendations on routine maintenance. He or she can determine how often your chimney needs cleaning, based on all the variables in your case. Select a sweep who belongs to the National Chimney Sweep Guild and is certified by the Chimney Safety Institute of America (CSIA). A chimney sweep must pass an examination to be certified. Remember that it's the worker, not the company, who should be certified. To find the names of certified members in your area, call the CSIA at (310) 963-6900.

"Rain" in the Fireplace

To avoid severe condensation problems that mimic rain in the fireplace, check the fit of the fireplace damper. If the damper leaks (or is left open) during the winter, warm moist air will flow up the chimney. This warm air will condense into water on the flue if the chimney is cold from lack of use; when temperatures are below freezing, the condensation will turn to ice on the flue. When you build a fire, this ice can fall like "rain."

"Rain" that falls onto your fire could also result from a leak in the flashing, a damaged cap, damaged

brick and mortar, or a liner problem. If the problem persists, hire a certified chimney sweep to do an inspection.

Wood Stoves

Wood stoves, wood heaters, wood-burning fireplace inserts and related wood-burning devices have become popular over the years. Many are well-designed and safe to use. Some are homemade contraptions that are not safe. Some are excellent factory-built units installed by amateurs in an unsafe fashion. **See Figure 7-6**.

If your home has any type of wood-burning device other than a professionally installed fireplace, have it checked by a professional before you use it. It may not be safe.

Figure 7-6.

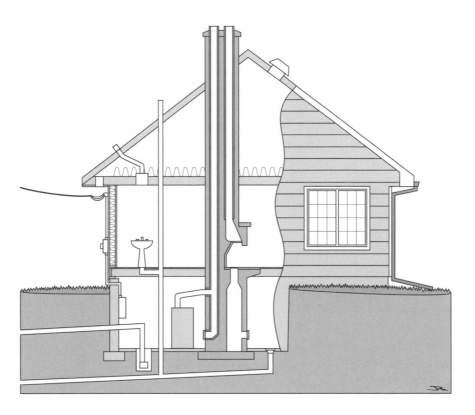

Service Requirements by the Calendar

Home operation and maintenance is easy if we understand our home systems and stay organized. A home operates just like a car—with the right maintenance, you can avoid major problems and efficiently run your home for many years. The key is preventing problems or catching small problems before they become home disasters.

If you don't change the filter on the furnace on a routine basis, you can freeze up the coil, and you will come home to a very warm house. If you don't turn off the exterior hose connection in the winter, you can come home to a flood.

This chapter provides that little bit of organization that helps us all remember to perform important preventive maintenance tasks. It offers lists of maintenance tasks to be performed on a routine basis. Refer to specific chapters in the book for detailed information on the specific tasks. Follow manufacturers' instructions for all service.

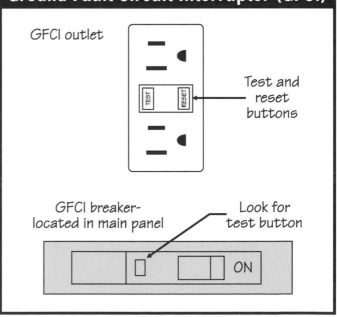

Ground Fault Circuit Interrupter (GFCI)

GFCI outlet

Test and reset buttons

TEST RESET

GFCI breaker- located in main panel

Look for test button

ON

Remember, not every maintenance item will be applicable to your home or its systems. You need to do the homework here—study and understand the systems in your home.

Exercise caution before attempting inspection, maintenance or repairs. Turn off the power and disconnect other utility services. Follow any owner's manual supplied by the equipment manufacturer. If you don't understand a problem or system, consult a professional.

Daily and Weekly

Be aware of any changes or strange sounds in your home. If the automatic garage door opener is groaning, the door and track may need lubrication,

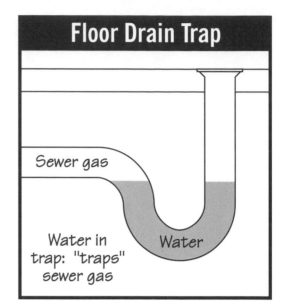

Floor Drain Trap

Sewer gas

Water in trap: "traps" sewer gas

Water

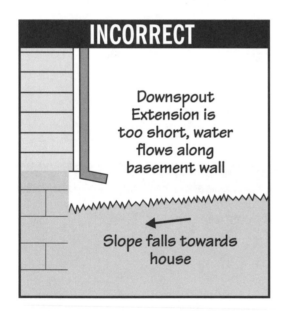

INCORRECT

Downspout Extension is too short, water flows along basement wall

Slope falls towards house

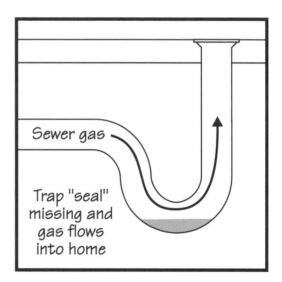

Sewer gas

Trap "seal" missing and gas flows into home

or perhaps a roller is broken. If you smell sewer gas in the basement, you may have a dried out floor drain trap. If the central air conditioner is squeaking, you may have a bad bearing on the fan motor. If a gutter is overflowing, expect water in the basement or crawl space. Just watch for changes, and address issues as they arise.

Be watchful during drastic weather changes. Weather can have a huge effect on our homes. A big snowstorm may make it necessary to clear your furnace's intake and discharge vent pipes. During periods of heavy rain, it is wise to check gutters and downspouts and make sure that the sump pump is working properly. If the furnace runs constantly or more often than you expect, check for a problem.

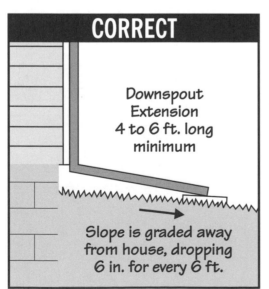

CORRECT

Downspout Extension 4 to 6 ft. long minimum

Slope is graded away from house, dropping 6 in. for every 6 ft.

Monthly

When these systems are in use, perform the following checks monthly.

System	Check Fire and smoke alarms. Test alarm.
Fire extinguishers	Check pressure; service as needed.
Carbon monoxide alarm	Test alarm, and check reading.
Warm air heating system	Check and change or wash filter (unless it is a special type). **See Figure 8-1**.
Furnace, high efficiency	Check condensate drain to make sure it is clear and draining.
Gas heat, water heater	Check flue pipe (smoke pipe) to chimney for damage, rust, condition.
Air conditioning	Check and change or wash filter (unless it is a special type); check condensate drain to make sure it is clear and draining.
Heat pump	Check and change or wash filter (unless it is a special type).
Steam heating system	Check water level and service as needed.
Shower and tub drains	Clear out hair and other debris.
GFCI	Test GFCI (Ground Fault Circuit Interrupter) outlets and breakers.
Plumbing	Check for any leaks at fixtures, traps and piping.
Water softener	Check salt supply.
Clothes dryer	Clean lint from filter (after every use) and check duct for lint.
Garage door operator	Test auto-reverse safety feature.

Spring

Air conditioning	Schedule professional service. Check that unit is level and clean and has proper clearance. Adjust main duct dampers if needed.

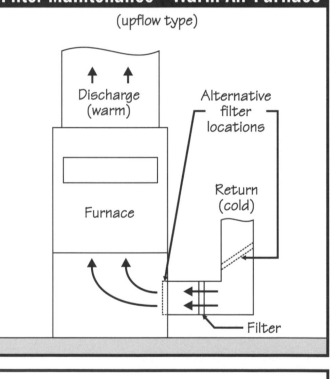

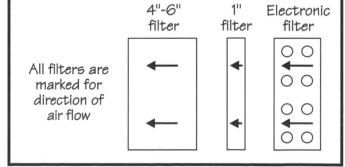

Figure 8-1.

Humidifier	Turn off unit and water supply. Switch humidifier's duct damper from winter to summer setting as needed.
Duct dampers	Adjust dampers for a switch from heating to cooling if necessary.
High and low returns	Open high returns and close low returns for cooling season. **See Figure 8-2**.
Whole house fan	Check belt, lubricate, clean.
Gutters, downspouts	Clean gutters and make sure downspouts are attached and extended.

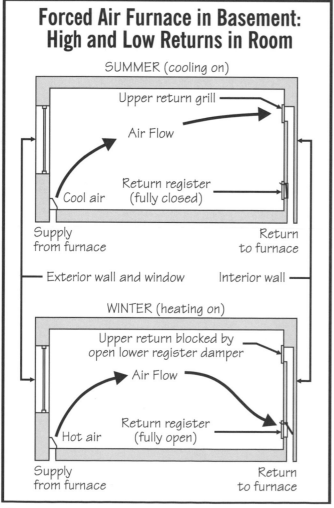

Figure 8-2.

Roof	Visually inspect for any damage. Trim trees if needed.
Roof vents	Inspect for damage or bird nests.
Chimney	Visually inspect for any damage to cap, flashing and masonry.
Sump pump	Test sump pump to make sure it removes water from the crock.
Exterior, general	Check condition of paint, caulk and putty.
Exterior, grounds	Check that grading of soil and hard surfaces slopes away from the basement. **See Figure 8-3**.
Attic	Check for signs of leaks, mildew, condensation.
Basement	Check for any signs of leaks, cracks, movement, rot, mildew.
Crawl space	Check for adequate ventilation to remove excess moisture.
Dehumidifier	Clean; start operation in basement as needed.
Plumbing	Open outside hose connection shutoff.
Clothes dryer	Clean lint from duct and from unit per manufacturer's instructions.
Refrigerator	Clean coil, clean drain pan, and check drain.
Range hood	Clean filter, wash fan blades.
Bathroom exhaust fans	Clean grill and fan.

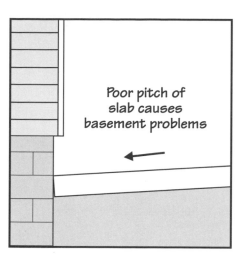

Figure 8-3. Grading Problems

Bathroom tile	Check grout, caulk and tile for damage.
Water heater	Draw sediment from tank as needed.
Sprinklers, irrigation	Service and start system.
Decks	Cleans and seal as needed.

Summer

Air conditioner	Keep bushes and plant material clear of unit. Maintain air conditioner's filter on furnace. **See Figure 8-4**.

Gutters & downspouts	Clean gutters, and make sure downspouts are attached and extended.
Sump pump	Test sump pump to make sure it removes water from the crock.
Exterior	Complete any major paint, putty, wood repair and caulking projects.
Fireplace	Schedule professional cleaning and service as needed.
Wood stoves	Schedule professional cleaning and service.
Chimney and roof	Schedule profession service as needed.
Exterior metal	Check metal railings, and paint as needed.

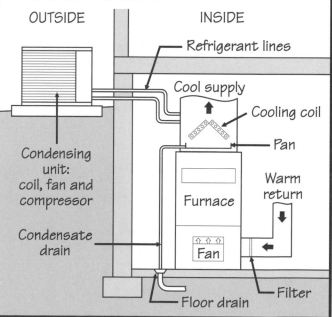

Figure 8-4.

Fall

Air conditioning	Cover top of unit if desired at end of cooling season.
Heating	Schedule professional service; lubricate fan, motor, and pumps.
Oil heat	Arrange for maintenance and oil delivery.
Water heater	Service gas and oil water heaters. Draw sediment from tank as needed. Check for carbon monoxide.
Humidifier	Service, clean, change water panel as needed. Switch duct damper as needed from summer to winter setting.
Duct dampers	Adjust dampers for the switch from cooling to heating if necessary. **See Figure 8-5**.
High and low returns	Open lower returns and close upper returns for heating season.
Gutters, downspouts	Clean gutters and make sure downspouts are attached and extended.
Roof	Visually inspect for any damage; trim trees as needed.
Roof vents	Inspect for damage or bird nests
Chimney	Visually inspect for any damage to cap, flashing and masonry. **See Figure 8-6**.
Sump pump	Test sump pump to make sure it removes water from the crock.

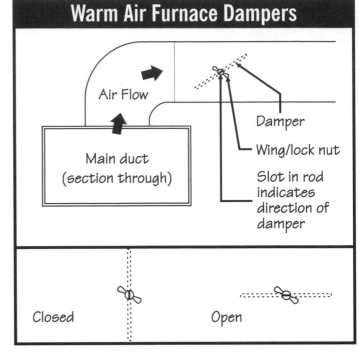

Figure 8-5.

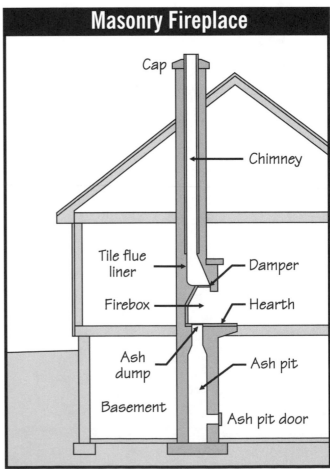

Figure 8-6.

Exterior, general	Check paint, caulk and putty condition.
Weatherstripping	Check and repair weatherstripping on windows and doors.
Exterior, grounds	Check that grading of soil and hard surfaces slopes away from basement.
Basement	Check for any signs of leaks, cracks, movement, rot, mildew.
Crawl space	Check for adequate ventilation to remove excess moisture.
Plumbing	Close outside hose connection shutoff
Clothes dryer	Clean lint from duct and unit per manufacturer's instructions.
Bathroom tile	Check grout, caulk and tile for damage.
Garage door	Tighten all hardware, and lubricate moving parts.
Fireplace	Check flue, damper, firebox.
Sprinklers, irrigation	Drain and service system.
Room air conditioner	Remove unit, or install cover.
Swimming pools	Service and close.
Hoses	Remove from hose bibs; drain to prevent freezing.

Winter

Fire and smoke alarms	Change batteries, vacuum to remove dust, and test.
Carbon monoxide alarms	Change batteries, and test.
Roof and gutters	Monitor for ice dams, and record problems for future corrective work. **See Figure 8-7**.
Sump pump	Test sump pump to make sure it removes water from the crock.
Furnace	Lubricate fan, motor, and pumps as required at mid-season
Washing machine	Check supply hoses for damage. Clean screens in hose connections.
Doors and hardware	Lubricate hinges and moving parts.

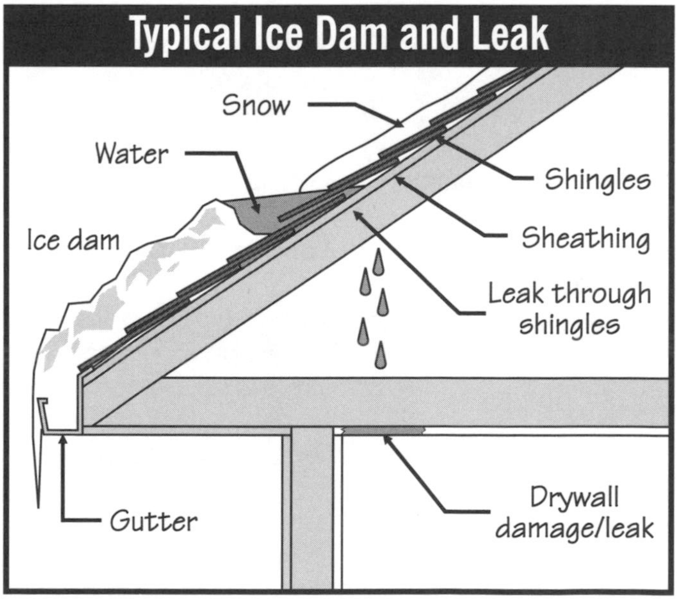

Figure 8-7.

Periodic Maintenance and Service As Needed

Septic system — Schedule professional pumping and inspection at least every 2 years. **See Figure 8-8**.

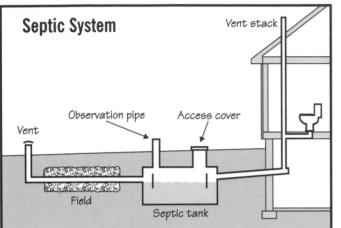

Septic System

Vent stack

Observation pipe

Access cover

Vent

Field

Septic tank

Figure 8-8.

Water softener — Clean brine tank and screens or filters as needed.

Well system — Test water for bacteria and other contaminants. Check pressure tank operation.

Fire and smoke alarms — Replace alarms every 10 years. **See Figure 8-9**.

Fireplace — Schedule cleaning and inspection as needed, depending on use.

Water filters — Replace as needed.

Water treatment units — Replace and service as needed.

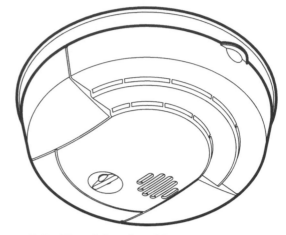

Figure 8-9. Fire / Smoke Alarm

Electric baseboard — Vacuum and clean based on usage.

Gas appliances — Check flexible gas connectors for stove, dryer, etc., yearly.

Range hood — Clean filter and fan.

Shutoffs — Periodically have your whole family review all utility disconnects.

Termites and other pests — Schedule professional inspections and service as needed.

Electrical — Eliminate extension cords. Check for damaged cords, plugs or outlets.

Water heater — Test pressure and temperature relief valve. Replace leaking valves.

Plumbing — Test main water shutoff. If it is hard to operate, call a plumber.

No Heat

What can you do if you wake up to a cold house and the furnace will not run? Follow these checklists before you call a service company.

For a Gas-Fired Furnace or Boiler

1. Check the thermostat. Is it set to "heat"? Is it set higher than the room temperature indicated on the dial? If it's a digital thermostat, is the battery dead? **See Figure 9-1**.

2. Check the on-off switch on the side of the furnace or near the furnace. **See Figure 9-2**.

3. Check the furnace pilot light. If it's out, light it, following the instructions on the furnace. If there is no pilot light, you have spark ignition

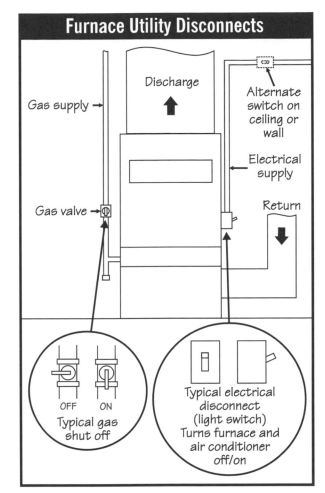

Furnace Utility Disconnects

Figure 9-2.

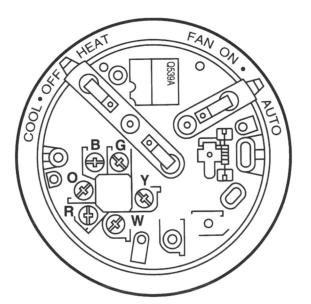

Figure 9-1. Heat-Cool Thermostat (Top Removed)

or a hot surface igniter; the igniter should be hot or sparking as the furnace attempts to fire.

4. Is the gas off at the furnace or to your home? If you have a gas stove, you can check this by seeing if the stove's gas supply is on.

5. Is the breaker or fuse to the furnace turned off? Reset the breaker or replace the fuse; but if it trips again, call a service technician.

6. Check the furnace fan compartment door. Some units have a safety switch that turns the furnace off when the door is ajar.

7. Check for a broken belt or a severely clogged air filter.

For an Oil-Fired Furnace or Boiler

1. Check the thermostat. Is it set to "heat"? Is it set higher than the room temperature indicated on the dial? If it's a digital thermostat, is the battery dead? **See Figure 9-1**.

2. Check the on-off switch on the side of the unit or near the unit. **See Figure 9-3**.

3. Is the breaker or fuse to the furnace turned off? Reset the breaker or replace the fuse; but if it trips again, call a service technician.

Warm Air Furnace with Oil Burner

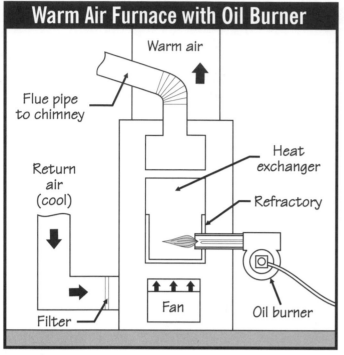

Figure 9-3.

4. Check the fan compartment door. Some units have a safety switch that turns the furnace off when the door is ajar.

5. Check for a broken belt or a severely clogged air filter.

6. Check the oil supply in the storage tank. If you are out of oil, arrange for oil delivery and burner service. An oil burner that runs out of oil will need service to restart.

7. Check the valve and filter on the tank

8. Press the reset button of the ignition safety control on the stack or burner. (Try this once only.)

9. Press the restart button on the motor. (Try this once only.)

For a Heat Pump

1. Check the thermostat. Is it set to "heat"? Is it set higher than the room temperature indicated on the dial? If it's a digital thermostat, is the battery dead? **See Figure 9-1**.

2. Check the on/off switch on the side of the furnace or near the furnace. **See Figure 9-2**.

3. Check the fan compartment door. Some units have a safety switch that turns the furnace off when the door is ajar.

4. Check for a broken belt or a severely clogged air filter.

5. Check whether the outside unit is iced up. If it is, call for service.

6. Check for tripped main fuses or breakers on the disconnect at the unit and at the main distribution panel.

No Air Conditioning

1. Check the thermostat. Is it set to cooling or AC? Is it set lower than the room temperature indicated on the dial? If it's a digital thermostat, is the battery dead?

2. Check the on/off switch on the side of the furnace or near the furnace. (Remember, the furnace distributes air for the air conditioning and must be switched "on".) **See Figure 9-2**.

3. Is the disconnect switch outside at the AC unit switched off, disconnect pulled or fuse blown? **See Figure 9-4**.

4. Is the main breaker or the 220-volt breaker or fuse for the air conditioner off? Reset the breaker or replace the fuse; but if it trips again, call a service technician.

5. Check the fan compartment on the furnace door. Some units have a safety switch that turns the furnace off when the door is ajar.

6. Check for a broken belt or a severely clogged air filter on the furnace.

7. Is the coil above the furnace iced up? Call for service.

8. Is the exterior coil dirty or blocked by plants? Service the unit.

No Electricity

1. Find out whether the outage affects only your home. Check with your neighbors. If the whole area is without power, notify the electric utility.

2. If your whole house is without power but your neighbors have power, you may have tripped

Air Conditioning – Exterior Electrical Disconnect
(To turn off electrical power to unit)

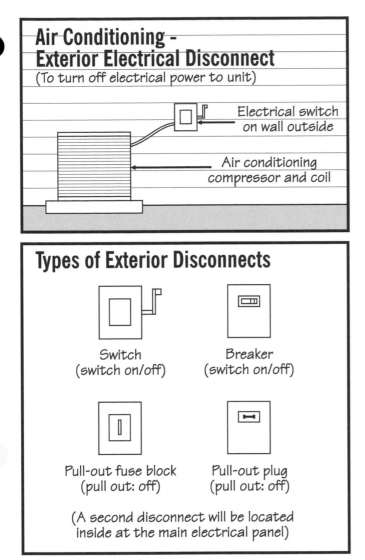

Electrical switch on wall outside

Air conditioning compressor and coil

Types of Exterior Disconnects

Switch
(switch on/off)

Breaker
(switch on/off)

Pull-out fuse block
(pull out: off)

Pull-out plug
(pull out: off)

(A second disconnect will be located inside at the main electrical panel)

Figure 9-4.

the main breaker or fuse. Inspect the panel to make sure there is no water or visible signs of damage. Then try to diagnose the problem; disconnect any heater or electrical device that may have tripped the breaker. Reset the main breaker or replace the main fuse. If it trips a second time, call an electrician. **See Figure 9-5**.

3. If only a part or section of your home has no power, one of the branch circuits has tripped. Check the main box for signs of water or damage. Disconnect a heater or electrical device that may be causing the problem. Reset the tripped breaker or replace the blown fuse. If it trips again, call an electrician, and temporarily disconnect electrical devices connected to that circuit. **See Figure 9-5**.

4. If power is out in the bathrooms, near the kitchen sink, in the garage, or at the exterior outlets, this indicates that a Ground

Fault Circuit Interrupter (GFCI) has been tripped. You will find the reset button on the affected outlet; or there may be a reset button on a single bathroom outlet that controls all bathroom and exterior outlets; and occasionally a GFCI breaker is located in the main circuit panel (it will have a "test" button). Try resetting the GFCI once or twice; after that, replace the appliance that is causing the problem, or call an electrician. The usual procedure is to turn a GFCI breaker fully off, then on again. **See Figure 9-6**.

Electrical Main Circuit Breaker Panel

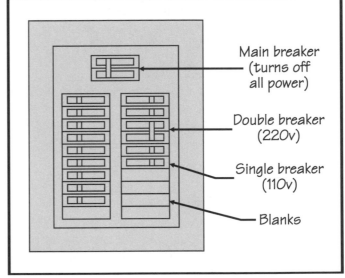

Main breaker
(turns off all power)

Double breaker
(220v)

Single breaker
(110v)

Blanks

Figure 9-5.

Ground Fault Circuit Interrupter (GFCI)

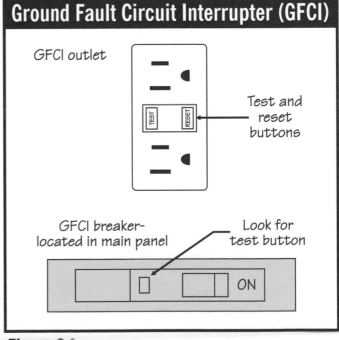

GFCI outlet

Test and reset buttons

GFCI breaker– located in main panel

Look for test button

ON

Figure 9-6.

No Water / Frozen Pipes

1. If you're on a municipal system, check with the neighbors to see if the whole area is out of water. Call the water utility.

2. If you have a private well system, check the switch and breaker or fuse for the well pump. Check the pump if it is accessible. If the pump is hot, you need professional repair. If the pump seems okay, try resetting the breaker or replacing the fuse. If the overload device trips again, call for service.

3. In very cold weather, suspect a frozen pipe—either a main line or a smaller line inside your home. Turn off the water to a frozen pipe, because the pipe may be broken and will sprout a major leak when it thaws. Call a plumber.

4. If there is water flowing near the main or from the pressure tank on a private system, this indicates a major leak or damaged piping. Turn off the water and/or the pump, and call for service.

No Hot Water

1. If you have a gas water heater, check the pilot light. If you smell gas, turn off the gas supply to the water heater and call for service. Never,

ever attempt to light a water heater pilot if you smell gas. If you do not smell gas, you may attempt to re-light the pilot, following the instructions on the water heater. If the pilot light keeps going out, the unit needs service. **See Figure 9-7**.

2. Check to make sure the gas supply is on. Check other gas appliances in your home, or ask your neighbors if their gas supply is working. **See Figure 9-8**.

3. For an electric water heater, check the circuit breaker or fuse. Reset the breaker or fuse once if there is no visible damage at the water heater or the electrical panel. If the overload trips again, call for service.

4. An electric water heater has a high-limit switch under the heater's top cover on the upper thermostat. You can remove the upper cover and reset this switch once by pushing in the button. You should only attempt this if you feel confident opening the panel and possibly exposing live electrical connections. **See Figure 9-9**.

Leaking Water Heater

1. If water is leaking from the tank on the floor, the water heater has failed. Turn off the water supply, the electrical power and/or the gas

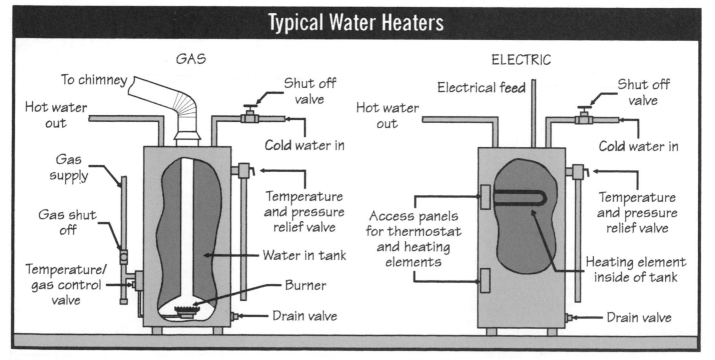

Typical Water Heaters

GAS

To chimney
Hot water out
Gas supply
Gas shut off
Temperature/ gas control valve

Shut off valve
Cold water in
Temperature and pressure relief valve
Water in tank
Burner
Drain valve

ELECTRIC

Electrical feed
Hot water out
Access panels for thermostat and heating elements

Shut off valve
Cold water in
Temperature and pressure relief valve
Heating element inside of tank
Drain valve

Figure 9-7.

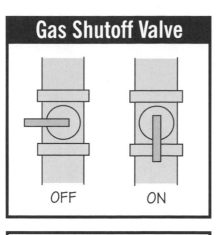

Figure 9-8.

water continues to leak or spray from the unit, open the lowest hot faucet in the system to attempt to drain water and relieve pressure.

2. If the water is leaking from the temperature and pressure (T and P) valve and running down the pipe on the side of the unit, the water heater may be overheating or the valve may have failed. Carefully open a hot water faucet and check for overheated water or even steam. If the water is excessively hot, disconnect power and gas to the unit and call for service. **See Figure 9-10**.

3. If there is a slow leak from the T and P valve drain line and the water is not excessively hot, have the valve replaced soon. Once the valve has leaked, it needs replacement; sediment may have built up in the valve.

4. If there is a small drip from the drain valve on the side of the unit, try screwing a hose cap and washer on the fitting to stop the leak. Normally, this valve does not need to be replaced.

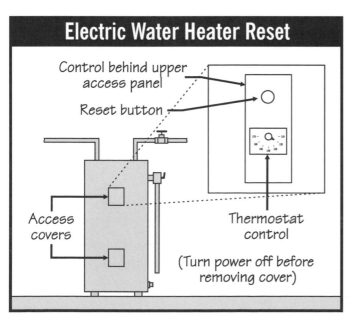

Figure 9-9.

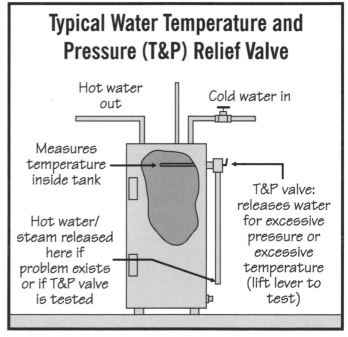

Figure 9-10.

supply and call for service. The supply valve is usually found on the piping on top of the water heater. You will still have cold water in your home when you turn off this valve. If

Gas Odors

If you smell gas anywhere in your house, take the following steps.

1. Get everyone out of the house.

2. Don't light matches or use electrical switches or devices.

3. Call the gas (or propane) company from a neighbor's house.

4. Once outside, turn off the gas main. It is located near the meter. Give the valve a quarter-turn with a wrench until the valve is perpendicular to the piping. **See Figure 9-8**.

5. Wait for help from the gas company.

Wobbling Ceiling Fan

When properly installed and balanced, a ceiling fan should not wobble excessively. Make sure your fan has been mounted properly; there should be an electric box or special bracing to support the fan's weight and movement. **See Figure 10-1**. You may be able to stop the wobble by switching blade positions and balancing the fan (see below). Contact the manufacturer of your fan for specific instructions, and ask if a balancing kit is available.

For information on how to contact the manufacturer, see the References section.

Typical balancing instructions:

1. Check that the fan is properly installed and that the blades are securely attached.

2. Run the fan on high speed (set to downdraft) and observe the wobble. Stop the fan; switch positions of two adjacent blades. If this improves the balance of the fan, leave it as is and use balancing weights.

3. With the fan stationary, attach the manufacturer's balancing clip on the leading edge of one blade, halfway between the outer tip of the blade and the attachment bracket. (A balancing clip, available from most fan manufacturers, is a small plastic weight that firmly clips to the blade.)

4. Run the fan on high speed, set to downdraft, and observe the wobble. Stop the fan; move the clip to the next blade. Again run the fan and observe the wobble. Repeat this for all fan blades.

5. Move the clip back to the blade where you noticed the least wobble. This time, attach the clip to the leading edge of the blade near the blade bracket. Run the fan and observe the wobble. Stop the fan and move the clip outward toward the end of the blade in small increments until you find the position where the fan runs best.

6. Attach a permanent balancing weight on the blade next to the clip. (Weights are often self-stick lead strips provided by the fan manufacturer.)

7. Remove the clip and run the fan. If the wobble was not completely corrected, you may be able to further improve the balance by repeating the above steps and adding more weights.

Doorbell Problems

Don't be afraid to try to repair the doorbell. All of its parts are low voltage—12 to 24 volts—and can't really hurt you. However, you should not attempt to repair or replace the transformer for the unit, which will be located in the basement or near the main power panel. It converts a 110-volt supply to 12 or 24 volts.

Most often, the chime unit consists of an electro-magnetic plunger that strikes a chime when activated—one sliding movement (and one chime) for the rear door and two movements for the front door's double chime.

Some door chimes consist of a low-voltage buzzer or a vibrating hammer on a bell. Others have huge chimes and complicated parts best left to a service company.

If the doorbell thumps or hums when you press the button, you need to clean the chime and plunger.

If pressing the button doesn't trigger any sound, the button itself is probably at fault. The doorbell button is the most common source of problems because of its exposure to weather. For a button that's flush with the wood trim, slip a screwdriver or

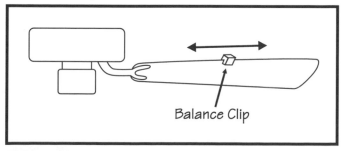

Balance Clip

Figure 10-1.

putty knife under the edge to pry the button out of its hole. If the button is screwed to the frame, remove the screws.

Now you can see the low-voltage wires. If they are loose or broken, this could be why the doorbell isn't working. **See Figure 10-2**.

If the wires look okay, disconnect their ends and touch them together to complete the circuit. If the doorbell rings now, you have found the problem— a bad button. You can easily replace the button with a matching button from the hardware store.

If the doorbell does not ring when you manually complete the circuit, the problem is in the chime or transformer.

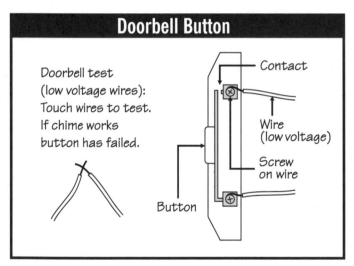

Doorbell Button

Doorbell test
(low voltage wires):
Touch wires to test.
If chime works
button has failed.

Contact

Wire
(low voltage)

Screw
on wire

Button

Figure 10-2.

Check the chime: remove the cover, and take a peek at the chime. Make sure it is level. Vacuum away any dust. You will see a round plunger that needs to move freely in the magnet surrounding it. Look for broken parts or damaged brackets.

After you have checked these items, the next step would be to use a voltmeter to analyze the transformer and wiring. This is a task you may wish to leave to a professional because it involves working with 110-volt power.

Or, for about $20, you can buy a new battery-operated chime/button set that needs no wires. The button is mounted anywhere within 100 feet of the chime. This is a great option when wires are damaged.

Removing Broken Light Bulbs

Sometimes, especially on exterior light fixtures, the glass bulb breaks away from the metal base. There is no best way to remove the base from the fixture, but here are several options.

Before replacing an exterior light, purchase a higher quality bulb with a brass-plated or copper-plated base that will not rust. You could coat the threads with a special dielectric grease available at automotive stores. Dry lubricant, Permatex Anti-Seize, and Vaseline will also work.

To remove the broken base, first make sure the power is off. Wear eye protection. Protect the immediate area from broken glass that may remain on the base. I like to use a needle nose pliers to grab the metal rim of the bulb and twist it. You can also jam the nose of the pliers into the base of the bulb to get a grip. Sometimes opening the pliers inside the metal threads will give you a grip.

If all else fails, use the needle nose pliers to collapse the metal threads until you can remove them.

Folks have phoned my radio show with the following suggestions for removal:

- Use your fingers, protected by heavy gloves.

- Use a fuse puller the same way I use a needle nose pliers.

- Jam into the broken base and turn with:

   – a large cork.

   – a wooden ruler.

   – a wad of white bread (perhaps you need some really heavy Italian bread).

   – a potato.

   – a trimmed paint-stirring stick.

Patio Screen Door Sticks and Rubs

Almost every sliding patio screen door in the world sticks, because few homeowners know they can adjust the rollers that run in the track. You still need to keep the track clean, but adjusting the rollers is the key.

Look at the base of the door; you will see two small Phillips screw heads. They will be above the frame or in the side of the door, near the bottom. Tightening these screws lowers the rollers and lifts the door so the door rolls on the rollers without rubbing the frame. **See Figure 10-3**.

Most doors have a similar roller adjustment for the top rollers. If the door is tight or bound in the frame, loosen these top screws to allow the door to be raised when lowering rollers and screws. Don't adjust the door to the point that it's squeezed between the top and bottom frame.

When you adjust the rollers, clean the track. Then spray a light lubricant on the frame and track.

Bathroom Paint and Mildew Problems

If your bathroom has problems with moisture, mildew and peeling paint, an exhaust fan is the best solution. You could have a fan installed in the ceiling or, if that's not practical, perhaps you can put a fan directly in an exterior wall.

Reduce bathroom moisture problems by wiping down wet surfaces after a shower and removing wet towels. Keep the bathroom door open after a shower. Consider using a small fan to circulate air into the hall.

You can also use a special paint that resists mildew and peeling. First, kill existing mildew with laundry bleach and water. Scrape away any loose paint, and sand the surfaces smooth. Spackle as needed. Then paint with Zinsser brand Perma-White Bathroom Wall and Ceiling Paint. This is a self-priming paint, so apply two coats. **See Figure 10-4**.

Zinsser Perma-White is a white semi-gloss paint that can also be tinted. I have used it for several years with great success. It is guaranteed to resist mildew and peeling.

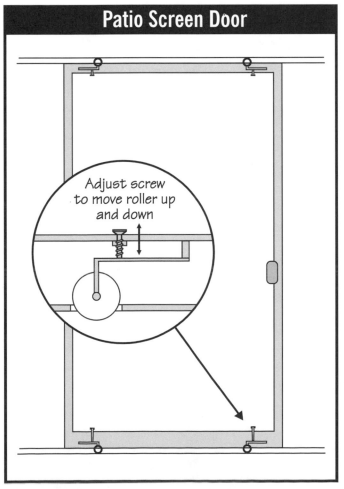

Figure 10-3.

Figure 10-4.

For information on how to contact the manufacturer of Zinsser Perma-White, see the References section.

Proper Venting of a Fireplace

The draft problem with most fireplaces in tightly-built homes is that the fire lacks sufficient air for combustion unless a window is open. Sometimes this produces smoke indoors. Fireplaces in older homes didn't have this problem because leaks around windows, doors and framing provided plenty of air for combustion.

A fireplace with an inadequate air supply can be dangerous. As a fire is starting or going out, it may back up dangerous carbon monoxide into your home. A fire with a strong draft can also interfere with the natural venting of a gas-fired water heater or furnace, causing a backdraft of combustion fumes into the home. Any gas-burning appliance vented by gravity up a chimney can have such a problem.

One good solution is to install small fresh-air vents that bring outside air directly in the firebox. A qualified brickmason, fireplace contractor, or chimney sweep must install such a system; it is definitely not a do-it-yourself project. The vent must penetrate an outside wall and the side or front of the fireplace. The vent may also need to be combined with fireplace doors. **See Figure 10-5**.

Remember that most natural fireplaces are heat losers when operated in cold weather. Most of the heat goes up the chimney. Fireplaces do work well at removing excessive moisture levels in the winter because they draw lots of air into your home for ventilation (provided a window is open!)

Gutter Leak—a Quick Patch

For quick repair of small holes in the rain gutters, try gutter repair or flashing tape. It's available in most hardware stores and is manufactured by several companies. This thick aluminum foil tape uses a mastic-type adhesive that's almost like thick tar. The tape comes in short rolls either 2" or 3" wide and costs just a few dollars.

To repair the gutter, clean away debris with a wire brush. Wash the area. Once it's dry, apply the tape, rubbing it well into the hole. The aluminum facing on the back side allows you to rub the tape securely onto the gutter. The foil also protects the patch from sunlight. The adhesive of the tape is thick enough to fill small holes and seams. This repair can easily last several years.

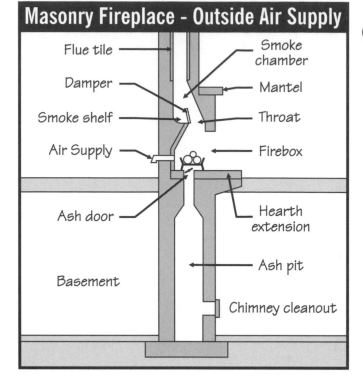

Masonry Fireplace - Outside Air Supply

Flue tile — Smoke chamber
Damper — Mantel
Smoke shelf — Throat
Air Supply — Firebox
Ash door — Hearth extension
Basement — Ash pit
Chimney cleanout

Figure 10-5.

Black Stuff Growing on the Roof

If your roof has light-colored shingles, you may see black streaks on them, especially on the north side. The problem is caused by mildew or fungus growth. There is less sunlight on the north side, so the roof stays damp. Mildew loves a damp surface.

The best way to prevent this algae growth is to provide sunlight and natural ventilation to dry the roof. Obviously, this is not always possible. At least keep all tree branches and leaves about 4 feet away from the roof.

Short of replacing the roof, there is no good quick fix. You could try killing the mildew with a strong solution of laundry bleach and water. Spray or brush the solution on the roof and wait until the areas turn lighter. Then rinse well. You could also use a mildew wash that is sold in paint stores for washing painted wood siding.

Several cautions about using bleach: protect yourself, the gutters, and plant materials. Spilled bleach solution can kill grass and bushes. Use eye and skin protection. Do not walk on the roof while cleaning;

it will be slippery and dangerous. Work from a ladder or use other special equipment. Flush the gutters and metal flashing well to prevent damage.

I suggest you hire a professional roofer for the cleaning. You can also purchase a product called Shingle Shield, which consists of zinc strips that are placed under the shingles near the peak of the roof. The zinc reacts with rainwater to produce a chemical that prevents the growth of fungus and mildew. Again, consult a professional roofer. Although the product inhibits the growth of new algae, it may not remove existing algae.

If you ever plan to replace the roof or build a new house, keep in mind that several shingle manufacturers offer shingles with a built-in mildew-resistant chemical.

Peeling Varnish on Front Door

Many homes feature a beautiful wood front door that is stained and varnished. In time, though, the varnish begins flaking and peeling, especially if there's no storm door.

Sunlight is the culprit. Ultraviolet (UV) rays attack the cellular structure of the wood under the varnish, giving it a "sunburn." Varnish can't stick to damaged wood. UV rays also damage the clear finish.

The best solution is to paint the door. Paint has coloring pigment that blocks UV rays and protects the wood. But if you really like that stained and varnished look, it requires a little work.

First you must sand, scrape or strip the damaged finish. Where the finish is in good condition, you must sand and roughen the surface. If the color of the wood has changed, you will need to stain the door before varnishing.

How far you go with the refinishing depends on the condition of the door. If more than 25% of the finish is damaged, your best bet is to chemically strip the door and start with bare wood.

For a final clear finish, look for a UV-resistant varnish (often called spar varnish or marine finish). This finish is expensive and may only be available in a gloss formula. Follow the specific instructions for your varnish, and don't forget to finish all six areas of the door (front, back, top, bottom and sides).

A final option would be to install a storm door to protect the wood door. There are attractive storm doors available that are mostly glass so your wood door can still show through.

Opening the Garage Door During a Power Outage

Let's say you've got an automatic garage door opener. It's a great convenience, one you take for granted...until the power goes out. Now what do you do?

Your door opener came with an emergency release. This allows you to disconnect the door from the automatic opener unit and open the door manually. The release is a lever attached to the track and door arm connection. **See Figure 10-6**.

It's a good idea to test this emergency release before you need it, just to make sure it works properly. If you are confused by the procedure even after reading the following instructions, have someone show you how the release operates.

Start with the door closed. This is very, very important. If the springs are not adjusted properly, a door released in the up position may crash to the ground. Open the door manually. You should only need to apply a few pounds of lift, and the door should almost balance at any point as you raise and lower it. If you must use excessive force to open the door or if it closes very quickly, the balancing springs need to be adjusted.

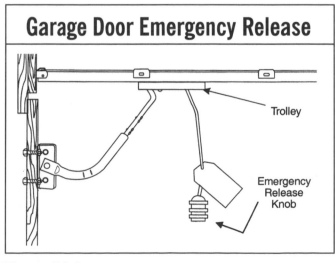

Garage Door Emergency Release

Trolley

Emergency Release Knob

Figure 10-6.

These springs have a tremendous amount of force, so have any necessary adjustment done by a professional. Sometimes the cable and pulley mechanisms also need adjustment or replacement.

If you have a detached garage without a service door (an ordinary-size door that provides alternate access without using the overhead door), you will be locked out of the garage when the power is off and the garage door is down. You need to find the special lock that releases the door from the outside. Hopefully, you door will have this feature – if not, you should add the release.

Find a circular lock at the top panel of the garage door, near the center, where the door connects to the operator track. **See Figure 10-7**. Open this lock and pull the attached cable through the opening. The cable attaches to the release that detaches the opener. You can now open the door manually.

Clean and Polish Brass Hardware

Real polished brass finishes on hardware and plumbing fixtures are preserved by the factory with a coat of clear lacquer finish. The lacquer prevents oxidation and tarnishing. Most of the shiny brass or antique brass finishes we see today feature a plated or painted finish, not real polished brass. You will find real polished brass only on very expensive hardware and old hardware.

If your fixtures have real polished brass, you can preserve the finish. First you must meticulously clean the surface with a cleaner or buffing compound. You can also clean and polish brass with 0000-grade steel wool and a paint stripper.

Once the brass is polished, apply a high-quality, non-abrasive, polymer-based car wax. If you prefer a more durable finish, apply lacquer or exterior polyurethane sealer. Wipe down the surface with lacquer thinner, and handle the surface only with clean cloths. Fingerprints contain skin oils that can damage the finish. After the surface is clean, apply the clear coating.

If your fixture has a brass finish with a polished, clear finish, don't use strong or abrasive cleaners. Instead, apply a coat of paste wax or automotive wax or a product like Faucet Bright to polish and protect the surface.

For information on how to contact the manufacturer of Faucet Bright (T.R. Industries), see the References section.

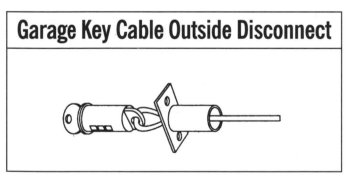

Garage Key Cable Outside Disconnect

Figure 10-7.

Garbage Disposal Out to Lunch

Two problems commonly occur with garbage disposals: (1) they make no noise and don't run at all, or (2) they "hum" without spinning. You can perform simple service on the unit yourself.

If the unit no longer "hums," the overload probably is tripped. First, switch the unit off. Then look under the sink and locate a small red button on the base of the unit. **See Figure 11-1**. This is the electrical reset. Push this button to reset the thermal overload/reset.

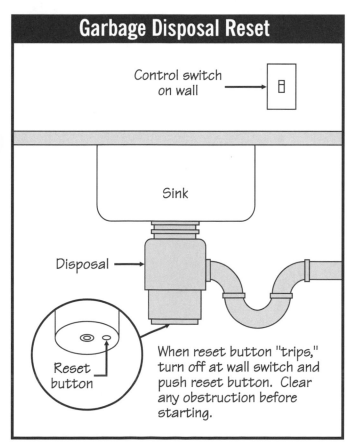

Garbage Disposal Reset

Control switch on wall

Sink

Disposal

Reset button

When reset button "trips," turn off at wall switch and push reset button. Clear any obstruction before starting.

Figure 11-1

Switch the unit on. If it "hums" but will not run, turn it off immediately—this indicates a jam in the disposal that needs to be cleared. The jam is what tripped the overload.

Look under the sink for a small L-shaped service wrench that looks like an Allen wrench with a bend on each end. It may be in a small plastic pouch stapled to the side of the cabinet. The bent end of this tool is a hex wrench. **See Figure 11-2**. Insert it into the hole you'll find under the disposal, at the center bottom. Work the wrench back and forth for several revolutions until the unit moves freely. As you move the wrench, you are moving the shaft of the disposal and clearing the jam.

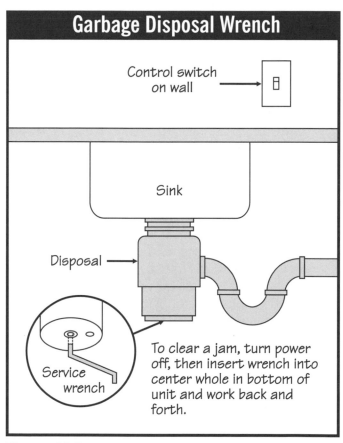

Garbage Disposal Wrench

Control switch on wall

Sink

Disposal

Service wrench

To clear a jam, turn power off, then insert wrench into center whole in bottom of unit and work back and forth.

Figure 11-2

If you don't find a service wrench in your cabinet, you can buy one at any hardware store. You can also free the disposal by working from above with a socket on the end of a long extension. The socket lets you turn a hex nut atop the shaft in the disposal.

Now look inside the disposal from above for any foreign objects and remove them with tongs. Run water and start the unit.

Frozen Pipes at the Kitchen Sink

A kitchen sink on an outside wall may be vulnerable to freezing during cold, windy conditions. The water supply and drain lines routed through the exterior wall can easily freeze when exposed to a small cold-air leak.

If the pipes are frozen, turn off the water supply, because when the ice begins to melt there may be a major leak. Thaw the pipes by opening the sink cabinet doors and directing a fan or a small space heater into the cabinet. In the basement or crawl space below the sink, place a small heater or heat lamp to warm the pipes.

You can also warm the pipes with a hair dryer or heat gun, but don't ever use a tool with an open flame. Take your time, and warm the pipes slowly. Periodically turn on the water supply to check for flow. Once the pipes are thawed, turn on the water and check for leaks. Remember that a small leak could be hidden in the wall.

You should also seek a permanent solution to the situation by looking for tiny holes that allow cold air to blow in and freeze a pipe. Start in the basement on a sunny day. Keep the basement lights turned off. See if sunlight leaks through the basement wall, sill area, foundation overhangs, or lower edge of the house siding. Caulk and fill any gaps; some may need to be filled from the outside. Remove existing insulation to expose the wood framing for inspection.

Next, make sure there is good insulation in the sill area above the foundation wall. Fill the area with tight-fitting fiberglass. Pack all areas between the outside framing and the top of the basement wall.

Insulate the supply pipe with plastic foam insulation (available at most building supply centers). Trim the insulation for a tight fit, and tape all joints.

If the problem persists, you may need to open kitchen sink cabinet doors during cold weather to allow for warm air circulation. You could also place a fan or small heater in the basement to help move and warm the air around the pipes.

As a last resort during very cold weather, leave the water running in a trickle at the fixture that freezes. The water circulation will warm the pipe and prevent freezing. This is a desperate measure, though, because it wastes a natural resource and puts an unnecessary load on sewage treatment facilities.

Frozen Sump Pump Lines

If your sump pump discharges through a 1¼" plastic pipe exposed to the weather, it could be vulnerable to freezing. A frozen pipe prompts the sump pump to run continuously until it fails, and then you can get water in the basement.

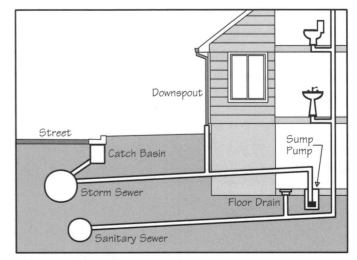

Figure 11-3

The best alternative is to have a storm sewer line installed underground into the basement and then connect the sump pump to this line but this is not practical with an existing home. **See Figure 11-3**. Your next best bet is to route the 1¼" pipe so it exits the basement at about 12" above grade if possible. Extend the pipe 12" away from your home and connect it to a 4"- to 6"-wide plastic drain tile, plastic pipe, or large downspout. **See Figure 11-4**. Extend this large pipe at a steep pitch so it discharges 6 to 8 feet away from your house. Water will drain through this large pipe with little chance of plugging and freezing.

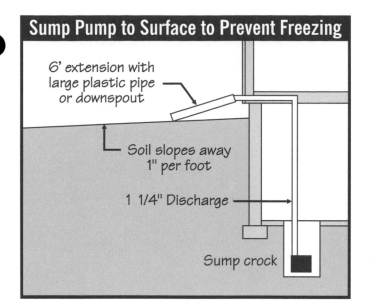

Figure 11-4

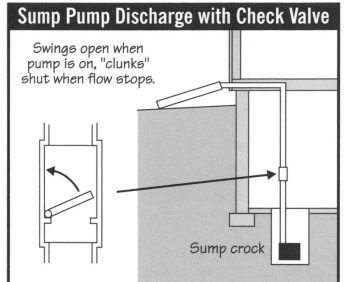

Figure 11-5

It's important to pitch the exposed 1¼" pipe in the right direction as it exits the house. The "right" pitch depends on whether your sump pump has a check valve. If there is a check valve, it will be on the vertical discharge pipe just above the pump. The check valve is slightly larger than the pipe. If the pipe is steel, the check valve is screwed in; if the pipe is plastic, the check valve is attached with rubber hose connections When the pump turns off, the check valve is the part that "clunks" shut.

If your sump pump has a check valve, pitch the pipe away from your home; otherwise the check valve will trap water in the pipe, where it could freeze. If your pump doesn't have a check valve, pitch the pipe slightly toward the inside, allowing water to siphon back into the crock when the pump turns off.

Thumping from the Sump Pump

The check valve is the culprit when you hear a loud noise as the sump pump shuts off. Every time the pump runs, it pushes open the check valve. **See Figure 11-5**. When the pump stops, the valve slams shut with a thump. This can be annoying at times.

Some clunking is normal as the check valve stops water from siphoning back down the discharge pipe into the crock. If there is a long pipe run, this siphoning water could fill the crock. The pump would start up again to remove the same water.

This could happen over and over. So—the check valve is important.

On a short pipe run that goes directly up and out of the basement with no horizontal section more than 5 feet long, it's less likely that water will flow back into the crock. In this case, you could remove the check valve. You could also experiment with adding a small hole or vent pipe at the top of the pipe run outside your home. This small hole will allow air into the top of the pipe and break the siphoning. The water below the vent will still flow back into the crock.

Or, consider installing a newer check valve that may be quieter.

Finally, try to isolate the piping from the wood framing of your home. If the piping is firmly attached to the wood framing, or wedged against the framing, the wood amplifies sounds and vibrations. Hang the piping with wire or metal straps and add foam insulation between the piping and the straps.

If Your Sump Pump Never Runs...

In some houses, the sump pump never seems to run. Is this a problem?

If your basement walls and floor are always dry, even during heavy rains, you don't need to do anything. Natural drainage around your home must be preventing water from reaching the drain tile system and sump crock. Test the pump several times a year by filling the crock with a hose until the pump turns on. That way, you know the pump will work if water ever does enter the system.

However, if there is dampness in your basement and your sump crock remains dry, there may be a problem with the tile system. Water around the foundation should reach the crock and get pumped out. This situation should be checked by a consultant or contractor because of the potential for excessive pressure that can cause extensive basement wall problems.

Leaking Air Gap ("Chrome Mushroom") on the Sink

The "chrome mushroom" next to the kitchen faucet is an air gap for the dishwasher drain line. When the dishwasher pumps out the dirty water, it flows up to this air gap, makes a U-turn, and is routed down a drain line. This "air gap" provides a physical break that keeps dirty water from flowing back into the dishwasher. **See Figure 11-6**.

Without an air gap, the drain line from the dishwasher would be connected directly to the garbage disposal or the side of the drain line below the sink. If the sink or disposal ever backs up with dirty water, this line could carry contaminated water into the dishwasher.

If the air gap leaks, remove the chrome or plastic cover and clean the plastic parts. The cover simply lifts off. You will find a plastic U-shaped tube that routes water back down a drain line. At the opening in the U, look for deposits that need to be removed.

Toilet Running at Night

Ah, yes! The mysterious toilet that runs in the night. If you hear this happening and want to check what's going on, place a few drops of food coloring in the tank, and soon color will appear in the bowl. This indicates a slight leak in the flush valve.

Water is slowly draining from the tank into the bowl, then down the sewer line. Because the excessive water in the bowl automatically flows through the trap into the sewer, you never see a leak. As the water in the tank slowly lowers, the float goes down and the fill valve automatically fills the tank.

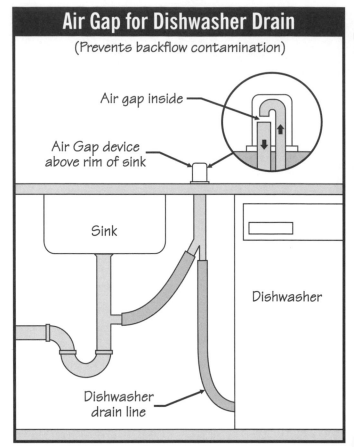

Figure 11-6

Check the fit of the flush valve to its seat. There may be a flapper valve or a ball valve. Dirt or rust that accumulates on the mating surfaces can cause a small leak; wipe the parts with a coarse cloth. Also, the parts may be out of alignment, or the rubber of the flush valve may be cracked and leaking. Replace the valve if it is damaged. **See Figure 11-7**.

Toilet with Poor Flush

You could try several things on a stubborn toilet:

1. Pour 2 or 3 gallons of water from a pail directly into the bowl. If it flushes well, the drain and vent are probably clear. If it does not flush, clear the trap with a plunger or snake. As a last resort, remove the toilet to clear the trap, or have a plumber clear the blockage.

2. Make sure that the water level in the tank is at the water mark or just below the overflow tube.

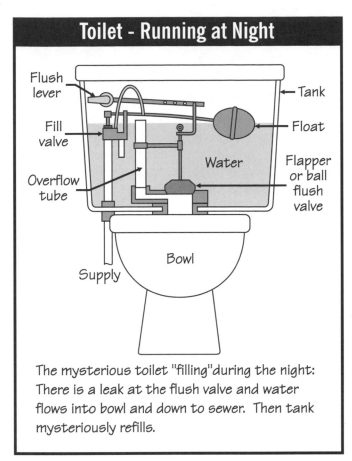

Toilet - Running at Night

Flush lever

Fill valve

Overflow tube

Supply

Tank

Float

Water

Flapper or ball flush valve

Bowl

The mysterious toilet "filling" during the night: There is a leak at the flush valve and water flows into bowl and down to sewer. Then tank mysteriously refills.

Figure 11-7

3. If there are rocks or bottles in the tank, throw them at the former homeowner. (Just joking!) Remove them, because they displace some of the water needed for a good flush.

4. Check the operation of the flush valve. Is it opening fully and staying open until all the water is out of the tank? Some valve balls or flappers become waterlogged and close too early. Hold the valve open and check the flush.

5. Check for a jet flush hole—a ¾" opening in the front edge of the toilet trap. Water flows from the jet to aid the flow down the trap. If there is a jet flush hole, it should be free of deposits. If necessary, use acid cleaner (available at plumbing supply stores) and a stick to clear the opening.

6. On an old toilet, the holes around the rim and the chamber leading to the holes may be blocked. Use acid cleaner to clean this chamber and the holes. Follow specific instructions on the product you buy. The usual procedure is to plug the holes with plumber's putty, pour acid into the overflow tube, and allow the acid to sit for a while to dissolve deposits.

7. Calling a plumber or installing a new toilet is my last suggestion.

Banging Pipes (Water Hammer)

Why do water pipes bang?

You might hear thumping or banging when water stops filling the toilet tank…or when you turn water off quickly at certain faucets…or after the washing machine draws water.

You may need a plumber to fix this problem, but first you can try a simple trick. Your plumbing system probably has air cushions. These cushions or shock absorber chambers, located near the laundry, the kitchen, or the main valve, were initially filled with air so that when a valve closed quickly, the force of the water movement bounced against the air cushion. This prevented the hammering. **See Figure 11-8, 11-9**.

Now these air cushions are probably filled with water. To solve the problem, you need to drain your plumbing system. Start by turning off the main water supply. Then open all the faucets in your home. Air will be drawn into the upper faucets. Water will drain from the lower faucets.

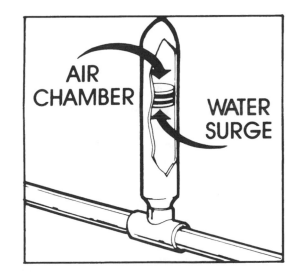

AIR CHAMBER

WATER SURGE

Figure 11-8.

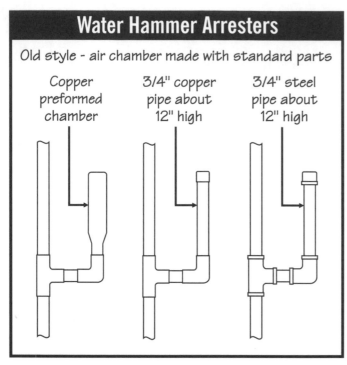

Water Hammer Arresters

Old style - air chamber made with standard parts

Copper preformed chamber

3/4" copper pipe about 12" high

3/4" steel pipe about 12" high

Figure 11-9.

When water stops flowing, slowly fill the system by opening the main valve slightly. Walk through your home closing each valve as air is eliminated and a solid stream of water flows through that faucet. After you have closed all the faucets, open the main valve fully.

Now you should have an air cushion in the shock absorber chambers. If this does not do the trick, call a plumber. Remember that sediment and air may come out of the faucets for a short time after you've performed this procedure.

The water-hammer effect can be especially severe with automatic washing machines that have electrically operated water valves which may close very quickly. If your washer doesn't have shock absorber chambers, a plumber can install them. To check whether yours does, look for a 12" tube or a 4" chamber extending above the hose bib connections for the water.

Also, check that piping to the washer is properly supported, because the banging can be compounded when pipes move around and hit wood framing or other objects. Adding a support may help correct the problem.

Don't ignore the problem. Eventually, water hammer can cause a break. Have a qualified plumber modify your system.

Two Sump Pumps?

Homeowners sometimes wonder whether their basement has two sump pumps. That's not really the case. The answer involves understanding the two types of water that must be removed from the home: wastewater and groundwater.

Your home's sanitary waste system routes wastewater from toilets, sinks, tubs and drains to a septic system or a sewage treatment plant. In homes with a private septic system, the main line to the septic tank usually exits the basement about 4 feet up from the basement floor.

Most wastewater flows by gravity through pipes to this main exit. However, water from the basement floor drain and any basement laundry tubs flows into a crock and must be pumped up to the main line. This is accomplished by a small pump called a lift pump or a gray water sewage ejector that looks like a sump pump. **See Figure 11-10.**

In older homes, this lift pump may have a loose-fitting cover, just like a sump pump. It may be a pedestal pump with the motor above the water

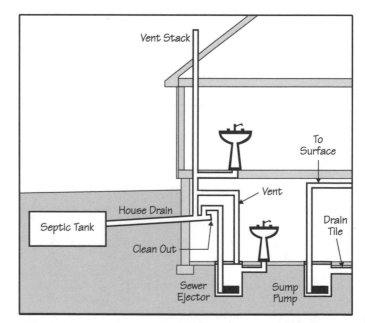

Figure 11-10 Sump Pump And Sewer Ejector

level or a submersible pump with the pump and motor below the water. Newer homes will have a tightly sealed crock and a submersible pump.

The other pump in your basement is a sump pump. Groundwater flows through a drain tile system below the basement floor and near the footings. As this groundwater collects in the sump pump crock, the sump pump ejects it up to the surface or to a storm sewer line. Eventually, storm sewers discharge to rivers and streams, not to the septic system or the municipal sewer treatment plant.

So, you may have two pumps—a lift pump removing sanitary sewer water, and a sump pump removing clear water. I suggest you check these pumps periodically to make sure they are moving water. The newer type of lift pump in a covered sump pit should be tightly sealed with cover gaskets and screws.

One word of caution: there is always an exception. In a very large basement, or a remodeled or repaired basement, you may find two sump pumps. The key to determining the type of pump is the source or type of wastewater and the final destination of the water.

"Slippery" Water

If you are accustomed to unsoftened water and move into a home with a water softener, you might find that softened water feels slippery, especially in the shower. This can take a little adjustment on your part. However, with softened water, clothes will be easier to wash and dishes will have fewer water spots. There is no method that allows you to partially soften water and make it less slippery.

Dripping Water Heater

On the side of the water heater is a temperature/pressure valve with a handle. This valve is designed as a safety measure—it will open if the water heater overheats and creates excessive pressure. **See Figure 11-11**.

When the valve develops a leak, though, water runs down the tube and drips on the floor. A leaky valve should be replaced. The leak can get worse at

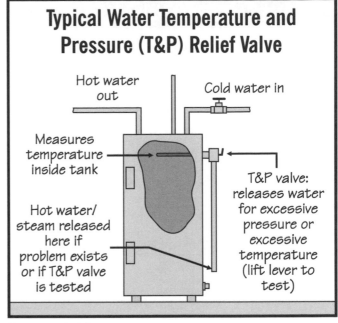

Figure 11-11

any time. More seriously, the constant flow of water may corrode or seal shut the valve with hard water scale, and that creates a potential danger. A new valve costs about $20 and take less than 30 minutes to install.

Dripping Valves—Interior

Sometimes an indoor valve—for example, a basement valve for an outside water connection—develops a slow drip. How can you fix the leak?

Examine the valve and you'll see that the handle is mounted on a round brass stem or shaft. The shaft enters the body of the valve through a hole in a hex nut. If you tighten this hex nut (packing nut), the leak should stop. You only need to tighten this packing nut slightly to stop the drip.

If you overtighten the packing nut, the valve will be hard to operate and you may not be able to turn the handle at all. If the valve is hard to operate, just loosen the nut. **See Figure 11-12**.

Globe Valve

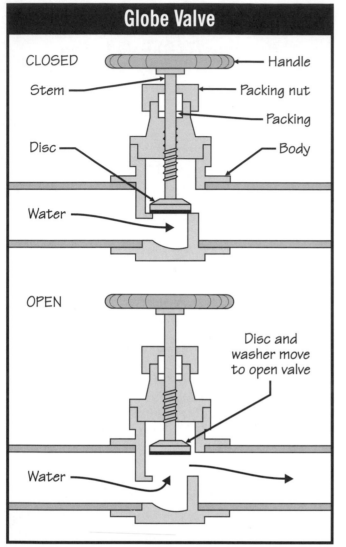

CLOSED

Handle

Stem

Packing nut

Packing

Disc

Body

Water

OPEN

Disc and washer move to open valve

Water

Figure 11-12

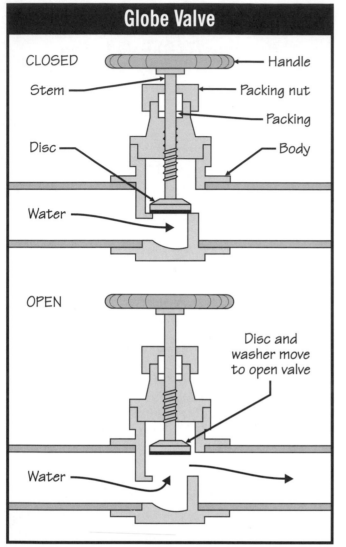

> **Caution**
>
> If the valve has a buildup of corrosion and hard water scale inside, tightening the nut may not solve the problem. You may need to dismantle the valve and replace a packing ring or washer below the nut. To rebuild the valve, you may need to clean the stem and/or replace parts.

Dripping Garden Hoses

Many of us have problems with garden hoses that leak at the fittings. This is easy to fix with the new products on the market. By paying attention to leaks and spending a few bucks and a few minutes, we can conserve water—a precious resource.

The most common problem is a missing or hardened washer. Open the fitting and look for the washer inside the female end of the fitting. If the washer is hard or damaged, replace it with a new washer.

While you have the fitting open, look at the male end of the fitting. It should have a relatively flat surface to contact the washer. Both of the threaded ends should be relatively round. **See Figure 11-13**.

Polymer Female Hose Menders	Polymer Male Hose Menders

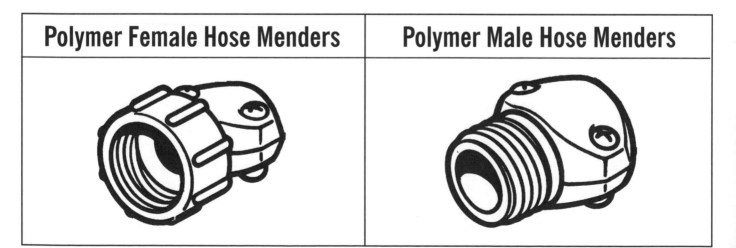

Figure 11-13

If the threaded ends are out of round, or if they're bent or cracked, replace them. You can buy great replacement ends at the hardware store. Cut off the old fitting with a sharp knife and take it to the hardware store to match the inside hose diameter with the new fitting. The best fittings are plastic with small plastic clamps. You slip the fitting into the hose and tighten down the clamp. If you have trouble slipping the hose over the fitting, warm it with hot water.

If there's a break or split in the hose, cut out the bad area and buy a fitting to connect the hose sections.

Name Game, Part 1: Hose Bib

"Hose bib" is a plumbing term for an exterior hose faucet or hose connection. I don't know where the term orginated, but a hose bib is just a faucet. **See Figure 11-14**.

Name Game, Part 2: Water Closet

Do you know what a water closet is? Sure, a toilet. Where did that name come from?

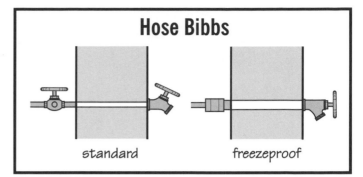

Figure 11-14

The modern toilet was invented by a English plumber named Thomas Crapper, who solved what was then a serious problem in London: the waste of clean water. He founded a large manufacturing company that produced toilets carrying his name. When our soldiers visited Europe during World War I, many of them saw a toilet for the first time. All the toilets were labeled Crapper. The rest is history.

Dishwasher Will Not Run

Let's say you've just moved into your home. You load the dishwasher for the first time, and it won't run.

Before you complain to the former homeowner or call a repair technician, try this:

There may be a switch on the wall above the kitchen counter. It looks like a light switch, but it turns electricity to the dishwasher on and off to prevent the dishwasher from being turned on when you don't want it on (for instance, when a toddler starts playing with the controls).

Every homeowner should know about this mystery switch. Even I had to learn about it from somebody else—and I'm "Mr. Fix-It."

Fuses or Breakers Which Is Better?

An older fuse system that is working well need not be replaced merely to convert to modern circuit breakers; it is a safe system. However, replacing it with circuit breakers will increase the value of your home and may be needed for increased capacity.

Both systems have pros and cons. **See Figure 12-1**. A fuse is the best protection for an overload—it will trip every time. A circuit breaker, on the other hand, is an electromechanical device that has a very slight chance of failure to trip.

On some fuse systems, a fuse can be replaced with a fuse that's too large, creating a potential overload of wiring.

If you are concerned about your system, hire an electrician or home inspector to do an inspection that includes:

- checking the wiring for signs of overheating.

- tightening of connections.

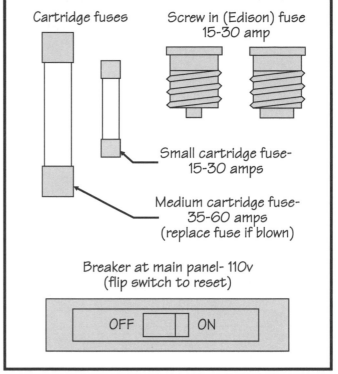

Fuses and breakers

Cartridge fuses

Screw in (Edison) fuse 15-30 amp

Small cartridge fuse- 15-30 amps

Medium cartridge fuse- 35-60 amps (replace fuse if blown)

Breaker at main panel- 110v (flip switch to reset)

OFF | ON

Figure 12-1.

- inspecting the main feed and ground.

- checking that all fuses and breakers are matched to the wire size they feed.

- inspecting feeds and grounds to subpanels.

- checking several typical outlets for proper wiring.

After this inspection, you can decide whether a new system is warranted. Systems are usually replaced when increased electrical service is required; 60-amp fuse systems have limited capacity.

Problems with Fluorescent Lights

Always switch off the fixture before you remove lamps (bulbs) from a fluorescent light.

Humming

Humming or buzzing in a fluorescent light fixture is usually caused by a ballast that's poorly built or improperly mounted. The hum occurs as electrical current moves through metal plates in the ballast. **See Figure 12-2**.

With the power off, open the fixture. The ballast is a metal box with wires leading to it. (In a 4'-long fixture, the ballast measures about 2" by 3" by 10".) Make sure that the mounting screws are tight. If there are vibration-isolation spacers, check them. Identify the problem by comparing this bad fixture to any similar quiet fixtures you may have. It may be necessary to replace the ballast.

Also check to make sure that the metal housing of the fixture is not amplifying the sound. You may need to change the mounting.

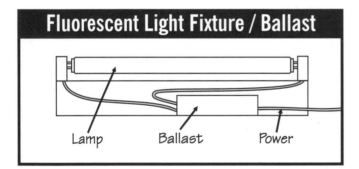

Figure 12-2.

Flashes and Intermittent Light

When a fluorescent fixture flashes and glows but don't fully light, or if one bulb works and the other doesn't, try these steps.

The electrical connections at the end of the bulbs (technically called lamps or tubes) may be dirty. Remove the lamps and inspect the the metal connectors at either end. If they are dirty, rub with a coarse cloth. If there is visible corrosion, lightly sand the metal until it is clean and shiny. Re-install the lamps and test the fixture.

If they still don't light, try replacing them. Worn lamps will have black marks inside, near the ends. Some of the white coating inside the lamps may be falling off. When a fixture has more than one lamp, replace all the lamps at once. Note the identification numbers on the ends of the lamps so you can buy matching lamps.

Also, inspect the lamps' mounting brackets. They may be loose or corroded; the metal parts may be damaged. Make sure that the metal conductors inside the brackets securely contact the metal tips of the lamps.

If the light still does not work, it may have a faulty ballast or starter. This type of replacement is best left to a professional, and often it's not worth the time and effort on a cheap shop-type fixture.

Attic Fan

On hot days during the summer, you might hear a faint noise coming from the attic. It's not your imagination—it's the attic ventilation fan.

This fan is designed to remove excessive heat from the attic during hot summer days. The fan unit includes an electric box with a commercial-type thermostat that must be set with a screwdriver. It will be set at about 100 degrees F.

The sun's rays can easily heat the attic to 100 degrees. At that point, the fan turns on, drawing cooler air through the attic vents. When the attic temperature drops below 100 degrees, the fan turns off.

Cooling the attic in this way limits the buildup of heat that would otherwise flow through the ceiling into your home's living spaces. **See Figure 13-1**.

Cool Air from the Furnace

If you were accustomed to an older furnace and now have a high-efficiency gas furnace, the air coming from the grills might feel cool and drafty.

Modern energy-efficient furnaces convert as much as 95% of gas energy into heat. Very old furnaces converted as little as 60% of the energy into heat.

This increase in efficiency means that newer furnaces can't heat the air to a high temperature the way the old furnaces did. To further increase efficiency, newer furnaces must also move more air across the heat exchanger surfaces. You may feel a draft as this cooler air discharges at a greater speed from the supply duct grills.

You could install plastic deflectors on the grills to redirect the air flow. When the air is not blowing across your skin, you will not feel the draft.

If you are still uncomfortable, ask your contractor to check whether the furnace was set up properly and that the fan speed is set correctly. If you notice a draft at one particular register, ask the contractor to lower the flow to that register.

Some top-of-the-line furnaces also have variable speed fans (variable air flow) and variable heating rates to adjust for this "draft" problem. Have the contractor check that all settings are correct.

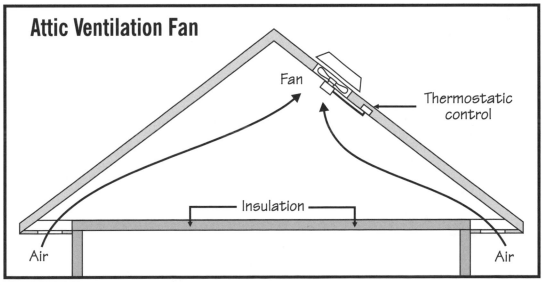

Attic Ventilation Fan

Fan

Thermostatic control

Insulation

Air

Air

Figure 13-1.

Most people don't find the new furnaces objectionable once they understand the operating principles. You may just need to get used to the cooler air discharge while you enjoy the 35% energy savings. And because this furnace uses less energy, now you can afford to set the thermostat higher for greater comfort.

One Cold Room

Suppose you notice, during your first heating season in a home, that one of the rooms is always cold and that there is little airflow through the heating duct even when the grill is fully open. The previous owner may have closed the heating supply duct to this room.

In the basement, look at the main warm-air supply duct. This duct originates directly above the furnace. Often it is a rectangular duct running down the center of the basement.

This rectangular duct may branch off into smaller circular ducts serving individual room registers. Where the round duct is attached to the rectangular main, look for evidence of a duct damper—a wing nut around the end of a ¼" threaded rod. There will be a screwdriver slot in the end of the rod. **See Figure 13-2**.

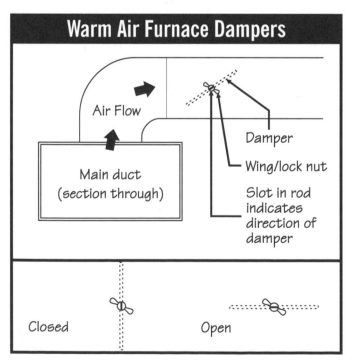

Warm Air Furnace Dampers

Air Flow

Damper

Wing/lock nut

Slot in rod indicates direction of damper

Main duct (section through)

Closed   Open

Figure 13-2.

If the slot is perpendicular to the small round duct, the damper is closed. If the slot is parallel to the duct, the damper is open. You can loosen the wing nut and change the position of the damper. Then secure it by retightening the wing nut.

The threaded rod might have a lever that indicates whether the damper is open or closed. Some rods have flat sides parallel to the duct damper.

Some room ducts may be rectangular rather than round, but they will have similar rods and controls.

If opening the damper solves the problem, great. If the room is still cold, you may need to partially close other dampers to direct more air to the cold room. Often, dampers fit loosely, and even when fully closed, they can leak substantial amounts of air.

Close Storm Windows with Air Conditioning

If possible, close storm windows when running your air conditioner. For some homes, this is impossible, because the storms are replaced with screens for the summer.

Adding that one pane of glass to a standard window increases the R value (insulation value) from 1 to 2, doubling the resistance to heat loss. The storm also helps stop infiltration of hot, moist air into your home. Closing blinds to block out the sun also greatly reduces heat gain.

Using storms in the summer is less important than using them in the winter because of temperature differentials. In the winter we can experience temperature differences between the inside air and outside air of 70 degrees or more. During the summer, the difference is rarely more than 20 degrees. However, storms are still important in summer, because running the air conditioner is more expensive per energy unit than running the furnace.

Clean the Heating Ducts

Cleaning the ductwork is not necessary in a newer home unless someone in the family has a respiratory problem. But in homes that are more than 25 years old, cleaning the ducts is a good idea, especially if you are considering a new furnace.

New energy-efficient furnaces move more air through the ductwork, stirring up old dust. Also, cleaning the ductwork helps keep the furnace clean, which prolongs its life and produces greater energy efficiency. You could clean the ductwork before you install the furnace or as the furnace is installed, when the ducts will be opened.

See the References section for information on a free booklet about cleaning ducts.

Dehumidifier Freeze-Up

Many homeowners run a dehumidifier in the basement. Sometimes the dehumidifier will freeze up and stop running. There are several causes to investigate.

The humidifier could have a dirty coil. Dirt slows air flow and limits heat transfer, causing the coil to ice up.

After disconnecting the power, clean the coils with a vacuum. Remember that there are two sets of coils to clean. Inspect the fan (you might need to remove a cover to reach it), because the fan blades may also need to be washed. **See Figure 13-3**.

It may be too cold in the basement. You can raise the temperature by providing heat to the basement. You can also keep the dehumidifier far above the floor so it operates in warmer air.

Finally, the unit may have a refrigeration or control problem that needs to be evaluated by a professional.

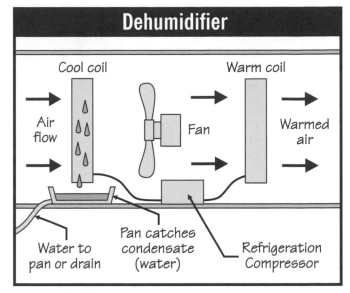

Figure 13-3.

Snow and Water in the Attic

Heavy wind during snowstorms or rain storms can carry snow or rain through attic vents at times. This is normal. Often, the moisture will evaporate before you notice it. However, if there are water stains on the insulation or ceilings, you should have a roofer move or modify the vent.

Placing a pan below the vent is a good option for an occasional small leak. **See Figure 14-1**. The water in the pan will evaporate without damage to your home. Don't try to get by using a pan for a large leak, though—it could lead to a large problem.

Ice Blocking the Gutters

In winter, ice can build up in the gutters, forming a condition called an ice dam. **See Figure 14-2**.

The process is triggered by excessive heat in the attic. The heat warms the roof deck, causing rooftop snow to melt. The slushy melted snow flows down the roof and into the gutters. Since gutters aren't warmed by the escaping heat, they remain cold, and the slush refreezes there. As the process continues, the ice gets thicker, forming a dam.

Eventually, water ponds behind the ice (the same way water pools behind a river dam), and this water can leak through an asphalt shingle roof. Roof shingles are designed to shed water but will not resist ponding water. The leaks will occur just above the ice dams, penetrating the overhangs.

Your best defense against ice dams is to keep the attic cool with good ventilation and adequate insulation. The attic should have about R-40 (about 15") of insulation. Close all air leaks into the attic, and insulate and seal all access doors.

Check ventilation openings. There should be about one square foot of ventilation per 150 square feet of attic floor space. Half the ventilation openings should be high in the attic and half should be in the overhangs. For homes with a vapor barrier below the insulation, the ventilation ratio is 1 per 300.

If ice dams persist even when there are no obvious problems with attic insulation and ventilation, you may need the help of a professional insulation contractor. Ventilation can be tricky with complicated roof designs. Air leaks from the heated space to the attic are a common cause of attic problems, but often they are hard to find.

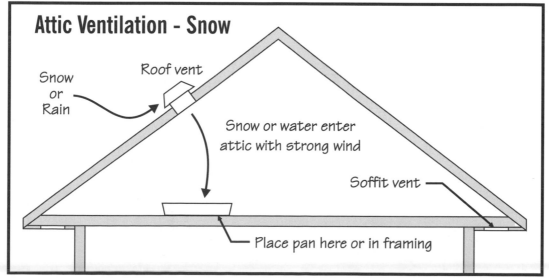

Attic Ventilation - Snow

Snow or Rain

Roof vent

Snow or water enter attic with strong wind

Soffit vent

Place pan here or in framing

Figure 14-1.

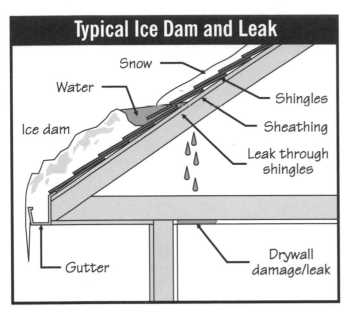

Figure 14-2.

Moisture on the Windows

Often, moisture ("steam") condenses on windows in the fall with the start of the winter heating season. As long as moisture condenses only occasionally and disappears after several weeks, you don't need to do anything.

Condensation requires a cool surface and moisture in the air. Inside your home, when the temperature of the glass drops below the dew point of the inside air, invisible water vapor in the air condenses on the cool glass. More condensation occurs when there is more water vapor in the air and/or when glass surfaces become colder.

Over the summer, moisture slowly accumulates in furniture, walls, woodwork, cloth and other surfaces. In the fall, as the exterior temperature drops for the first time, some of this moisture condenses on cold window glass. Most moisture leaks out of your home as your furnace runs and vent fans are used. Eventually, all the materials in your home dry out, and moisture stops condensing on the windows. This normally takes a few weeks.

If condensation continues to form on windows after several weeks, your home may have excessive moisture. Most moisture problems can be solved by limiting sources of moisture and improving ventilation.

Reducing Severe Dampness Throughout the House

Some homes have problems with excessive moisture. It's most noticeable as condensation on windows. If moisture is excessive and stays on your windows for several days…if water runs off windows and damages wood surfaces…if ice forms on windows and frames…or if storm windows remained fogged up and icy all winter, you need to reduce the humidity level inside your home.

Condensation requires a cool surface and moisture in the air. Inside your home, when the temperature of the glass drops below the dew point of the inside air, invisible water vapor in the air condenses as water on the cool glass. More condensation occurs when there is more water vapor in the air and/or when glass surfaces become colder.

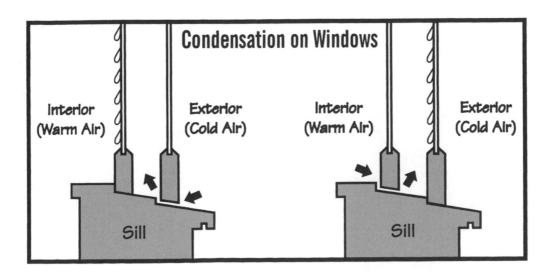

Evaluate changes you have made to your home—any effort to tighten up a home and reduce air infiltration will increase humidity levels. A high-efficiency furnace vented with two plastic pipes draws combustion air from outside and reduces ventilation. Weatherstripping, better windows, caulking, and any other measures you have taken to reduce air leaks will increase the amount of moisture retained inside your home.

Try to increase ventilation by running kitchen and bath exhaust fans whenever steam is produced by cooking or bathing/showering. In the bathroom, keep the fan running until the bathroom is dry. Add timer switches to the fans if necessary.

Limit the number of plants in your home. Look for plumbing leaks or damp areas in the basement. If basement crawl spaces have bare soil, cover the soil with a vapor barrier.

There are many other sources of moisture and ways to eliminate excess moisture. Often your local natural gas utility company can provide information on moisture problems. University extensions often have good booklets on solving moisture problems.

Excessive Winter Dryness Indoors

Humidification of air inside the home has been the subject of many articles and investigations. Manufactures of humidifiers have claimed that humidified air would protect us from health hazards, but there are no firm facts that humidified air is better for us. In fact, humidifiers can cause problems with excessive moisture and even mold or bacteria.

To decide on the need for a humidifier, evaluate the comfort of your home during the dead of winter. Many of today's tighter, energy-efficient homes don't need additional moisture. Condensation on windows indicates excessive humidity; in that case, you don't need a humidifier. However, if your nose and skin are dry, and static electricity is a problem, you may need a humidifier.

The best type is a central humidifier that mounts on a forced-air furnace. Look for one that flushes water over a panel and drains away excess water as it operates. It should be mounted on the return duct to prevent water leaks into the furnace, and it should have a humidistat control that automatically turns the unit on as needed.

Aprilaire is a quality brand of furnace-mounted humidifier. **See Figure 14-3**. Its newer models have a removable plastic cover that makes the unit easy to maintain. This type flushes water over a panel and doesn't require a water reservoir.

Portable humidifiers can operate with a reservoir and evaporative panel. To create mist, some use ultrasound, others use a spinning wheel (for a cool mist), and others use heat (making steam). I consider all of these types hard to maintain and difficult to control. Any unit with a water reservoir is a potential source of mold or bacteria and must be meticulously cleaned and disinfected on a routine basis.

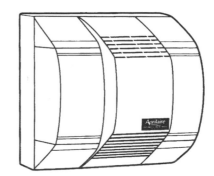

Figure 14-3.

15 MYSTERIOUS SOUNDS & SIMPLE SOLUTIONS

Strange Sounds Throughout the House

During the night, you may hear creaking, cracking and other strange sounds in various parts of your house. You might also hear sounds during the day when other noises have quieted. What causes the sounds?

Our homes are "breathing" and reacting to moisture and temperature changes.

Most of the noises you hear are natural, and you need not worry unless walls are leaning, doors are sticking, and floors are sagging. The noises are caused by the normal expansion and contraction of wood and manmade materials.

Some of the biggest offenders are wood framing, vinyl and metal siding, plumbing, and heating ducts. Wood can shrink 1/4" or more across 6" of wood grain as its moisture content changes with the seasons. This movement makes floors creak, move and crack.

As the drywall or plaster attached to the wood framing attempts to move, you can hear cracks and pops. You will often see drywall nails popping from the drywall surface as the wood shrinks or expands.

Masonry chimneys, tile chimney liners and the wood framing attached to them move at different rates, and this also creates noises. Imagine how hot that chimney liner can get and how much it may move in that cold masonry chimney.

Your basement has metal heating ducts and metal piping attached to wood framing. When you run hot water in the bathroom, the cool pipe becomes hot and expands significantly. This expanding pipe is attached to the wood frame of your home, and it must bounce and slide along the framing or hangers until the expansion is accommodated.

Outside your home, vinyl siding is often a culprit for clicks and thumps. Vinyl siding must be installed so it can move horizontally. As outdoor temperatures change, or when bright sunlight hits the siding on a cold day, you will hear movement noises.

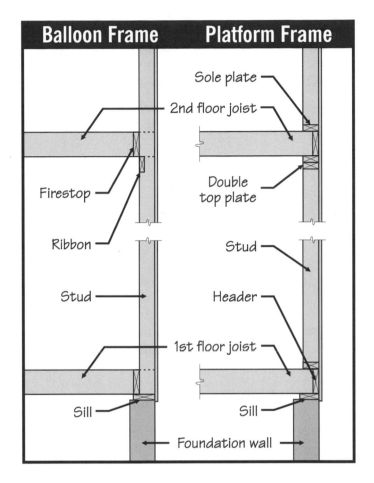

Aluminum siding, metal gutters, and metal flashing all move with temperature changes.

And boy, those water pipes pound, slush, and gurgle as water flows and drains. Pipes can pound loudly if the air cushion has been lost in the water hammer arresters—air chambers that absorb the energy when water changes direction. See the "Plumbing Mysteries" section for more detail.

Does your toilet run at night when no one is using the bathroom? There's a solution to this problem, too, in "Plumbing Mysteries."

Don't forget that the water softener and sump pump can run at almost any time with a spurt, whoosh or clunk as a valve closes.

Did I miss anything? Sure. Everything in your home that is hot, cool, dry or moist or that moves water or air can cause noises. Don't worry about the sounds. Just chalk them up to the personality of your living, breathing home.

Water Heater Popping and Pounding

If your gas water heater makes a popping and pounding sound when heating water, this indicates that sediment has built up on the bottom of the tank. When the gas flame is on, the water boils, just like water in a metal pan on the stovetop. The sediment at the tank bottom hinders heat transfer and releases steam bubbles, and when the bubbles rise into colder water in the upper part of the tank, they collapse as the steam turns back into water. Their collapsing makes the popping and pounding sounds. **See Figure 15-1**.

Often there is little you can do to remove the sediment from the bottom of the tank. Usually it consists of hard water scale that is literally bonded to the tank. This same scale sticks to the plumbing fixtures in your home. You could try draining several gallons of water from the drain valve near the bottom of the tank, which removes any loose sediment. To do this, attach a hose to the valve on the bottom of the tank and let 5 or 10 gallons of water drain out. Be careful—the water will be hot. If the drain water is full of sediment, you are having some success and you should repeat the procedure several times over several days. Often, though, little or no sediment will be removed.

Since the drain probably hasn't been operated for years, be prepared for leaks in the stem or valve. You can use a garden hose cap with a rubber washer to stop a drip from the valve. You can also tighten the valve stem to stop a leak at the stem. If there is excessive leaking, you will need to replace the valve.

The popping and pounding does little harm to the water heater or the piping. When a water heater gets to be about 10 or 20 years old, it has exceeded its normal lifespan, and you should plan for a replacement.

Banging / Clicking Heat Ducts

You might notice two distinct sounds coming from your warm air furnace and central air conditioner. When the air conditioning starts, the ductwork may produce a loud bang; this does not occur when the heat turns on. On the other hand, when the heating system starts and runs for a few minutes, you might hear clicking and slight pounding in the ductwork at the far end of the basement. Both problems have simple solutions. **See Figure 15-2**.

When the air conditioner runs, the furnace fan must move more air through the system than when the unit is used for heating. Often the fan will automatically run at a higher speed for greater volume and pressure.

Because air is moving through the system with greater speed, volume, and pressure, it is more likely that the ductwork will "pop" outward. Isolate the problem by listening for the sound and watching the ductwork when the air conditioner starts. You will probably find the sound coming from large, flat pieces of sheet metal near the furnace. Screw a lightweight angle iron over the part of the duct that is moving.

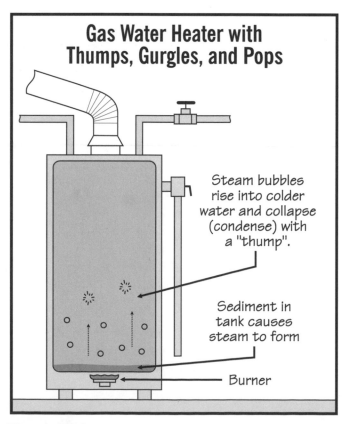

Gas Water Heater with Thumps, Gurgles, and Pops

Steam bubbles rise into colder water and collapse (condense) with a "thump".

Sediment in tank causes steam to form

Burner

Figure 15-1.

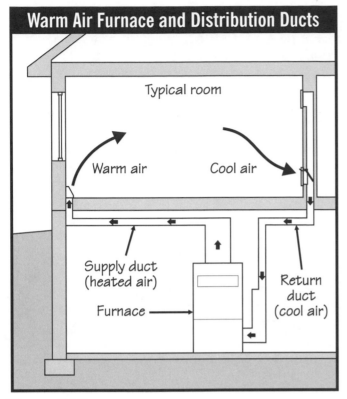

Warm Air Furnace and Distribution Ducts

Typical room

Warm air   Cool air

Supply duct
(heated air)

Return
duct
(cool air)

Furnace

Figure 15-2.

In the case of heating noises, the problem occurs as the metal ductwork heats up. Metal expands as it heats, so it needs room to move. If the ductwork is trapped within the wood framing in the basement, or if it's too tightly secured to the framing, this creates friction that causes the noise. Watch the ductwork and listen for the sounds as the furnace runs. You may need to loosen some mounting brackets or adjust duct work that's forced against wood framing.

Floor Squeaks

Floor squeaks are caused by loose floorboards and framing that move and rub as you walk on the floor. It could be wood rubbing on wood or wood rubbing on nails. Most often this occurs in the winter, because our homes dry out during the heating season. As wood dries, it shrinks, and gaps open up. A common 1 by 6 could shrink as much as $1/4$" across its 6" width when going from damp summer conditions to dry winter/heating conditions.

If the squeaks occur on the first floor and you can reach this area from the basement, try the following measures. (If you can't get underneath the squeaking floor, see the information below about a product called Squeeeek No More.)

Have someone walk on the offending floor while you listen for squeaks and watch for movement in the basement. Mark the problem areas.

If you can reach the joists and subflooring in the squeaking area, your best fix is to "sister" a 2 by 4 or 2 by 6 to the side of the joist and tight against the subfloor. "Sister" is a carpentry term meaning that the 2 by 4 is parallel to the joist with the wide, flat surfaces together. **See Figure 15-3**.

Use a short length—18" to 36"—and liberally apply construction adhesive to two adjacent 90-degree sides. Construction adhesive is dispensed from a caulking gun and has a caulk-like consistency. You then attach this board to the joist and the subflooring with several screws or nails driven into the joist at an angle.

The construction adhesive will effectively weld the wood to the joist and the subfloor, preventing movement. The adhesive fills voids and will not release as the wood shrinks and moves. Construction adhesive is the key—it will not shrink as it cures. Use as many short lengths as you need to stop the movement and squeaks.

Although many home improvement books recommend driving small shims between the joists and floorboards, I think this can complicate the problem. How far do you drive the shims into the gap? If you drive them in too far, you can loosen the subfloor.

Two products on the market work well to eliminate floor squeaks. Squeak-Relief from Accuset Tool Co., Troy, MI, provides a small aluminum bracket and

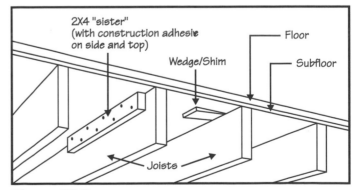

2X4 "sister"
(with construction adhesive
on side and top)

Floor

Wedge/Shim

Subfloor

Joists

Figure 15-3.

specially sized screws. The bracket takes the place of the 2 by 4. It effectively secures the floor to the bracket and the joist. **See Figure 15-4**.

Squeeeek No More from O'Berry Enterprises, Crystal Lake, IL, works from above the squeak through carpeting or hardwood flooring. It is a special bracket that holds and drives a long notched screw. Once driven into the offending area, the screw disappears. The bracket ensures that the screw is driven to the right depth. Then you use the bracket to break off the head and shank of the screw just below the wood. If you use this on a finished wood floor, it will create a tiny hole that should be patched with wood putty. **See Figures 15-5.**

For information on how to contact the manufacturers of Squeak-Relief and Squeeeek No More, see the References section.

Fluorescent Light That Hums

For solutions to a loudly humming fluorescent light, see "Problems with Fluorescent Lights" in "Electric Mysteries and Secret Solutions."

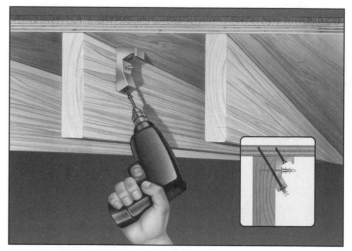

Figure 15-4. Squeak-Relief

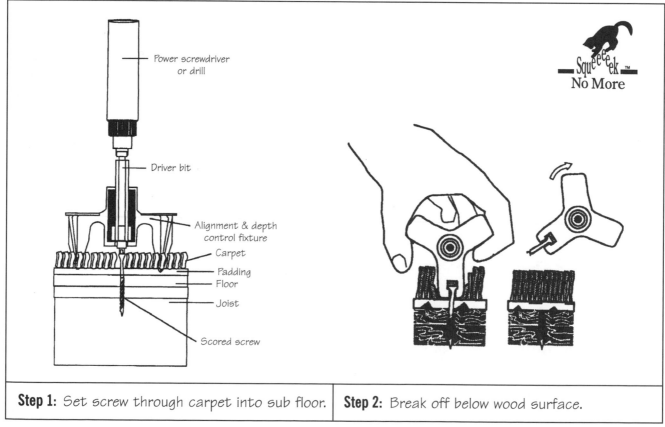

Step 1: Set screw through carpet into sub floor.   **Step 2:** Break off below wood surface.

Figure 15-5. Squeeeek No More

Sewer Smell in Home

When you detect a sewer smell in your home, there may be a dry trap in the drainage system. Often the smell comes from a seldom-used floor drain in the basement.

All drains to a sewer system have a P-shaped trap which is usually filled with water. The trap provides a seal to keep out sewer gas. **See Figure 16-1**. If your basement floor drain is rarely used, water evaporates from the trap over time. Eventually the seal is eliminated, allowing sewer gas (and smell) into your house. The solution is easy: pour water into the drain.

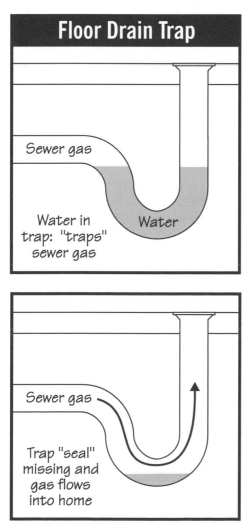

Figure 16-1.

If the trap is okay and the smell is noticeable mainly around a sink, try flushing a strong cleaner and bleach down the sink's overflow—the small hole(s) inside the bowl near the rim. This area may have an odor because when the sink fills to near overflowing, water is routed through an inner chamber to the drain. Debris can collect inside the inner chamber, causing odor.

If neither of these measures solves the problem, there may be a small leak in one of the vent lines of the plumbing system, or a small leak around the base of a toilet or other fixture. You may need the help of a plumber. Check for loose fittings, corrosion, or holes in vent piping. Also, check the top side of horizontal drain pipes. If the top is rusted, it may never leak liquid, but it will leak sewer gas. Drain lines made of copper, steel or cast iron may all exhibit this problem.

Sewer Smell from Toilet

When urine and sewer smells persist near a toilet despite careful cleaning, identify the source of the smell. Is it from the hot water? Is it from the floor around the toilet? Is it from the sink or tub?

Smells from the hot water may be caused by bacteria in the water heater and the anode rod. Smells from the floor area may indicate that the toilet is leaking, wetting the subfloor. Traps in sinks and tubs also can give off odors from time to time. Once you know the source, you can track down a solution

If the smell comes from the area around the toilet, there may be an air leak at the wax ring of the toilet or in the vent pipe. **See Figure 16-2**. Check to see if the toilet is tightly sealed to the floor. Grab the bowl of the toilet and try to slide it from side to side. It should resist a few pounds of pressure. If the toilet rocks from side to side, the wax ring has failed.

To replace the wax ring, hire a professional plumber. It's necessary to check the spacing between the pipe flange and the toilet base, and it is difficult to properly secure a toilet in place.

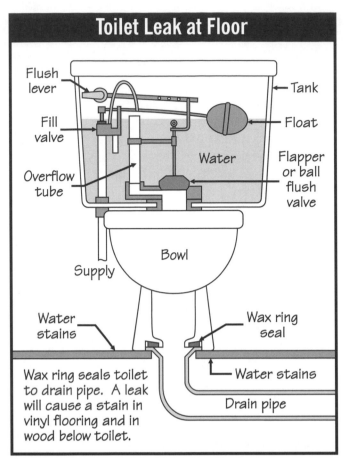

Toilet Leak at Floor

Flush lever

Tank

Fill valve

Float

Water

Overflow tube

Flapper or ball flush valve

Bowl

Supply

Water stains

Wax ring seal

Water stains

Drain pipe

Wax ring seals toilet to drain pipe. A leak will cause a stain in vinyl flooring and in wood below toilet.

Figure 16-2.

Water Supply Smells Like Rotten Eggs

Some homeowners have recurring problems with bad odor in the water supply—especially the "rotten egg" smell of sulfur. Water odors are a tough problem to solve, but I suggest you follow up on these ideas.

First, check whether your neighbors are experiencing similar problems. If your water comes from a municipal well, maybe your local water utility can help.

If your home has its own well, the smell may originate in the well system. There could be sulfate-reducing bacteria in the water supply. While the smell is bad, it usually is not a health risk. However, excessive sulfur bacteria can damage your water system.

It is relatively common to have this rotten egg odor in hot water only. In that case, the water heater's "sacrificial" anode rod is to blame. This rod, made of

magnesium, helps protect the tank lining from corrosion; instead, the rod itself corrodes. Unfortunately, as it does, the magnesium gives off electrons that nourish sulfate-reducing bacteria. Removing this rod may eliminate the problem (although it may also void the warranty for the water heater). The anode rod may be replaced with an aluminum rod.

If odor exists in both hot and cold water systems, you may need to treat the well with a shock chlorination. I suggest you use a contractor for this service. The contractor will add a strong chlorine solution to your well and circulate it through the system. The solution must remain in the well and piping for at least 24 hours and then be flushed out. The chlorine solution must be removed carefully because it will kill grass and shrubs and should not run into a lake or stream. This process may need to be repeated more than once. Equipment is available for automatic and routine addition of chlorine to the well if needed.

If you are concerned whether your water is safe to drink, have it tested. Often your city or county's health department or building inspection department or your state's department of natural resources will perform tests and explain the results. A local well service company can also test your water.

Also, most local water treatment contractors or the local health department will know about the common problems with water in your area. Your neighbors probably have the same water problems and can share their solutions or the names of good resources.

One final tip—the water holding/pressure tank can be a source of odor problems. Most modern tanks have a rubber bladder that holds the water away from the air cushion in the tank. This bladder may increase odor. An air-over-water tank with an air release system can help. In this system, the pump adds air to the tank each time it runs, and a float in the tank releases excess air. There is no rubber bladder.

Does this all sound complicated? It is. I suggest you consult a professional who has experience in your specific area. If you choose this route, interview several water specialists. Make sure the one you choose will investigate your problem fully and isn't just selling you a standard package of expensive water treatment equipment. Find out how your neighbors solve the problem.

Smoke Smells from the Fireplace—Without a Fire

A smoky smell coming from a fireplace that's not in use is probably caused by negative pressure that draws air down the chimney, past the stinky ashes, and into your home.

First, check that the damper is in good condition and is tightly closed. If there are fireplace glass doors, close them. Close any outside air supply to the fireplace.

Now think about what may be causing the pressure that draws air down the chimney. Clothes dryers and kitchen exhaust fans are notorious for this. Bathroom fans and other ventilation fans also remove air. A whole-house ventilation fan is another likely culprit. A naturally drafted gas appliance like a water heater or furnace also removes air from your home and sends it up a different chimney along with combustion gas. Some high-efficiency furnaces and water heaters have a draft fan that draws air.

Analyze this problem carefully, because the negative pressure could also cause a gas furnace or water heater to backdraft, sending combustion gas into your home. Backdrafting is a serious safety concern. You may need to have a heating contractor or an engineer analyze the problem.

The solution may also be simple: open a window slightly when running the clothes dryer or kitchen exhaust fan to provide another air source so air won't be drawn down the fireplace chimney.

Removing Smoke Smells from Home or Car

Cigarette Smoke

Once cigarette smoke smell has penetrated finish materials in a home or car, it is difficult to remove. Professional cleaners or scents to cover the smell don't always work.

Have the carpets and furniture or car seats professionally cleaned. Also, scrub all washable surfaces.

One great way to remove or cover smoke smells is with Pine-Sol cleaner. Place several small bowls of Pine-Sol in the problem area and close it off overnight or for several days. Pine-Sol's detergent smell is very strong and will cover the smoke smell. Afterward, open the area and ventilate with outdoor air. As fresh air removes the detergent scent, most or all of the smoke odor will be gone, too.

Smoke Smells from a House Fire

If part of the house has been damaged by fire, obviously you'll need to replace carpeting and drapes in affected areas. Standard repainting may not be sufficient to seal the smoke/burn smell; many times a special primer/sealer like Kilz or Bin is required.

Before replacing carpeting, clean the wood underneath, then seal with Bin or Kilz. Even though wood may not look damaged, it may still retain a smoke smell. You might also need to clean the ductwork and the furnace.

Finally, check the attic above the fire area. Is there a smoke smell or damage in the insulation, ceiling or roof? You may need to seal these surfaces and remove damaged materials.

See the References chapter for information about the manufacturers of Bin and Kilz.

Burning Odor from Light Fixture

If a light fixture gives off a burning smell, disconnect the fixture until you have determined the source of the odor. Overheating electrical wires and devices often emit a burning smell. Don't use the fixture again until it has been repaired by a professional.

A fluorescent fixture may have a ballast that has failed and is spilling tar.

For typical incandescent light fixtures, the burning smell may occur if you're using an oversized bulb. Check the rating of the fixture and the wattage of the bulb. Never exceed the wattage recommended.

There might also be a loose electrical connection at the splice or in the outlet box, or a loose screw or lamp base. A loose connection creates excessive resistance to electrical flow, and the resistance builds up heat. Excessive heat makes metal connections expand and contract, loosening them further. This heat can damage insulation and even start a fire. Sometimes, when such excessive heat melts plastic, the problem area emits a misleading "dead animal" smell.

If you notice any strong smells near outlets, electrical boxes, or light fixtures, they may be due to an electrical problem. Call an electrician to evaluate and fix the problem. In the meantime, do not use electrical power in that area.

When To Call a Professional

Many of us successfully complete home repair and improvement projects with a feeling of great accomplishment. Some of us approach a project out of necessity: we just can't afford to hire a contractor or we can't find a contractor for a small job. Some of us love the challenge. Some of us love the diversion from our day to day work. Whatever the reason, home repairs and remodeling can be a great source of satisfaction and pride.

Most of us will start with simple projects like painting, wallpapering and related decorating. We may attempt simple carpentry and refinishing furniture or woodwork. Eventually we get involved in building a deck or installing a garage door operator.

How do you know when to hire a professional and when you can do it yourself? This question comes up all the time on my radio show. And the answer depends on your skill level, your level of interest and how willing you are to seek professional help. The answer varies for each person.

You can't get in much trouble with painting, decorating and simple carpentry. But what about electrical, plumbing, heating and structural work? Where should we draw the line?

I think you should consider the complexity of the project and ask your local municipal building inspector if a permit is required for the work. When a permit is required, this often means a professional trade person would normally do the work. Once a permit is "pulled," the work is subject to local building codes and controls. You must conform to codes and safety requirements. A code official will check your work.

I suggest that most average handy-people stay away from electrical, plumbing, roofing and structural work because of the complexity. If you must try this type of work, I suggest you ask yourself the following questions. If you can't pass the test, don't attempt the work.

Can You Handle Advanced Projects? Take This Quiz and Find Out!

ELECTRICAL

1. Explain polarity. **See Figures 17-1, and 17-2.**

2. On a lamp cord, how is the neutral wire marked?

3. In a main electrical panel, what two colors are ground wires?

4. Can a white neutral wire give you a shock?

5. What size wire is used for a 30-amp line for a clothes dryer?

PLUMBING

1. Explain how a trap works. **See Figure 17-3.**

2. What does the T and P valve on the water heater or boiler do?

3. How many fixtures can be served by a $1/2''$ copper line?

4. What type of solder must be used today for copper pipes?

5. Explain water hammer and how to eliminate it.

ROOFING

1. How many layers of shingles will you find in one layer of a three-tap asphalt shingle?

2. What is the lowest slope roof for a standard asphalt shingle application?

3. Describe roof slope and define the terms used.

4. Why must an attic be ventilated?

5. What is a step flashing?...counter flashing?

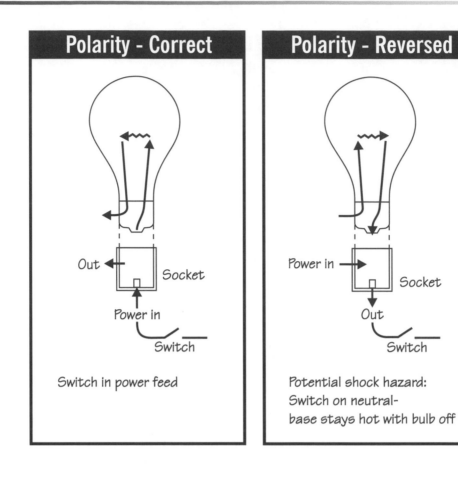

Figure 17-1.

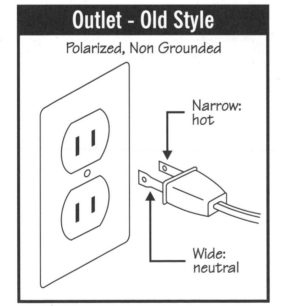

Figure 17-2.

STRUCTURAL

1. What is the normal span for a 2 by 10 on 16" centers?

2. Explain "16" on center."

3. How does a cap flashing work at a window?

4. Why are joist hangers used on a deck?

5. How deep must deck posts go into the soil?

MECHANICAL

1. Explain a condensing, high efficiency warm air furnace. **See Figure 17-4.**

2. Why can a "orphaned" gas water heater be a problem in a masonry chimney?

3. Do you need a check valve on a sump pump?

Floor Drain Trap

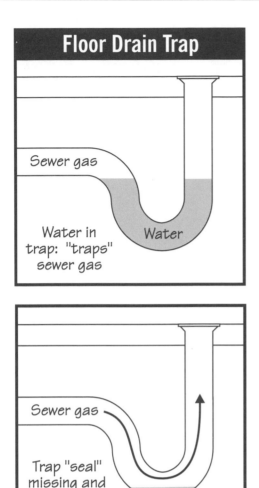

Figure 17-3.

High Efficiency Warm Air Furnace

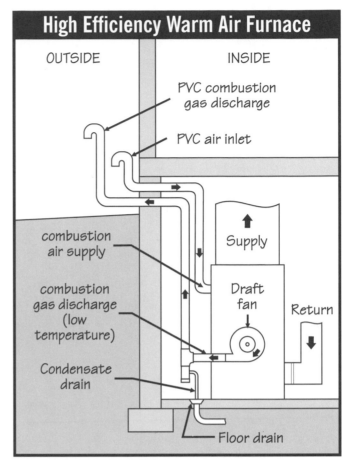

Figure 17-4.

4. What are the symptoms of a waterlogged pressure tank on a private well system?

5. Where is the evaporator coil in a central air conditioning system? **See Figure 17-5.**

If you can pass the test, perhaps you can try your hand at more complicated repairs. Some of the answers are in this book, but others are beyond the scope of this book and the knowledge of most homeowners. You need to know all the answers before you attempt extensive home repairs.

Remember to follow all safety precautions and man-ufacturers' instructions. Take out a building permit and follow the advice of the local building inspector. Have your work inspected. Consult a professional as needed or whenever you have any questions.

Good luck!

Air Conditioning System with Warm Air Furnace

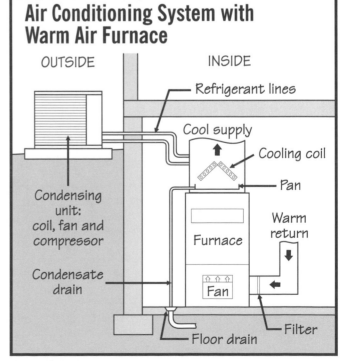

Figure 17-5.

Short Trips

It's good to think ahead if you're going to leave your home unoccupied for a while. Most people don't think about what could happen to their home during vacation until they come home to a disaster.

For a short (3- to 5-day) absence during the summer, turn off the main water supply valve. **See Figure 18-1**. (If you've asked a neighbor to come in and water your house plants, fill the bathtub with water first to provide water for the task.) Also, turn the water heater and water softener to a "vacation" setting if there is one.

Any minor plumbing leak can cause a major disaster. One of my friends came home to a $20,000 problem because a second-story toilet supply line had sprung a leak; by the time the family came home, the kitchen cabinets were on the floor.

One caution: inspect and test the main water valve long before you plan to shut it off. Because the valve is rarely used, it may be corroded and can even be stuck in the open position. If the valve looks clean and is easy to operate, turn it off as a test. If the valve is corroded and the handle seems hard to turn, don't force it; get a plumber to replace or repair the valve. Once you move the handle, the valve may leak, and it could become impossible to shut it off all the way. Don't use a wrench or pliers on the handle or stem, and don't test the valve on a Sunday or holiday when you can't get help or parts.

If you have central air conditioning, set it to a high temperature (85 degrees or above), or just turn it off. If there is a sump pump in the basement, test it before you leave. (For instructions, see "Sump Pump Maintenance" in the chapter "Little Problems That Become Big Problems in a Hurry.")

For a short trip during the summer, leave the rest of the utilities on. Set up timers on some interior lights. Ask a neighbor or friend to check on the house. Don't forget to have someone pick up your mail and newspaper to make the house look "lived in."

For short winter absences, set the heating temperature to 55 or 60 degrees but no lower. Don't risk frozen pipes in your home. Also, make sure that all widows and doors are tightly closed—even a small draft can freeze a pipe.

Shutting Down for a Whole Winter

The chief risks associated with leaving a home unheated over a cold winter season involve freezing water and the movement of framing, drywall, plaster and flooring.

Properly securing the water system involves much more than turning off the water. You must also secure anything that may contain water, including drain traps, all piping, water heater, dishwashers, and clothes washers. You must actually open up the

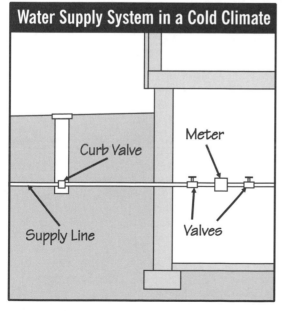

Water Supply System in a Cold Climate

Curb Valve

Meter

Supply Line

Valves

Figure 18-1.

piping at several locations to drain water. Then you must fill drain traps and toilets with antifreeze to keep sewer gas from entering your home. It's important to use a special type of antifreeze, designed for use in motor homes, to prevent damage to the sewage system.

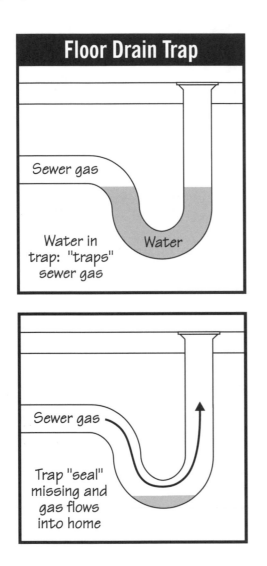

Turn off the washing machine supply lines and remove and drain them. To clear water from the washing machine pump, run the washer on the fill part of its cycle, set to warm water. For a dishwasher, remove the inlet hose and open the supply valve after you have turned off the water supply to the house. Operate the dishwasher to clear the valve; remove the drain hose.

Unplug all electrical appliance to prevent any damage from power surges or lightning strikes.

Another serious potential problem is expansion and contraction of the structure of your home from changes in temperature and humidity. Expansion and contraction may cause cracks in plaster, tile, flooring, wood trim and other components that would be expensive to repair. Keep the heat turned on, at a low setting. The risk of structural damage isn't worth the relatively small amount you would save by turning off the heat altogether.

Damage from animals and insects is another potential problem. With no people around, pests can have free run of the house.

Rain gutters, downspouts, sump pumps, and appliances can malfunction during a long winter absence. Security is also a major concern—someone could break in, or that beautiful oak tree could fall on the roof or the picture window.

In short, if you plan to leave your home for the winter, turn the water off, secure the plumbing, and leave the heat on at a low setting. Also, find someone to check on the house weekly.

Floor Stains Around the Toilet

A small leak can seriously damage floor covering and framing if not repaired promptly.

The most likely source of water or water stains around the base of a toilet is a leaky seal between the toilet outlet and the toilet drain flange. Grab the toilet and gently try to move it slightly from side to side or rock it back and forth. If there is any movement, the toilet needs to be reset to the drain line.

When the toilet was installed, a wax ring was placed between the base of the toilet and the drain pipe. **See Figure 19-1**. Eventually, the toilet and piping can move, and this seal can be broken, allowing a small leak every time someone flushes the toilet. If the floor framing is visible in the floor below (for instance, in the basement), you will also see stains and dampness below the toilet.

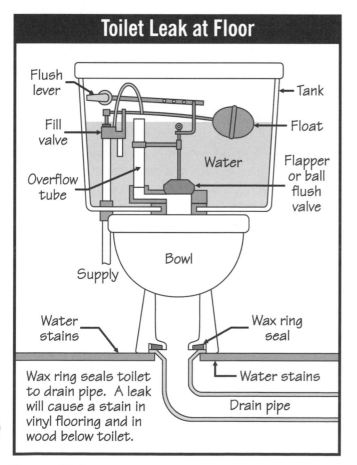

Toilet Leak at Floor

Flush lever

Tank

Fill valve

Float

Water

Overflow tube

Flapper or ball flush valve

Bowl

Supply

Water stains

Wax ring seal

Water stains

Drain pipe

Wax ring seals toilet to drain pipe. A leak will cause a stain in vinyl flooring and in wood below toilet.

Figure 19-1.

Replacing the wax ring requires removing the toilet. In most cases, I suggest you hire a plumber to do this, because many problems can occur and most households can't afford losing the use of a toilet for too long.

Here is what's involved in the repair. You will need to obtain a new wax ring and probably new bolts, too.

First, disconnect the water supply and drain all water from the tank and bowl. Remove the bolts on either side of the toilet, and lift the toilet from the floor. Because the old bolts may be almost impossible to remove, often they're just cut off. The new replacement bolts should be cut to the required length.

Clean away the old wax ring and place a new one on the base. Carefully set the toilet in place over the bolts. Gently tighten the bolts until the toilet is secure.

Rusted Metal Lintels (Beams) at Windows

Rusted lintels can create serious cracks and masonry failure.

A brick or stone home may have steel angles over windows and doors. These angles, called lintels, hold up the brick and stone over the openings. **See Figure 19-2**.

Most people don't realize that the lintels are there, and they allow them to rust away. When the lintel eventually fails, the wall may split apart at the mortar joints. Over large openings, the brick and rusted lintel can sag into the opening, requiring a major repair.

Treat this steel lintel like any exterior metal. Remove the rust down to bare metal, prime with a metal primer, and paint with an exterior metal paint.

An option to cleaning down to bare metal is to remove most of the rust, then paint/prime the remaining solid rust with a product like Rust-Oleum Rust Reformer or a rusty-metal primer. Reformer transforms the existing rust to stop the rusting action and provides a primer for the finish coat.

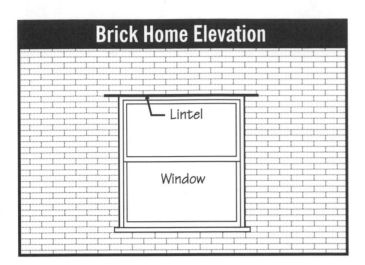

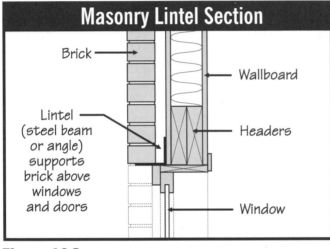

Figure 19-2.

Often, latex exterior house paint is mistakenly applied to the metal lintels when the wood siding and trim are painted. Latex paint will not hold up over the long run and can allow the metal to rust.

There may also be small openings between the top of the lintel and the brick. These openings allow condensation (water) in the wall to drain away. Do not seal these openings, and don't caulk this joint. Sealing the openings will cause excessive rust and wall damage.

Garage Door—Paint It to Save It

If you don't paint all sides of a wood garage door, it will fail.

When your wood or wood-product garage door needs painting, your first step is to clean the door with detergent and a scrub brush. Rinse well, then allow the door to dry for several days.

Wipe the cleaned surface with your finger. If the paint leaves a chalky deposit on your finger, you need to prime the surface.

To determine if the paint is loose, try this cellophane tape test. Cut a shallow "X" in the surface and rub tape over the X. Lift the tape quickly. If paint comes off in chunks, it's loose. Loose paint must be removed and primed, or at least primed. Sand the door first if necessary.

Prime the surface with an exterior oil-based primer. If you wish to change the door to a lighter color, prime with a special stain blocker/ primer such as Bin or Kilz. (For more information about the manufacturers of Bin and Kilz, see the References chapter.)

If the existing paint surface is solid and not too "chalky," paint directly over it with a high-quality 100% acrylic latex paint.

When painting a garage door, remember that each door panel has six sides that need painting. To reach areas between panels at the hinges, you must paint with the door partially open. The most common mistake people make when painting a garage door is to skip the other five sides of the panels.

Drainage Problems

Ignoring improper drainage allows serious basement leaks to create structural problems.

Most basements in the Midwest have a drainage system designed to remove groundwater near the floor and walls. There are exterior tiles at the base of the wall and interior tiles just beneath the concrete floor. These systems are connected under the foundation wall by bleeder tiles through the footings. Bleeder tiles direct the water to a sump pump, which pumps the water out. **See Figure 19-3**.

If the gutters or the sump pump discharge their water near the foundation wall, the soil can become saturated, pushing inward on the foundation. Water seeps into the block or concrete and eventually flows inside at the top or midpoint of the basement wall.

It's essential to direct surface water at least 6 feet from the foundation to a point where the water naturally flows away from your home.

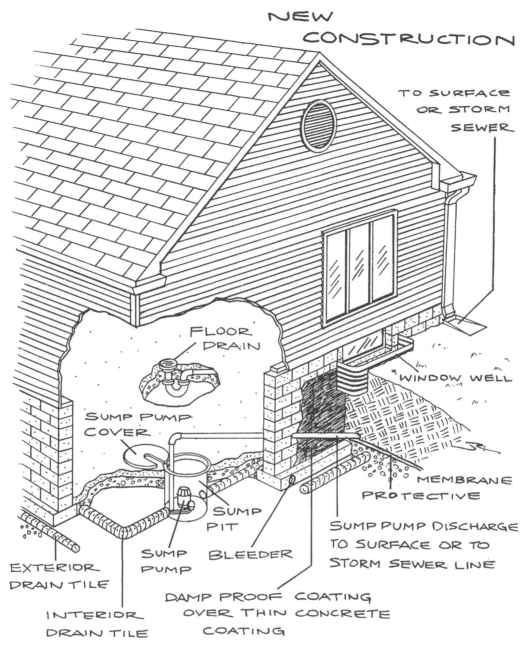

NEW CONSTRUCTION

TO SURFACE OR STORM SEWER

FLOOR DRAIN

WINDOW WELL

SUMP PUMP COVER

MEMBRANE PROTECTIVE

SUMP PIT

SUMP PUMP DISCHARGE TO SURFACE OR TO STORM SEWER LINE

EXTERIOR DRAIN TILE

SUMP PUMP

BLEEDER

INTERIOR DRAIN TILE

DAMP PROOF COATING OVER THIN CONCRETE COATING

Figure 19-3.

Drainage problems are compounded in the spring when there is a large snow meltdown and most of the ground is still frozen. Ice and snow piles may also trap water against your home. The soil next to your home thaws before the rest of the soil because of heat from your basement, and this thawed soil accepts water while the frozen soil rejects water.

Monitor these conditions, and correct problems at the surface of the soil. If leaks continue or cracks develop in basement walls, contact a basement specialist.

Grading Soil and Hard Surfaces

Improper grading contributes to basement leaks and serious structural problems.

More than 90% of basement dampness and seepage problems are caused by poor grading or poor maintenance of gutters and downspouts.

When your home was built, the excavation was dug larger than the basement to allow space for workers to construct the walls. Often, the hole is backfilled with native soil that settles quickly for up to 5 years and then more slowly after that. If the fill contains debris or organic materials, settling is even more pronounced.

Soil and soft surfaces such as grass should always be pitched away from the foundation with a minimum 5% slope—about 1/2" of drop for every 12 linear inches. A better slope would be 1" to 2" every 12". This slope should extend at least 6 feet from the basement wall to an area where water will naturally flow away from your home.

When regrading your landscaping, it is a good idea to exceed the minimum requirements, because the soil will continue to settle for a long time afterward.

Hard surfaces such as concrete need less slope than soft surfaces, because water runs freely on the hard surfaces, but they still need a minimum slope of 1% to 2%. That is about 1/8" to 1/4" of drop for every foot of horizontal run—so in 4 feet, the patio should slope 1/2" to 1" away from your foundation. These hard surfaces should route water to a location that will naturally drain it away. **See Figure 19-4**.

Sagging Patio or Sidewalk

Improper surface-water flow can damage the basement or crawl space.

Any hard surfaces pitched toward your home present a problem. They allow water to pond next to the foundation wall. Water will flow to the lowest level—into your basement or crawl space, or below the patio slab.

As noted above, saturated soil exerts excessive horizontal pressure that can crack basement walls and move them inward. Water collecting below a patio slab makes the soil move and heave until the slab breaks.

If the patio or sidewalk is poorly pitched but otherwise in good condition with few cracks, mudjacking can help. Mudjacking involves drilling several holes, about 2" in diameter, in the low end of the slab. You probably have seen similar holes or patches on commercial properties. "Mud" (actually a mixture of ground stone, water and a little Portland cement) is forced into the hole under pressure by a pump. The pressure raises or levels the slab. **See Figure 19-5**.

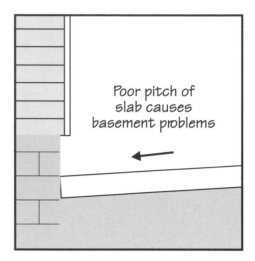

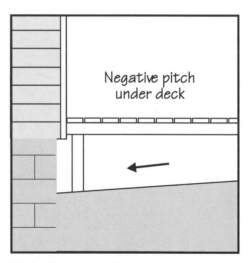

Figure 19-4. Poor Grading

This repair will not be permanent, because the slab will continue to settle. However, mudjacking is much less expensive than replacing the concrete and allows you to "recycle" an otherwise good concrete slab.

Mudjacking is desirable only if the slab is in good condition with little cracking. If not, the concrete should be replaced.

How Important Is Furnace Servicing?

Neglecting routine service ignores safety and efficiency measures.

Generally, forced air furnaces will run for many years without a dramatic breakdown or loss of heat. However, for safety, energy efficiency and extended life of the furnace, you should have it serviced every year.

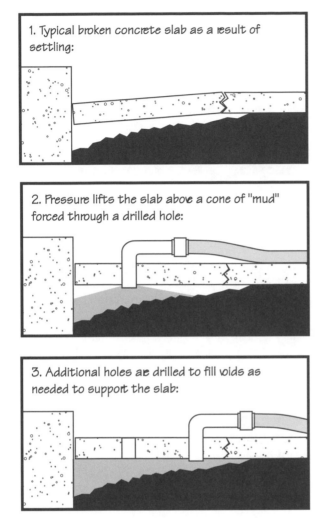

1. Typical broken concrete slab as a result of settling:

2. Pressure lifts the slab above a cone of "mud" forced through a drilled hole:

3. Additional holes are drilled to fill voids as needed to support the slab:

Figure 19-5.

Proper service includes cleaning the burner and heat exchanger and inspecting for cracks or other damage. A dirty or mis-adjusted burner can produce carbon monoxide, a dangerous gas that you can't see or smell. Carbon monoxide inside your home can make you sick and can even kill you.

When a burner is tuned properly, it works with maximum efficiency. This will save you money. And a properly tuned burner is less likely to produce dangerous carbon monoxide.

Good servicing also includes testing of all safety controls; lubrication; belt maintenance; and inspection of the combustion flue pipe or discharge piping. Other areas to check include gas piping and electrical components. The service technician should also check the humidifier, air conditioning coil, drain pan, and all drain lines.

Have a professional service the furnace yearly. A good time for service is in the spring—you can have both the furnace and the air conditioner serviced at a reduced cost.

For more detailed information, see the Service Checklists chapter.

Deteriorating Ceramic Tile at Tub or Shower

Damaged or loose ceramic tile or grout can lead to extensive damage to tiles and walls.

If ceramic wall tile around a tub or shower starts coming loose, don't delay the repair. Once water finds its way behind the tile, the drywall or plaster will start to deteriorate. If drywall is the backing material, large chunks of the wall can be damaged, and tile and drywall will fall off the wall. In addition, water will leak into the surrounding wall and floor.

Even a small break needs immediate repair. Replace the loose grout. If the break is near a spout or faucet, caulk around it, creating a tight seal. If tile is loose, remove it from the wall and then re-secure it with tile adhesive or waterproof construction adhesive.

If the wall is damaged behind the tile, remove the soft material and patch with plaster, wood bracing and/or cement board. You may need to cut out enough material to reach the wood studs to support the patch.

What if you can't fix the break immediately? Cover the area with plastic sheeting taped or caulked tightly to the good tile around the damaged area. This little "umbrella" over the damage will keep the water out until you can do a total repair.

Cleaning Fireplace and Flue

Failing to clean the fireplace and flue can lead to a serious chimney fire.

A fireplace requires routine maintenance to prevent safety problems and expensive repairs. The frequency and type of maintenance depends on the type of fireplace and how often you use it. There are two basic types of fireplaces: metal fabricated and masonry (brick). **See Figure 19-6.**

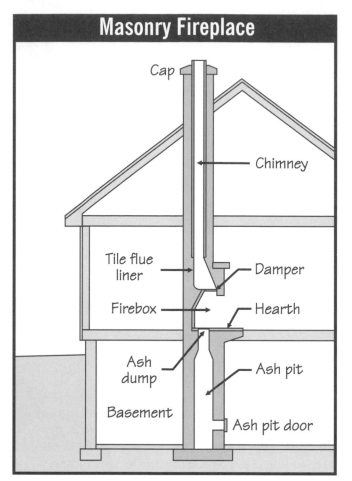

Masonry Fireplace

Cap

Chimney

Tile flue liner

Damper

Firebox

Hearth

Ash dump

Ash pit

Basement

Ash pit door

Figure 19-6.

Even if you never use the fireplace, have the exposed chimney inspected and maintained to prevent weather damage.

If you just purchased your home, have a professional clean and evaluate the fireplace before you use it. The professional should check the damper and flue for proper construction, look for any creosote or soot buildup, make sure the fireplace operates properly, and evaluate clearances to combustibles. Outside, the inspector should evaluate the cap, screen, flue, flashings, and chimney structure.

If you hire a professional chimney sweep, he or she should take the time to explain the basic construction and operation of the fireplace. A thorough sweep will also give you information on building a safe fire and maintaining your chimney. Consider hiring a chimney sweep who is a member of the Chimney Safety Institute of America (CSIA).

The CSIA has great brochures on fireplace maintenance and operation, and will also provide a list of certified chimney sweeps in your area.

See the References section for information on how to contact the CSIA.

Inspecting a Masonry Chimney

Failing to maintain the exposed parts of a masonry chimney can lead to expensive damage. See Figure 19-7.

You can, if you wish, inspect your own chimney. A masonry chimney should be inspected every year. Outside, masonry surfaces take a beating from the weather. Inside, we often start with cold chimney surfaces and heat them with a roaring fire in the fireplace—pretty tough on the materials. Chimneys are also subjected to moisture and acid from the combustion of natural gas or fossil fuels.

You can inspect the chimney from the ground (with binoculars) or from the roof if you can safely reach the roof area around the chimney. Don't go on a roof that is steep or slippery. If there is a question of safe access or potential damage to roofing surfaces, leave the inspection to a professional.

Start your inspection with the top of the chimney. The clay tile should be solid with no major cracks, gaps, or broken sections. The tile should extend above the top cap. Use a flashlight to peer down into the tile. You can also view the inside of the tile from the fireplace or the cleanout door in the basement. Look up at the tile with a bright light and a mirror. There should be no obstructions inside the tile.

Around the clay tile, on the top of the chimney, there will be a cap made of stone, cast concrete or mortar. The cap seals against the tile and covers the top of the masonry surfaces, keeping moisture out. If you see minor cracks in the cap or the joint, caulk them with masonry or silicone caulk. Major cracks or broken sections dictate replacing the cap.

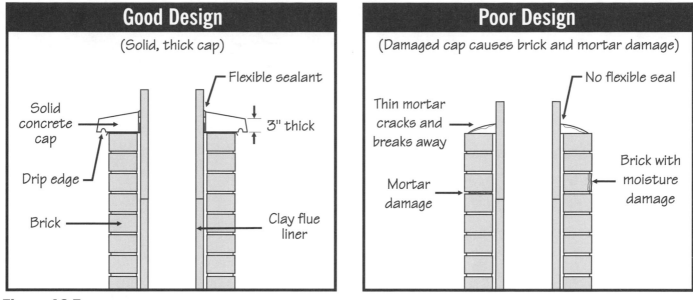

Figure 19-7.

The cap is essential. Fixing a minor cap problem will prevent a major failure down the road. Any moisture that bypasses the cap will destroy the masonry surfaces in time as freeze-and-thaw cycles ruin the brick and mortar.

Inspect the brick or stone and mortar. Minor cracks can be caulked; monitor them thereafter to make sure they don't grow. Major cracks, spalling (flaking) brick surfaces or loose bricks require the attention of a professional. See below for more information on how to recognize and repair spalling brick.

Simple maintenance can prevent huge repair bills. Rebuilding the top of a small chimney will cost about $200 per linear foot—which can add up to over $1,000 for a small chimney.

Check the metal flashing where the brick meets the roofing material. The top flashing or counter flashing should be sealed tightly into the mortar joints. Often this joint "steps" down the mortar joint and is actually cut into the mortar. To prevent water penetration, seal any gaps at this joint with either caulk or mortar, depending on the existing conditions.

Some flashings will be sealed with tar or roofing cement. If there are gaps or cracks in the roofing cement, re-seal the surface. With this type of coating, it is often impossible to see the type or condition of the actual flashing, so sealing any open areas is often the only alternative.

If the chimney has a metal cap, make sure it is securely fastened and not blocked by debris. Normally a metal chimney cap is a good idea because it deflects rain and snow away from the clay tile. The cap also keeps animals out of the chimney.

Finally, your inspection should include all connections to the chimney. Metal fittings should be tightly mortared and sealed to the chimney. Minor cracks and openings can be filled with fireplace mortar or with furnace and fireplace cement. You can purchase this material in caulking tubes or in small tubs to be applied with a putty knife. Follow the instructions for the material you purchase.

Any rusted or loose flue pipes leading to the chimney should be repaired and securely supported. This includes the flue pipe from the water heater and the furnace. A chimney flue used for natural-gas-fired appliances should not be shared with a fossil fuel burner such as a wood stove or an incinerator.

Inspecting a fireplace chimney should include a check inside the fireplace with a bright light. Open the damper and look up the flue. The brick and mortar should be sound, without gaps. There should be very little buildup of shiny creosote or fluffy soot. If the buildup exceeds 1/4", the chimney needs cleaning. The damper should open fully and latch securely in the open position.

If any of this is confusing, or if you suspect a problem, contact a profession chimney sweep, heating contractor, or roofing contractor. Chimney and flue connections are designed to safely remove the products of combustion from your home. Don't risk any chance of smoke, fire or carbon monoxide entering your home.

Spalling (Flaking) Chimney Brick

Flaking bricks that aren't repaired promptly can lead to structural failure. See Figure 19-7.

When the face of a brick breaks away, the brick is said to be "spalling." Usually, this happens when water penetrates the brick and the freeze/thaw cycle separates the surface from the brick. Moisture problems can also lead to mortar cracking around the brick.

Inspect the cap of the chimney. Moisture problems are most often caused by a failing cap. The cap is supposed to seal the flue, covering the top of the brick and protecting the structure below from water. Many caps are a "mortar wash" type that provide only a thin coat of mortar; the mortar is higher and thicker near the flue and tapers to a thin covering near the edge of the chimney. A better cap is made of pre-cast concrete or cast-in-place concrete that is about 3" thick with a tapered top surface.

If there is any damage to the cap or the flue, or any source of water leakage above the brick, you have found the problem. Eliminate the source of the moisture as soon as possible to prevent serious damage to the chimney. Once deterioration starts, it can progress rapidly.

Chimney sweeps and brickmasons will perform chimney repair. If your chimney has one of those cheap mortar wash caps, consider having it replaced. It is common for caps to deteriorate after 10 years or less.

Sump Pump Maintenance

A failed sump pump = water in the basement.

To understand why it's important to maintain your sump pump, first you should know what the sump pump does. Groundwater flows through drain tiles around and below the basement floor. After the water collects in the sump pump crock, the pump

lifts it to the surface outside or into an underground storm sewer pipe draining away from your home. This system is separate from the sanitary sewer system that drains wastewater from toilets, sinks, the washing machine, and so on, routing it to the sanitary sewer treatment plant. **See Figure 19-8**.

Test your sump pump every few months. Add water to the crock; the pump should switch on when the water is 8" to 12" below the top of the concrete floor. You could also start the pump by lifting the float. Watch to make sure the pump removes water from the crock. If groundwater has collected in the crock, the water should be clear. The crock should be free of roots or debris.

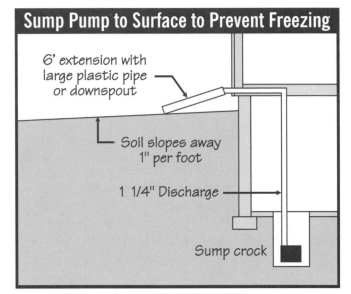

Sump Pump to Surface to Prevent Freezing

6' extension with large plastic pipe or downspout

Soil slopes away 1" per foot

1 1/4" Discharge

Sump crock

Figure 19-8.

If the pump has a float on a metal rod, check that the float operates easily and doesn't rub against the crock or the cover. If a float sticks, the pump will not run, and your basement could flood.

The pump should be securely mounted in the crock. Its plug should be securely fastened in an outlet, not an extension cord. Replace the pump if it is old and worn, rusty, or noisy.

If the pump runs more than several times per day and runs often during heavy rain, purchase a spare pump, or mount a second pump in the crock. The second pump could have its float set for a higher water level so it will run only if the first pump fails.

20 MY TOP ENERGY-SAVING AND COMFORT TIPS

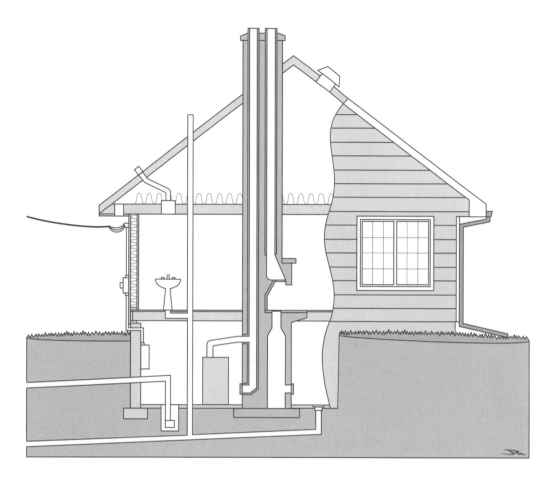

General Philosophy

Energy efficiency with comfort is a goal I learned from my energy buddy Clyde Rymer more than 20 years ago when we were trying to save energy at a large college facility. No one gets excited about simply saving energy, but if you can combine energy conservation with comfort improvements, everyone is happy.

These are my top tips on saving energy and improving comfort in your home. (By the way, at the college we reduced energy bills every year for 14 years straight and saved over $10 million during a period when energy costs were increasing!)

1. Insulate the Attic Trap Door

Insulating and weatherstripping the trap door to the attic is one of the best energy-saving measures you can take. It costs little and will eliminate a large heat loss and potential attic moisture problems.

You don't feel cold air at the trap door because warm house air pushes up through cracks and gaps into the cold attic. Weatherstripping will stop these air leaks, and a few layers of insulation will prevent heat transfer through the door.

2. Water Heater Temperature

Lower the water heater temperature to the lowest setting you find comfortable. This saves energy by reducing the continuous heat loss that occurs when storing a tank of hot water. It will also reduce the chance that anyone may be scalded by hot water.

How low can you set the water temperature? Normally 120 degrees is the recommended temperature for energy savings. Water feels hot at 105 degrees. At 115 degrees, water can cause first-degree burns. Gas water heaters will not have an actual temperature indicated on the dial, so set the heater to the lowest or "warm" setting and check the temperature at a hot water faucet the next day. It will take some time for the water in the tank to cool. **See Figure 20-1**.

Electric water heaters may have a setting that indicates the actual temperature. **See Figure 20-2**. Sometimes the dial is exposed on the side of the heater, but most often it is under the top cover. Be careful when you open the cover, since there may be some "hot" exposed wires beneath. Check the actual water temperature after you reset the unit. If the water feels too cold, you can always increase the temperature.

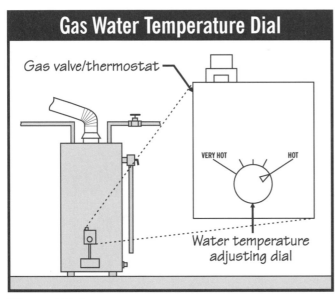

Figure 20-1.

Note: some dishwashers require 140-degree water. Check the directions for the dishwasher and for the detergent you are using. Consider switching to a detergent that works better at a lower temperature.

Also, try to conserve hot water. Wash clothes in cool, cold or warm water. Take a quick shower and use a low flow showerhead.

3. Thermostat Settings

You can save a substantial amount of energy by lowering the temperature setting for your heating system in the winter and raising the temperature for the air conditioning in the summer. By dialing back your heating system 1 degree, you can save up to 3% on your heating bills.

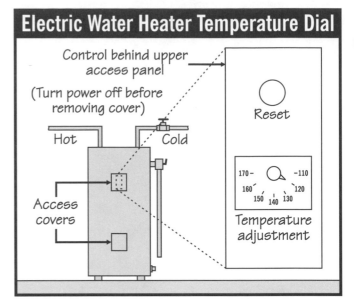

Figure 20-2.

In the winter, try to live with the thermostat set at 68 degrees. This may require wearing a sweater if you are older or don't move around much. In the summer, try setting the thermostat at 78 degrees for cooling.

During a period of hot weather, leave your air conditioning system on throughout. Don't turn it on and off from day to day. The air conditioning system removes moisture from the interior air, and this helps you feel comfortable. If you open the windows for a few hours to air out your home, you will immediately lose all that dry air.

Consider installing a setback (programmable) thermostat to control your heating and cooling systems. **See Figure 20-3**. Programmable thermostats have come a long way in the last 20 years. Now they are electronic wonders – easy to install, easy to program and very inexpensive (about $50 to $100). Properly used, these thermostats can save you 10% of your heating and cooling bill.

Programmable thermostats allow you to set back the heating temperature during the evening when you are sleeping or during the day when no one is home. You program the unit to increase the temperature before you wake up or before you come home from work. This results in substantial energy savings with no loss in comfort. You can also program the temperature setting for your air conditioning.

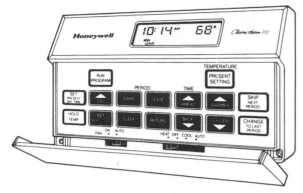

Figure 20-3. Digital, Setback Thermostat

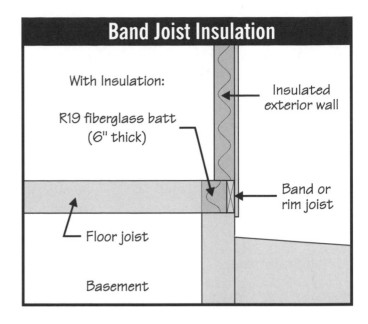

Band Joist Insulation

Programmable thermostats come with complete installation instructions, and most handy people can install them. The only wiring involved is low-voltage control wiring, and you just need to match the wire colors. When looking for a thermostat, remember that there are heating-only units and combination heating-cooling units.

4. Band Joist (Sill Plate) Insulation

You may have one large bare area around your home that allows a huge heat loss—the area at the band joist or sill plate. This is the area just above the basement wall, between the joists of the first floor of your home. On the outside, this area is near the ground but still exposed to weather. **See Figure 20-4**.

In this area, you may have no insulation, just the wood frame (a $1\frac{1}{2}''$-thick band joist) and the siding. An area like this has less insulation value than a common insulated glass window.

To insulate this area, first look for any gaps or cracks. Study the area when the sun is bright outside; keep the basement lights low. The gaps will be obvious. Seal them with caulk or a foam sealant.

Insulate with 6"-thick unfaced fiberglass insulation. Buy insulation that is designed to fit between the spacing of the joists—normally between 16"-on-center joists. (The actual space is $14\frac{1}{2}''$ wide once you subtract for the $1\frac{1}{2}''$-thick lumber.) Cut the insulation by compressing it against a board with a straightedge. It will slice easily with a utility knife. Cut the insulation slightly larger than the opening so that friction will hold it in place.

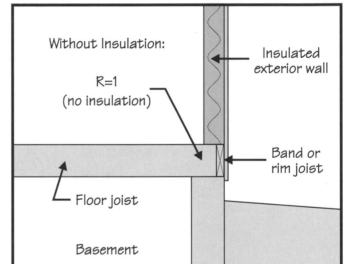

Figure 20-4.

5. Weatherstripping and Caulking

In general, it makes a lot of sense to seal up the exterior envelope of your home. This eliminates heating and cooling losses and seals your home against potential pests. Every year you should check caulking and sealant used around any penetration through the exterior wall of your home. Check window and door caulking. An investment of a few dollars and a few hours can eliminate drafts and make your home more comfortable.

Weatherstripping around windows and doors can also help stop cold drafts and save energy. There are many, many types of door sweeps, strips, foam strips, rubber tapes, closed-cell foam tape, tubular vinyl, felt, bronze strips, open-cell tape, vinyl clad foam—the list goes on. Visit the hardware store and choose the product that is right for your application.

My favorite product for weatherstripping is 3-M brand V-Seal. **See Figure 20-5 and 20-6**. This is a very thin vinyl that folds along its length to form a V, similar to the age-old bronze metal strips. The key to this product is its size, ease of use, and effectiveness. It has an adhesive strip on one edge. You just cut it to the length you need with a scissors, peel off the backing tape and place the V-Seal in the opening. Because the product is so thin, it fits easily around doors and windows.

Figure 20-5. 3m V-Seal

I actually used V-Seal to "double weatherstrip" all my doors. It is easy to use and inexpensive, and it will last a long, long time. You can find it at all hardware stores.

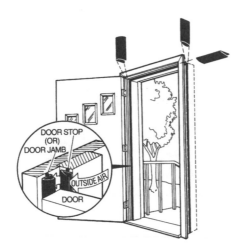 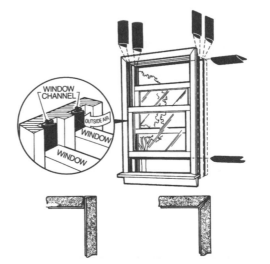

Figure 20-6.

6. Temporary Caulking and Storms

If you need a quick fix for air leaks, consider removable caulks and sealant. You can place these around offending windows to effectively seal them in place for the winter. In the spring, remove the caulk. These work great on drafty old windows you don't plan on opening for a season or two.

Also consider temporary inside or outside storms. These are great products first introduced by the 3-M Company. You place two-sided tape around the inside of the offending window or door, then place clear plastic on the tape. When you heat the plastic with a hair dryer, it stretches to become an invisible storm window. A similar product can also be used outside.

I have saved my kids several times in their old, drafty, dumpy, awful college rentals with these sealers and inside storms.

7. Showerheads

A low flow showerhead can give a good shower while saving a substantial amount of water as well as energy used to heat the water. I understand that this technology was perfected in submarines, where conserving water was an absolute necessity. Low flow heads have suffered a bad reputation for several years, but now many options and good showerheads are available.

You can also add a flow control valve at the showerhead. This allows everyone to adjust the flow to his or her preference.

If you want to test your showerhead, put a bucket below the showerhead and turn the water on full force. After 30 seconds, measure the amount of water in the bucket. Double that amount to determine the flow per minute. A good low-flow showerhead uses well below 2.5 gallons per minute. (You can also measure the flow for a full minute if you have a large bucket and a strong arm.)

A low flow showerhead will cost from $5 to $20 and can easily save more than that amount each year in reduced energy, water and sewer costs.

8. Lighting Controls

Teens or younger children seldom remember to turn lights off. From personal experience, I know that the best way to keep the lights off in a home shared with teenagers is to send them away to college. If that is not practical, here are several aids I have used successfully.

For walk-in closets or storage areas, replace the switch with a 15-minute timer. The maximum the light can be on is 15 minutes, and often the kids will switch the timer off because of its annoying ticking. This also works in bathrooms and bedrooms, but there you will need a longer (1- or 2-hour) timer.

For exterior lights, I always use fixtures with a built-in photo-eye control so the light only operates after dark. Fluorescent and sodium lights are also big energy savers for outdoor fixtures.

For bathroom and bedrooms, I have had mixed results with motion sensor switches. They can be hard to adjust and may turn off at inappropriate times. Ask yourself: would waving your hands in the dark while taking a shower be fun or frustrating? Despite some problems with adjustment, though, I think motion sensors generally work well.

9. Stop All Water Leaks

Any small drip or water leak will waste a huge amount of water and energy. Energy is required to pump the water and heat it. Once the water is in the sewer, it must be treated by the sewer system.

A small drip that fills a coffee cup in a 10-minute period wastes about 3,280 gallons of water per year. A drip rate of one per second can waste up to 200 gallons of water per month or 2,400 gallons per year.

Repair any leaking faucet or fixture to save energy and our precious resources.

10. Switch to Fluorescent Lamps

Now here is where I get in trouble. I love fluorescent light fixtures and the small fluorescent bulbs that can be used in standard lamps. I love the energy they save, but I get in trouble because my wife and kids have complained about these fixtures in our home for the last 20 years.

I will admit that 20 years ago, these fluorescent lights produced a poor, harsh color, and they often failed prematurely. But they have come a long way in 20 years, and come to think about it, I have not had a complaint at home for about 5 years. Perhaps my family has adjusted to my favorite lights, maybe because the lights have improved greatly.

I started using fluorescent and compact fluorescent bulbs in my commercial building projects 20 years ago and often brought home a few trial fixtures. I also consistently bought and received fixtures through utility company programs designed to save energy.

Today the fluorescent fixtures are great! You can buy color-corrected lamps that give off a warm light that is close to the color of natural sunlight. You can buy fluorescent bulbs that will fit in most lamps and fixtures. These fluorescent bulbs typically last 10 times as long as standard incandescent bulbs and produce the same amount of light for one-quarter the cost. Give them a try—at least in fixtures you use a lot or in your security lights.

11. Maintain Heating and Cooling Equipment–Yourself

Basic maintenance of heating and cooling equipment can easily save you up to 5 % of your heating and cooling bill and will help avoid a potentially expensive outage. **See Figure 20-7.**

What can you do? What must you do? Read the specific recommendations elsewhere in this book for the specific type of equipment in your home. Remember: change filters, keep coils clean, and keep plants away from air conditioners and heat pumps. Simple steps can save lots of money.

12. Maintain Heating & Cooling Equipment–Professionals

Don't forget to schedule professional service for your home's main heating and cooling equipment. Professionals can keep your equipment is top shape and can tune the equipment for energy efficiency. Have them follow the guidelines provided in this book.

For more information, see the References section.

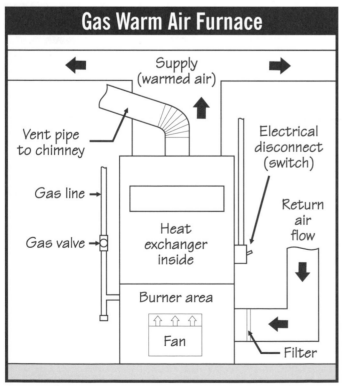

Figure 20-7.

13. Seal Heating and Cooling Ducts

Recent studied have confirmed that there is a huge potential for energy savings by sealing heating and cooling ducts in unconditioned spaces. Recent studies and airflow evaluations have found energy losses and comfort problems due to losses from distribution ducts.

These problems typically occur when heating and cooling ducts are run in unheated attics or crawl spaces. Any hole or crack in a heating/cooling duct will dump energy to the outside, reducing comfort inside your home. **See Figure 20-8.** Leaks are often found at joints that are not sealed or those sealed with duct tape that has failed. Duct tape is only a temporary fix; it will eventually dry out.

I have performed thousands of home inspections over the years and have often found damaged, uninsulated, disconnected ductwork in attics and crawl spaces.Why? Well, whoever looks in the attic or the crawl space?

Inspection and sealing is not easy but can produce great savings. Hire a professional home inspector or heating contractor to inspect your system, and plan on corrective work based on the inspection. Use special duct sealant to seal small cracks. Repair larger openings or gaps with special sealing mesh and duct sealant and a putty knife. Repair disconnected ducts.

14. Seal Openings Into the Attic

This is another tough problem. Many homes were built with poor sealing between the conditioned living space and the attic. This results in extensive air leaks and loss of heat and moisture. There may even be moisture damage in the attic due to leaks around pipes, electrical wiring, and vents routed through the ceilings.

Spotting this type of problem requires a throrough inspection of the attic—perhaps a task best left to an insulation firm or a professional home inspector. A professional will look for gaps around any penetration through the ceiling envelope of your home.

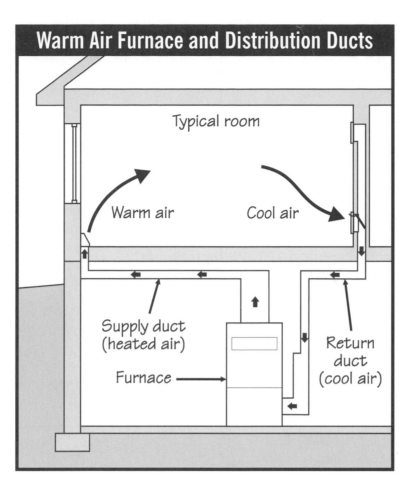

Warm Air Furnace and Distribution Ducts

Typical room

Warm air

Cool air

Supply duct
(heated air)

Furnace

Return
duct
(cool air)

Figure 20-8.

Gaps may occur around piping, wiring, fans, chimneys and other penetrations. Often an air leak will leave telltale signs such as mildew, moisture stains or dirt stains from air movement.

All of these gaps and holes can be filled with caulk, foam sealant or sheet metal caulked in place. Often a professional should do this work because of the hazards of working in an attic.

One word of caution: don't seal around standard recessed light fixtures. They need air movement to dissipate heat. Special sealed light fixtures can be installed to prevent air movement and heat loss.

15. Fireplaces: Warm and Romantic, But...

I hate to tell you this, but I have to: your standard masonry fireplace is a big, big heat loser. When you build a fire, a tremendous amount of air that

was heated by your furnace goes up the chimney. **See Figure 20-9.**

You can help this situation by using glass fireplace doors and having a contractor install an outside air supply for the fireplace. You can also help by closing the damper and doors when the fire is completely out.

Notice that I have been talking about standard masonry fireplaces. Modern metal-framed fireplaces with an outside air supply and the ability to heat some of the room air are much more efficient.

Modern gas-fired, sealed-combustion, direct-vented fireplaces are great! Consider one of these if you are building or remodeling. Their efficiency rivals that of furnaces, and they can heat a room or a portion of your home.

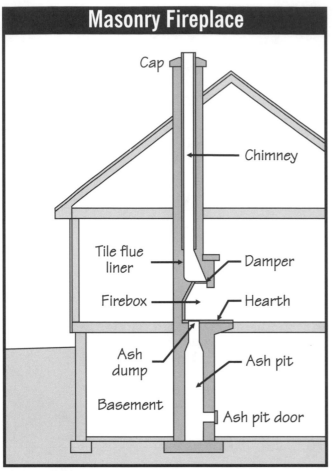

Figure 20-9.

Energy: A Quick Summary

You will notice that I have not addressed replacing furnaces, replacing windows, or insulating attics as my top energy-saving and comfort tips. While these are all fine approaches to saving energy, most of us complete these projects because of other concerns: the furnace is failing, the windows don't work, or there is no insulation in the attic.

I have addressed simple energy-saving ideas that you can easily work into your everyday routine and budget—things that work and provide substantial savings compared to the cost involved, and things that improve the comfort of your home.

Don't get hung up on big, expensive projects like a furnace replacement or insulation project until you have addressed the simple fixes. Also, consider contacting your local utility, which may offer a free or low-cost professional energy evaluation of your home.

CHAPTER 21 RECOMMENDED BOOKS AND MAGAZINES

For Most Homeowners

I have collected almost all the available books on home repair, and I do have several favorites. The best books provide accurate information on how systems work, give repair information, and offer lots of pictures or sketches.

One of the best home repair books is The New Complete Do-It-Yourself Manual from Reader's Digest. A great review of systems in a home is How A House Works by Duane Johnson (which is a series of articles from The Family Handyman magazine, reprinted in book format by Reader's Digest). Other good books include The Stanley Complete Step-By-Step Book of Home Repair and Improvement, Ortho's Home Improvement Encyclopedia, and the home repair and improvement book series published by Time-Life Books. Another of my favorites—no surprise here—is my own Just Fix It, which provides hundreds of answers to common home problems; ordering information appears at the end of this book.

Look for a reference work that focuses on the type of work you plan to perform. Some books are strong in painting and refinishing, others in mechanical and electrical repairs. Don't start with big, complicated home repairs and improvements if you've never done small jobs. You need to experience success on small projects and build from there.

My favorite magazines for the typical homeowner include The Family Handyman, Consumer Reports, Home Mechanics, Today's Homeowner and Practical Homeowner.

For Restoration

Folks involved in restoration of older homes can certainly use the books listed above, and should add the following:

Magazines

Old-House Journal

Books

The Old-House Journal Guide to Restoration (Dutton)

The Old-House Journal Restoration Directory (an annual sourcebook of suppliers)

Caring for Your Historic House edited by Charles E. Fisher (Harry N. Abrams)

Directory of Building Preservation by Ward Butcher (Wiley)

For Experts

Here are sources of info for experts and for amateurs with a special interest in residential construction:

Magazines

Fine Homebuilding

Fine Woodworking

The Journal of Light Construction

Books

Residential & Light Commercial Construction Standards (Robert S. Means Co.)

Builder's Guide to Cold Climates by Joseph Lstiburek (Taunton)

Builder's Guide to Mixed Climates by Joseph Lstiburek (Taunton)

Troubleshooting Guide to Residential Construction (from the editors of The Journal of Light Construction)

CHAPTER 22 REFERENCES

Quick Index For Catagories Listed:

Home related associations and manufacturers with addresses,
800 numbers and web site information.

Adhesives

DAP

888-327-8477
www.dap.com

Elmer's Products

180 E. Broad St.
Columbus, OH 43215
www.elmers.com
888-543-6377

Franklin Int't Titebond

800-347-4583
www.titebond.com

Gorilla Glue

800-966-3458
www.gorillaglue.com

Loctite Corp.

1001 Trout Brook Crossing
Rocky Hill, CT 06067
203-571-5100

Luzaire-Fraser-Johnston

P.O. Box 1592
York, PA 17405-1592
717-771-6130

Macco Adhesives

Liquid Nails
800-634-0015
www.liquidnail.com

Ohio Sealants

PL and Quickbond
800-321-3578
www.osisealants.com

Air Conditioning (See Heating)

Air Quality

Allergy and Asthma Network

800-878-4403
www.aanma.org

American Lung Association

800-586-4872
www.lungusa.org

Asthma and Allergy
Foundation of America

800-727-8462
www.aafa.org

Asthma Information Center

www.ama-assn.org/special/asthma

Indoor Air Quality Information
Clearinghouse

www.epa.gov/iaq

Appliances

Amana Refrigeration

Amana, IA 52204
800-843-0304
www.amana.com

American Whirlpool

800-327-1394
www.americanwhirlpool.com

Association of Home
Appliance Manufacturers

20 North Wacker Drive
Chicago, IL 60606
312-984-5822

Black & Decker

6 Armstrong Road
Shelton, CT 06484
800-552-0553

Caloric Corporation

Amana Refrigeration
Amana, IA 52204
319-662-5800

Eureka

800-282-2886

Frigidaire Home Products

6000 Perimeter Drive
Dublin, OH 43017
800-685-6005
800-FRIGIDAIRE
www.frigidaire.com

GE Appliances

Appliance Park
Louisville, KY 40225
800-626-2000

Gibson

6000 Perimeter Drive
Dublin, OH 43017
800-458-1445

Hamilton Beach
Proctor-Silex

800-851-8900
www.hambeach.com

HotPoint Appliances

800-626-2000
www.hotpoint.co.uk

In-Sink-Erator Division

Emerson Electric Co.

4700 21st Street
Racine, WI 53406
800-558-5712

Jenn-Air

3035 Shadeland
Indianapolis, In 46226
317-545-2271
800-536-6247
www.jennair.com

Kelvinator

6000 Perimeter Drive
Dublin, OH 43017
800-323-7773

Kenmore/Sears

847-286-2500
www.sears.com

KitchenAid

701 Main Street
St. Joseph, MI 49085
800-422-1230
www.kitchenaid.com

Maytag Corporation

800-688-9000
www.maytag.com

Sanyo Corporation

21351 Lassen Street
Chatsworth, CA 91311
818-998-7322

Sears / Kenmore

Sears Tower
25th Floor Brand Central
Chicago, IL 60684
312-875-1385
www.sears.com

Sub-Zero Freezer

800-222-7820
www.sub-zerofreezer.com

Tappan

6000 Perimeter Drive
Dublin, OH 43017
800-685-6005

U-Line Corp.

414-354-0300
www.u-line.com

Whirlpool Corporation

2000 M63 North
Benton Harbor, MI 49022
800-253-1301
www.whirlpool.com

White Westinghouse

6000 Perimeter Drive
Dublin, OH 43017
800-245-0600

Associations: Contractor, Supplier, and Builder

Adhesive and
Sealant Council

7979 Old Georgetown Rd.
Suite 500
Bethesda, MD 20814
301-986-9700

American Forest and
Paper Association
American Wood Council

1111 Nineteenth St.
Suite 800
Washington, DC 20036
www.awc.org
202-463-2766

American Gas Association

1515 Wilson Boulevard
Arlington, VA 22209
703-841-8667
www.aga.com

American Hardboard Assoc.

B520 N. Hicks Road
Palatine, IL 60007
708-934-8800

American Hardware Mfg

www.ahma.org
888-424-7458

American Homeowners
Association

www.ahahome.com

American Lighting Association

Box 420288
Dallas, TX 75342-0288
www.americanlightingassoc.com
800-274-4484

American Plywood Assoc.

Box 11700
Tacoma, WA 98411
American Red Cross
www.redcross.org

American Society for Testing
& Materials (ASTM)

100 Barr Harbor Dr.
West Conshocken, PA 19428
610-832-9500
www.astm.org

American Society of
Home Inspectors

800-743-2744
www.ashi.com

American Wood
Preservers Institute

1945 Old Gallows Rd.
Suite 550
Vienna, VA 22182
www.awpi.org
703-893-4005

Architectural
Landscape Lighting

2930 S. Fairview St.
Santa Anna, CA 92704
www.alllighting.com
800-854-8277

Asphalt Roofing
Manufacturers Assoc.

P.O. Box 3248
Grand Central Station
New York, NY 10163

Association of Home
Appliance Manufacturers

20 North Wacker Drive
Chicago, IL 60606
312-984-5822

Bat Conservation Int'l

www.batcon.org
512-327-9721

Brick Institute of America

114490 Commerce Park Drive
Reston, VA 22091
703-620-0010

California Redwood Association

888-225-7339
www.calredwood.org

The Carpet & Rug Institute

800-882-8846
www.carpet-rug.com

Cedar Shake &
Shingle Bureau

515 116th Avenue, N.E.
Bellevue, WA 98004
206-453-1323

Cedar Shingles

www.cedarbureau.org

Chimney Safety
Institute of America

16021 Industrial Drive, Suite 8
Gaithersburg, Maryland 20877
301-963-6900
Fax: 301-963-0838

Garage Door
Hardware Association

2850 S. Ocean Blvd.
Suite 311
Palm Beach, FL 33480
407-533-0991

Gas Research Institute

   8600 W. Bryn Mawr
   Chicago, IL 60631
   312-399-8249

Hardwood Council

   www.hardwoodcouncil.com
   412-281-4980

Hardwood Manufacturers
Association

   400 Penn Center Boulevard
   Suite 530
   Pittsburgh, PA 15235
   412-829-0770

Hardwood Plywood & Veneer
Association

   703-435-2000
   www.hpva.org

Home Ventilation Institute

   30 West University Drive
   Arlington Heights, IL 60004
   312-394-0150

Hydronics Institute

   35 Russo Pl.
   P.O. Box 218
   Berkeley Heights, NJ 07922
   908-464-8200

International Association of
Lighting Designers (IALD)

   800-423-6587
   www.iald.org

International Staple, Nail, and
Tool Association

   (ISANTA)
   512 W. Burlington Ave.
   Suite 203
   LaGrange, IL 60525
   708-482-8138

Maple Flooring Manufacturers
Association

   847-480-9138
   www.maplefloor.com

The Marble Institute
of America

   33505 State Street
   Farmington, MI 48024

National Association of the
Remodeling Industry

   1901 N. Moore Street
   Suite 808
   Arlington, VA 22209
   703-276-7600

National Association
of Brick Distributors

   212 South Henry St.
   Alexandria, VA 22314
   703-549-0437

National Concrete
Masonry Association

   2302 Horse Pen Road
   Herndon, VA 22071-3406
   703-713-1900

National Fire Prevention
Association-NFPA

   1 Batterymarch Park
   Quincy, MA 02269-9101
   617-770-3000
   www.nfpa.org

National Oak Flooring
Manufacturers Association

   Box 3009
   Memphis, TN 38173
   901-526-5016
   www.nofma.com

National Paint &
Coatings Assoc.

   1500 Rhode Island
   Washington, DC 20005
   202-462-6272
   www.paint.org

National Pest
Management Association

   www.pestworld.org

National Propane Gas
Association

   1600 Eisenhower Ln
   Suite 100
   Lisle, IL 60532
   708-515-0600

National Spa &
Pool Institute

   703-838-0083
   www.resourcecenter.com

National Wood
Flooring Association

   1688 Westwoods Business Park
   Ellisville, MO
   63021-4522

Painting & Decorating
Contractors of America

   800-332-7322
   www.pdca.com

Plumbing Heating Cooling
Contractors – National
Association

   800-533-7694
   www.naphcc.org

Plumbing, Heating
& Cooling Information Bureau

   303 East Wacker Drive
   Chicago, IL 60601
   312-372-7331
   www.phcib.org

Portland Cement Association

   5420 Old Orchard Road
   Skokie, IL 60077-4321
   708-966-6200

Red Cedar Shingle and
Handsplit Shake Bureau

   515 – 116th Avenue NE
   Suite 275
   Bellevue, WA 98004

Resilient Floor
Covering Institute

   966 Hungerford Drice
   Suite 12-B
   Rockville, MD 20850

Southern Forest
Products Association

   Box 641700
   Kenner, LA 70064
   504-443-4464
   ww.southernpine.com

Southern Pine
Marketing Council

   P.O. Box 52468
   New Orleans, LA 70152
   504-443-4464

Vinyl Siding Institute

888-367-8741
www.vinylsiding.org.

Western Wood Products Association

Yeon Building
522 S.W. Fifth Avenue
Portland, OR 97204-2122
503-224-3930
www.wwpa.org

Building Code

BOCA International
Building Officials Code
Administrators International

4051 West Flossmoor Rd.
Country Club Hills, IL 60478
www.bocai.org
708-799-2300

ICBO International Conference of Building Officials

5360 Workman Mill Rd.
Whittier, CA 90601
www.icbo.org
562-699-0543

SBCCI Southern Building Code Congress International

900 Montclair Rd.
Birmingham, +AL 35213
www.sbcci.org
205-591-1853

Building Products

Alcoa Building Products

2600 Campbell Rd.
Sydney, OH 45365-0132
800-962-6973
www.alocoahomes.com

California Closets

888-336-9702
www.calclostets.com

Cemplank

P.O. Box 99
Blandon, PA 19605
www.cemplank.com
877-236-7526

Certainteed

750 E. Swedesford Rd.
Valley Forge, PA 19482-0101
www.certainteed.com
800-233-8990

DOW Chemical USA

2020 Willard H. Dos Center
Midland, MI 48674

Gentek Building Products

29325 Chagrin Blvd.
Cleveland, OH 44122-4613
www.gentekinc.com
800-548-4542

Georgia-Pacific

133 Peachtree St.
Atlanta, GA 30303
www.gp.com
800-284-5347

Gutter Helmet

888-4-HELMET

Homasote Co.

P.O. Box 7240
West Trenton, NJ 08628-3300

James Hardie Industries

26300 La Alameda
Suite 250
Mission Viejo, CA 92691
www.jameshardie.com

Johns Manville

800-654-3103
www.jc.com

Louisiana-Pacific Corp.

111 SW Fifth Ave.
Portland, OR 97204
www.lpcorp.com
800-547-6331

Masonite

1 S. Wacker Dr. Suite 3600
Chicago, IL 60606
800-323-4591
www.masonite.com

Norandex-Reynolds

8450 S. Bedford Rd.
Macedonia, OH 44056
www.norandex.com
800-528-0942

Owens Corning

800-GET-PINK
Simpson Strong Tie
4637 Chabot Dr.
Suite 200
Pleasanton, CA 94588
www.strongtie.com
800-999-5099

Swan Secure Systems

7525 Perryman Ct.
Baltimore, MD 21226
www.swansecure.com
800-966-2801

Tyvek

800-44-TYVEK
Weyerhaeuser
800-869-3667
www.doors.wy.com

Brick

Brick Institute of America

114490 Commerce Park Drive
Reston, VA 22091
703-620-0010

National Association of Brick Distributors

212 South Henry St.
Alexandria, VA 22314
703-549-0437

Carpet

3M

800-433-3296

Allied Signal

800-441-8185

ANSO

800-441-8185

BASF

800-652-9964

The Carpet & Rug Institute

800-882-8846
www.carpet-rug.com

DuPont

800-4DU-PONT

Carpet Cleaning

Host Products

800-558-9439

Monsanto

800-633-3208

Caulks and Sealants

Adhesive and
Sealant Council

7979 Old Georgetown Rd.
Suite 500
Bethesda, MD 20814
301-986-9700

DAP Inc.

855 N. Thrid St.
Tipp City, OH 45371
800-543-3840

Dow Corning Corp

Box 994
Midland, MI 48686-0994
www.dowcorning.com
800-248-2481

Elmer's Products Inc.

180 E. Broad St.
Columbus, OH 43215
www.elmers.com
888-435-6377

Franklin Int't Titebond

800-347-4583
www.titebond.com

Geocel Corp

53280 Marina Dr.
Elkhart, IN 46514
219-348-7615
800-433-9517

Ceiling Fans

Casablanca Fan Co.

761 Corporate Center Dr.,
Pomoa, CA 91768
888-227-2178

Emerson Ceiling Fans

8400 Pershall Rd.
Hazelwood, MO 63042
800-237-6511
www.emrsonfans.com

Hunter Fan Company

2500 Frisco
Memphis, TN 38114
800-4Hunter
www.hunterfan.com

Red Devil

Union, NJ 07083
800-4-A-DEVIL

Cement, Concrete

National Concrete
Masonry Association

2302 Horse Pen Road
Herndon, VA 22071-3406
703-713-1900

Portland Cement Association

5420 Old Orchard Road
Skokie, IL 60077-4321
708-966-6200

Chimneys

Chimney Safety Institute
of America

16021 Industrial Drive, Suite 8
Gaithersburg, Maryland 20877
301-963-6900
Fax: 301-963-0838

Countertops

DuPont Corian

Barley Mill Plaza
Pricemill Bldg.
P.O. Box 80012
Wilmington, DE 19880
800-426-7426
www.corian.com

Formica Corporation

1504 Sadlier Circle South Drive
Indianapolis, IN 46239
800-367-6422

Nevamar Corp.

8339 Telegraph Road
Odenton, MD 21113
301-551-5000

Pionite Plastics Corp.

P.O. Box 1014
Auburn, ME 04211
207-784-9111

Ralph Wilson Plastics

600 General Bruce Drive
Temple, TX 76503
817-778-2711

Surrell Formica.

1504 Sadlier Circle
South Drive
Indianapolis, IN 46239
800-367-6422

Wilsonart

800-433-3222
www.builderonline.com/~wilsonart

Doors (See Windows)

Electrical

AMP

800-522-6752

GE Wiring

225 Service Ave.
P.O. Box 1050
Warwick, RI 02886
401-886-6200

Murray/Siemens Electrical

P.O. Box 9050
Charlottesville, VA 22906
800-548-6405

Square D

3201 Nicholasville Rd.
Suite 300
Lexington, KY 40503
800-392-8781
www.squared.com

Westinghouse

1090 W. Thorndale Ave.
Bensenville, IL 60106
800-443-3342

Energy, Energy Conservation

American Gas Association

1515 Wilson Boulevard
Arlington, VA 22209
703-841-8400
www.aga.com

Energy Efficiency
and Renewable
Energy Clearinghouse (EREC)

800-363-3732
www.erecbbs.nciinc.com

Home Energy

2124 Kitredge St. No. 95
Berkeley, CA 94704
www.homeenergy.org

Gas Research Institute

www.gri.com

Honeywell

www.honeywell.com
800-251-5423

National Appropriate
Tech Assistance Service
NATAS

U.S. Dept. of Energy
P.O. Box 2525
Butte, MT 59702-2525
800-428-2525

Epoxy Repair Products

Abatron Inc.

5501 95th Ave.
Kenosha, WI 53144
800-445-1754
www.abatron.com

Advanced Repair Tech

P.O.Box 510
Cherry Valley, NY 13320
607-264-9040
www.advancedrepair.com

Bondo/Mar-Hyde Corp.

3700 Atlanta Industrial Pkwy
Atlanta, GA 30331
www.bondomarhyde.com
800-421-2663

Cabot

800-US-STAIN

Minwax Wood Hardener
Minwax High Performance
Wood Filler

800-462-0194

Mr. Mac's Wood Fix
Mr. Mac's Concrete Fix

800-348-3571

Exhaust Fans

Broan

962 W. State St.
P.O. Box 140
Hartford, WI 53027
800-558-1711
www.broan.com

NuTone

Madison and Red Banks Rd.
Cincinnati, OH 45227
800-543-8687
www.nutone.com

Research Products

800-545-2219
www.spaceguard.com

Therma-Stor

1919 S. Stoughton Rd.
P.O. Box 8050
Madison, WI 53708
800-533-7533

Fireplaces

Chimney Safety Institute
of America

16021 Industrial Drive, Suite 8
Gaithersburg, Maryland 20877
301-963-6900
Fax: 301-963-0838

Heat-N-Glo Fireplace
Products, Inc.

6665 West Highway 13
Savage, MN 55378
800-669-4328
www.heatnglo.com

Heatilator

1915 W. Saunders Street
Mt. Pleasant, IA 52641
800-669-4328
www.heatilator.com

Kozy Heat

204 Industrial Park Dr.
P.O. Box 577
Lakefield, MN 56150
507-662-6641

Majestic Products

1000 E. Market St.
Huntington, IN 46750
800-525-1898

Superior Fireplace Co.

4325 Artesia Ave.
Fullerton, CA 92633
714-521-7302

Temco Fireplace

301 S. Perimeter Park Dr.
Suite 227
Nashville, TN 37211
615-831-9393

Vermont Castings

Prince Street
Randolph, VT 05060
800-728-3181

Floor Covering-
See Carpet, Vinyl, Wood

Garage Doors and Openers

Chamberlain/Lift Master

845 Larch Ave.
Elmhurst, IL 60126
800-528-9131

Garage Door Hardware
Association

2850 S. Ocean Blvd.
Suite 311
Palm Beach, FL 33480
407-533-0991

Genie Industries

22790 Lake Park Blvd.
Alliance, OH 44601
800-OK –GENIE
800-843-4084
www.genielift.com

Overhead

6750 LBJ Fwy.
Suite 1200
Dallas, TX 75240
800-543-2269

Stanley

800-447-3853
Wayne Dalton
1 Door Dr.
Mt. Hope, OH 44660
800-827-DOOR

Windsor Door

5800 Scott Hamilton Dr.
Little Rock, AR 72209
501-562-1872

Government Agencies

Chemical Referral Center

800-CMA-8200

**Environmental
Protection Agency**

EPA Region 5 (Midwest)
230 S. Dearborn Street
Chicago, IL 60604
www.epa.gov
312-353-2205
312-886-6165

Federal Information Center

414-271-2273

FEMA National Flood Insurance

800-CALL-FLOOD, ext. 180

**Forest Products Laboratory
Forest Service USDA**

One Gifford Pinchot Drive
Madison, WI 53705
608-231-9200

Lead Safety

www.leadsafeusa.com
www.leadlisting.org
www.epa.gov/lead
www.hud.gov.lea

**National Small Flows
Clearinghouse**

(Septic Information)
800-624-8301

**National Technical
Information Service (NTIS)
U.S. Department of Commerce
(Energy Related Information)**

5285 Port Royal Road
Springfield, VA 22161
703-487-4650

**Preservation Assistance Division
U.S. Department of Interior
National Park Service**

P.O. Box 37127
Washington, DC 20013-7127
202-343-9573

**Superintendent of Documents
U.S. Government Printing
Office (GPO)**

Washington, DC 20402
202-783-3238

**University of Illinois at
Urbana – Champaign
Small Homes Council**

Building Research Council
One East Saint Mary's Road
Champaign, IL 61820-6995
800-336-0616

**U.S. Consumer Product
Safety Commission**

Washington, DC 20207
800-638-CPSC
www.cpsc.com

Hardware Specialties

**ATCI Consumer Products
(Squeak-Relief)**

5873 Patterson Dr.
Troy, MI 48098
810-879-0030

**American Hardware
Manufacturers Association**

847-605-1025
www.ahma.org

Baldwin Hardware Corp.

841 E. Wyomissing Blvd.
P.O. Box 15048
Reading, PA 19612
610-777-7811

**Blaine Window Hardware
(Replacement Hardware)**

17319 Blaine Dr.
Hagerstown, MD 21740
800-678-1991

**Johnson Products, Inc.
(Pocket Door Hardware)**

2100 Sterling Ave.
Elkhart, IN 46516
219-293-5664
www.johnsonhardware.com

Kemp and George

800-343-4012

Kwikset Corporation

1 Park Plaza, Suite 1000
Irvine, CA 92714
800-327-5625

Larsen Products

800-633-6668
www.larsen products.com

Master Lock

2600 N. 32nd St.
Milwaukee, WI 53210
414-444-2800

**O'Berry Enterprises
(Squeeeeek No More)**

664 Exmoor Ct.
Crystal Lake, IL 60014
800-459-8428

**Renovators Supply
Renovators Old Mill
(Reproduction Hardware)**

Miller Falls, MA 01349-1097
413-659-2211

Schlage Lock

2401 Bayshore Blvd.
San Francisco, CA 94134
800-847-1864
www.schlagelock.com

Stanley Tools

600 Myrtle St.
New Britain, CT 06053
www.stanleyworks.com
860-225-5111

Weiser Lock

6660 S. Broadmoor Rd.
Tucson, AZ 85746
800-677-5625
www.weiserlock.com

Weslock National

13344 S. Main St.
Los Angeles, CA 90061
310-327-2770

Yale Locks and Hardware

P.O. Box 25288
Charlotte, NC 28229
800-438-1951

Heating and Air Conditioning

Air-Conditioning & Refrigeration Institute

4301 N Fairfax Dr.
Suite 425
Arlington, VA 22203
703-524-8800

American Standard Heating and Air Conditioning

800-752-6292
amstd-comfort.com

Bryant

P.O. Box 70
Indianapolis, IN 46206
800-468-7253
www.thermacool.com/bryant.htm

Carrier

7310 W. Morris St.
Indianapolis, IN 46231
800-4-CARRIER
www.carrier.com

Gas Research Institute

8600 W. Bryn Mawr
Chicago, IL 60631
312-399-8249

Goodman Mfg. Co.

1501 Seamist
Houston, TX 77008
713-861-2500

Heil Heating & Cooling Products

650 Heil-Quaker Ave.
Lewisburg, TN 37091
615-359-3511
www.heil-hvac.com/heil

Honeywell Consumer Products

800-468-1502
www.honeywell.com

Hydronics Institute

35 Russo Pl.
P.O. Box 218
Berkeley Heights, NJ 07922
908-464-8200

Jameson

708-963-2850

Lennox

P.O. Box 799900
Dallas, TX 75379-9900
214-497-5000
www.davelennox.com

Magic Chef

800-536-6247

National Propane Gas Association

1600 Eisenhower Ln
Suite 100
Lisle, IL 60532
708-515-0600

Payne

P.O. Box 70
Indianapolis, IN 46206
800-227-4633

Plumbing Heating Cooling Information Bureau

303 E. Wacker Dr.
Chicago, IL 60601
312-372-7331
www.phcib.org

Research Products (Humidifiers, Dehumidifiers, Filters)

800-545-2219
www.spaceguard.com

Rheem

5600 Old Greenwood Rd.
Fort Smith, AR 72917
501-646-4311
www.rheem.com

Robertshaw

(Controls)
800-468-1317

Ruud Air Conditioning

P.O. Box 17010
Fort Smith, AR 72917
501-646-4311
www.ruudac.com

Slant/Fin Corp.

100 Forest Dr.
Greenvale, NY 11548
516-484-2600

Tempstar Heating and Cooling Products

650 Heil Quaker Ave.
Lewisburg, TN 37091
800-434-4345
www.tempstarcom/tempstar

Therma-Stor

1919 S. Stoughton Rd.
P.O. Box 8050
Madison, WI 53708
800-533-7533

Trane

6200 Troup Hwy.
Tyler, TX 75707
www.trane.com

Weil-McLain

500 Blaine St.
Michigan City, IN 46360-2388
219-879-6561
www.weil-mclain.com

WIRSBO

800-321-4739
www.wirsbo.com

York International

P.O. Box 1592
York, PA 17405-1592
717-771-6225
www.york.com

Insulation

Celotex

www.celotex.com

Certainteed

800-782-8777
www.certainteed.com

Johns Manville

800-654-3103
www.jm.com

Owens Corning

800-GET-PINK
www.owenscorning.com

Lighting

American Lighting Association

Box 420288
Dallas, TX 75342-0288
www.americanlightingassoc.com
800-274-4484

Architectural Landscape
Lighting

2930 S. Fairview St.
Santa Anna, CA 92704
www.alllighting.com
800-854-8277

Catalina

800-523-5702
www.catalinaltg.com

GE Lightning Nela Park

1975 Noble Rd.
Cleveland, OH 44112
800-626-2000
www.gelighting.com

Greenlee Lighting

1300 Hutton Dr.
Suite 110
Carrollton, TX 75006
www.greenleelighting.com
972-466-1133

Halo Lighting System

770-486-4800
www.cooperlighting.com

Intermatic Malibu
Intermatic Plaza

Spring Grove, IL 60081-9698
www.intermatic.com
815-675-2321

International Association of
Lighting Designers (IALD)

800-423-6587
www.iald.org

Lights of America

800-321-8100
www.lightsofamerica.com

Osrom Sylvania

100 Endicott St.
Danvers, MA 01923
www.sylvania.com
800-544-4828

Philips

200 Franklin Square Rd.
Somerset, NJ 08873
800-555-0050
www.lighting.philips.com

Sylvania

GTE Products Corp.
Winchester, KY 40391
800-LIGHTBULB
www.sylvania.com

Lubricants

WD 40

Box 56436
Sherman Oaks, CA 91413
www.wd40.com

Marble, Synthetic Marble

Avonite

1945 Highway 304 South
Belen, NM 87002
800-428-6648

Cultured Marble Institute

435 Michigan Avenue
Suite 1717
Chicago, IL 60611
312-644-0828

Dupont Co.

Corian Products G51519
Wilmington, DE 19880-0010
800-426-7426

The Marble Institute of America

33505 State Street
Farmington, MI 48024

Surrell

1504 Sadlier Circle
South Drive
Indianapolis, IN 46239
800-367-6422

Nails (fasteners)

Jamestown Distributors

28 Narragansett Ave.
Jamestown, RI 02835
800-423-0030
www.jamestowndistributors.com

Independent Nails

30 Mozzone Blvd.
Taunton, MA 02780
www.mazenails.com

Maze Nails

100 Church St.
Peru, IL 61354
www.mazenails.com
800-435-5949

Swan Secure Products

7525 Perreyman Ct.
Baltimore, MD 21226
800-966-2801
www.swansecure.com

Tremont Nail Co.

P.O. Box 111
Wareham, MA 02751
(508)295-0038
www.mazenails.com

USP Lumber Connectors

703 Rogers Dr.
Montgomery, MN 56069
800-328-5934
www.uspconnectors.com

Paints and Related Products

3M Consumer Relations 3M DIY Division

Box 33053
St. Paul, MN 55133
800-842-4946

Ace Hardware

800-223-8663
www.acehardware.com

AKZO Coatings

1845 Maxwell
Troy, MI 48007
800-833-7288

American Wood Preservers Institute

1945 Old Gallows Road
Suite 550
Vienna, VA 22182
703-893-4005
www.awpi.org

Behr

800-854-0133
www.behrpaint.com

Benajmin Moore & Co.

51 Chestnut Ridge Road
Montvale, NJ 07645
800-826-2623
www.benjaminmoore.com

Bondex

3616 Scarlet Oak Blvd.
St. Louis, MO 63122
800-225-7522
www.bondex.com

Cabot

800-US-STAIN
www.cabotstain.com

Citristrip

www.citristrip.com
800-782-9926

Color Putty

www.colorputty.com
608-325-6033
Coronado
904-428-6461
www.coronadopaint.com

Daubert Coated Products

1 Westbrook Corp Center
Suite 1000
Westchester, IL 60154
800-634-1303

DAP Inc.

Box 277
Dayton, OH 45401-0277

Dutch Boy

800-828-5669
www.dutchboy.com

Flecto

P.O. Box 12955
Oakland, CA 94604-2955
800-6-FLECTO

Flood Co.

P.O. Box 339
Hudson, OH 44236-0399
800-321-3444
www.floodco.com

Fuller O'Brien

800-368-2068

General Finishes

800-783-6050
www.generalfinishes.com

Glidden

800-221-4100
www.gliddenpaint.com

Homer Formby's Help Line

800-FORMBYS

Home Right Paint Tools

800-264-5442
www.homeright.com

Insl-X

800-225-5554

Klean-Strip

Box 1879
Memphis, TN 38101
800-235-3546
www.kleanstrip.com

Krylon

800-4-KRYLON
www.krylon.com

The McColskey Corp.

7600 State Road
Philadelphia, PA 19136
800-345-4530

Minwax Company Inc.

Box 426
Little Falls, NJ 07424
www.minwax.com

National Paint & Coatings Assoc.

1500 Rhode Island
Washington, DC 20005
202-462-6272
www.paint.org

Olympic

800-441-9695

Osmose

800-522-WOOD

Painting & Decorating Contractors of America

800-332-7322
www.pdca.com

Parks Corporation

P.O. Box 5
Somerset, MA 02726
800-225-8543

Pittsburg, Olympic, Lucite

800-426-6306

Pittsburgh Paints

800-441-9695
www.ppgaf.com

Pratt & Lambert

75 Tonawanda Street
Buffalo, NY 14207
800-289-7728
www.prattandlambert.com

Rustoleum

www.rustoleum.com

Savogran

800-225-9872

Sears

800-972-4687

Sherwin Williams

101 Prospect Ave.
Cleveland, OH 44115
800-622-8468
www.sherwin-williams.com

Thompsons Help Line
(and Formby)

800-367-6291

True-Test Supreme

800-922-0061

UGL – United Gilsonite
Laboratories

800-272-3235
800-UGL-LABS
www.ugl.com

Wagner

Box 9362
Minneapolis, MN 55447
800-328-8251

Wm. Zinsser & Co.
(BIN, 1-2-3, Perma-White)

173 Belmont Dr.
Somerset, NJ 08875
908-469-4605
www.zinsser.com

Wolman-Loppers

800-556-7737

Wood Finishers Pride

800-45-PRIDE

Zar (See UGL)

Pests

Pest Facts

www.pestfacts.org

Bat Conservation International

www.batcon.org
512-327-9721

National Pest Management
Association

www.pestworld.org

Plastic Laminate
(See Countertops)

Plumbing

American Standard

One Centennial Plaza
Piscataway, NJ 08855-6820
800-524-9797, ext. 4023

Bemis Manufacturing Company

800-558-7651
www.bemismfg.com

Chicago Faucets Co.

2100 S. Nuclear Drive
Crane Plumbing / Fiat Products
1235 Hartrey Avenue
Evanston, IL 60202
708-864-9777

Delta Faucet

800-345-3358
www.deltafaucet.com

Chicago Faucets

Des Plaines, Il 60018
847-803-5000
www.chicagofaucets.com

Eljer Plumbingware

800-4-ELJER-2
www.eljer.com

Elkay Mfg. Co.

2222 Camden Court
Oak Brook, IL 60521
630-574-8484
www.elkay.com

Franklin Brass

800-421-3375
www.franklinbrass.com

In-Sink-Erator

(Garbage Disposals)
4700 21st St.
Racine, WI 53406
800-252-5254
www.insinkerator.com

Jacuzzi Whirlpool Bath

100 N. Wiget Lane
Walnut Creek, CA 94596
800-678-6889
www.jacuzzi.com

Kitchenaid

800-422-1230
www.kitchenaid.com

Kohler Co.

Kohler, WI 53044
800-546-4537
www.kohlerco.com

KraftMaid

800-571-1990

Moen Faucet

25300 Al Moen Dr.
North Olmstead, OH 44070
800-626-2000
www.moen.com

Moon Incorporated

377 Woodland Avenue
Elyria, OH 44035
800-321-8809

National Spa & Pool Institute

703-838-0083
www.resourcecenter.com

Peerless Products

800-279-9999
www.peerlessproducts.com

Plumbing Heating Cooling
Contractors – National
Association

800-533-7694
www.naphcc.org

Plumbing Heating Cooling
Information Bureau

303 E. Wacker Dr.
Chicago, IL 60601
312-372-7331
www.phcib.org

Price Pfister

www.pricepfister.com

Sinkmaster

800-345-8881
www.anaheimmfg.com

Sloan Flushmate

847-671-4300
www.flushmate.com

Sterling

800-STERLING

US Brass

800-US-BRASS

Pumps

Flotec

293 Wright St.
Delavan, WI 53115
262-728-7435
www.flotecpump.com

Little Giant Pump Co.

3810 North Tulsa
Oklahoma City, OK 73112
405-947-2511
www.littlegiant.com

Sta-Rite Industries

800-752-0183
www.starite.com

United Pump Inc.

1772 Buerkle Circle
White Bear Lake, MN 55110
651-770-7810
www.unitedpumpinc.com

Zoeller Pump

800-928-PUMP
www.zoeller.com

Remodeling

National Association of the
Remodeling Industry (NARI)

800-966-7601
www.ncma.org

Roofing

Air Vent

3000 W. Commerce
Dallas, TX 75212
800-247-8368

Alcoa Building Products

P.O. Box 716
Sidney, OH 45365
800-962-6973

Asphalt Roofing
Manufacturers Assoc.

P.O. Box 3248
Grand Central Station
New York, NY 10163

Cedar Shake & Shingle Bureau

515 116th Avenue, N.E.
Bellevue, WA 98004
206-453-1323

Cedar Shingles

www.cedarbureau.org

CertainTeed Corp

P.O. Box 860
Valley Forge, PA 19482
215-347-7000
www.certainteed.com

ELK Corp

800-650-0355
www.elkcorp.com

GAF Building Materials Corp.

1361 Alps Road
Wayne, NJ 07470
201-628-3000

Georgia Pacific

133 Peachtree Street N.W.
P.O. Box 105605
Atlanta, GA 30348
404-521-4000

Masonite Building
Products Group

1 South Wacker Drive
Chicago, IL 60606
312-750-0900

Red Cedar Shingle and
Handsplit Shake Bureau

515 – 116th Avenue NE
Suite 275
Bellevue, WA 98004

Vande Hey-Raleigh

1565 Bohm Drive
Little Chute, WI 54140
800-236-8453

Safety

National Lead Information
Center and Clearinghouse

800-424-5323
www.leadsafetyusa.com

Screen Material

Phifer Wire Products

Pet Proof Screens
P.O. Box 1700
Tuscaloosa, AL 35403-1700
800-874-3007
www.phifer.com

Screen Tight

(Porch Screening System)
407 St. James St.
Georgetown, SC 29440
800-768 7325

Sealers (See Paints)

Septic Information

National Small Flows
Clearing House

West Virginia University
P.O. Box 6064
Morgantown, WV 26505
800-624-8301
www.nsfc.wvu.edu

Small Scale Waste
Project Management

University of Wisconsin
1 Agriculture Hall
Madison, WI 53706
Bob.soils.wisc.edu

Siding

Alcoa Building Products

P.O. Box 716
Sidney, OH 45365
800-962-6973

Cedar Shake & Shingle Bureau

515 116th Avenue, N.E.
Bellevue, WA 98004
206-453-1323

Cemplank

P.O. Box 99
www. cemplank.com
877-236-7526

CertainTeed Corp.

P.O. Box 860
Valley Forge, PA 19482
215-341-7000
www.certainteed.com

Dryvit Systems, Inc.

One Energy Way
West Warwick, RI 02893
800-556-7752
www.dryvit.com

EIFS Industry
Manufacturers Association

3000 Corporate Center
Suite 270
Morrow, GA 30260
www.eifsfacts.com
800-294-3462

GAFBuilding Materials Corp.

1361 Alps Road
Wayne, NJ 07470
201-628-3000

Georgia-Pacific Corp.

P.O. Box 2808
Department M-WDS
Norcross, GA 30091
404-521-4000
www.gp.com

James Hardie Industries

26300 La Alameda
Suite 250
Mission Viejo, CA 92691
www.jameshardie.com
888-542-7343

Louisiana-Pacific Corp.

111 S.W. Fifth Avenue
Portland, OR 97204
503-221-0800
www.lpcorp.com

Masonite Building
Products Group

1 South Wacker Drive
Suite 3600
Chicago, IL 60606
312-750-0900
800-323-4591
www.masonite.com

National Fire Prevention
Association-NFPA

1 Batterymarch Park
Quincy, MA 02269-9101
617-770-3000
www.nfpa.org

Norandex-Reynolds

8450 S. Bedford Rd.
Macedonia, OH 44056
www.norandex.com
800-528-0942

Sto Corporation

6175 Riverside Dr.
Atlanta, GA 30331
www.stocorp.com
800-221-2397

Vinyl Siding Institute

888-367-8741
www.vinylsiding.org.

U.S. Consumer Product
Safety Commission

Washington, DC 20207
800-638-CPSC
www.cpsc.com

U.S. Gypsum

Box 806278
Chicago, IL 60680-4124
www.usgeifsnews.com
800-874-4968

Weyerhaeuser

800-869-3667
www.doors.wy.com

Skylights

Solatube

800-966-7652
www.solatube.com

Sun Tunnel

800-369-3664
www.suntunnel.com

Velux-America, Inc.

P.O. Box 5001
Greenwood, SC 29648
800-283-2831

Small Engine

Briggs and Stratton

414-259-5572
www.briggsandstratton.com

Stains (See Paints)

Tools

AEG

800-414-6527

American Tool

92 Grant St.
Wilmington, OH 45177
www.americantool.com
800-866-5740

Arrow Fastener

271 Mayhill St.
Saddlebrook, NJ 07663
www.arrowfastener.com
201-843-6900

Black & Decker

800-54-HOW-TO
www.blackanddecker.com

Bosch

800-301-8255

Craftsman

800-377-7414
www.sears.com/craftsman

Cooper Tools

Box 728
Apex, NC 27502
919-781-7200
www.coopertools.com

Delta International Machinery

412-963-2400
www.deltawoodworking.com

DeWalt

800-433-9258
www.dewalt.com

Dirt Devil

800-362-5509
www.dirtdevil.com

Dremel Tools

800-4-DREMEL
www.dremel.com

Grizzly Industrial

800-523-477
www.grizzlyindustrial.com

Hitachi

800-546-5482
www.hitachi.com

Klein Tools

800-553-4676
www.klein-tools.com

Leatherman

www.leatherman.com
800-847-8665

Makita

800-462-5482
www.makita.com

Milwaukee Electric Tool

13135 W. Lisbon Rd.
Brookfield, WI 53005
800-729-3878
www.mil-electric-tool.com

Panasonic

800-338-0552

Porter Cable

800-3219443
www.porter-cable.com

Powermatic

800-248-0144
www.powermatic.com

Ridgid

800-4-RIDGID
www.rigidwoodworking.com

Ryobi

800-525-2579
www.ryobi.com/powertools

Sears-Craftsman

3333 Beverly Rd.
Hoffman Estates, IL 60179
www.sears.com
800-364-3577

SK Hand Tool

800-822-5575
www.skhandtool.com

Skil-Bosch

773-286-7330
www.skiltools.com
www.bosch.com

Stanley Tools

600 Myrtle St.
New Britain, CT 06053
www.stanleyworks.com
860-225-5111

Starrett Co.

121 Crescent St.
Athul, MA 01331
978-249-5330
www.starrett.com

Vermont American Tool

800-742-3869
www.vermontamerican.com

Wagner

Box 9362
Minneapolis, MN 55447
800-328-8251

Ventilation

Broan Mfg. Co., Inc.

P.O. Box 140
Hartford, WI 53027
414-673-4340
www.broan.com

Home Ventilation Institute

30 West University Drive
Arlington Heights, IL 60004
312-394-0150

Nutone Inc.

Madison & Red Bank Roads
Cincinnati, OH 45227
800-543-8687

Vinyl Flooring

Armstrong World Industires Inc.

P.O. Box 3001
Lancaster, PA 17604
800-233-3823
www.armstrong.com

Armstrong Customer
Response Center

800-233-3823

Azrock Industries Inc.

P.O. Box 696060
San Antonio, TX 78269
512-558-6400

Congoleum Corp.

3705 Quakerbridge Road
Mercerville, NJ 08619
800-447-2882

Mannington Flooring

P.O. Box 30
Salem, NJ 08079
800-FLOOR-US

Resilient Floor Covering Institute

966 Hungerford Drice
Suite 12-B
Rockville, MD 20850

Wilsonart

800-710-8846

Tarkett

P.O. Box 264
Parsippany, NJ 07054
800-367-2774

Vinyl Siding Institute

355 Lexington Avenue
New York, NY 10017

Water Heaters

American Water Heater

800-999-9515

A.O. Smith

600 E. John Carpenter Frwy.
Suite 200
Irving, TX 75062
800-323-2636
www.aoswpc.whc.net

Bradford-White

800-531-2111

Rheem

5600 Old Greenwood Rd.
Fort Smith, AR 72917
501-646-4311
www.rheem.com

State Industries

800-821-2019
www.stateind.com

Water Softeners

Bruner Corp.

800-5-Bruner
www.brunercorp.com

Culligan

www.culligan.com
800-CULLIGAN

Rainsoft Water
Treatment Systems

800-860-7638
www.aquion.com

Windows and Doors

Allied Windows

(Invisible Storms)
800-445-5411
www.invisiblestorms.com

Anderson Windows Inc.

P.O. Box 3900
Peoria, IL 61614
800-426-4261
www.andersonwindows.com

Bilco Co.

Basement Access
P.O. Box 1203
New Haven, CT 06505
203-934-6363

Blaine Window Hardware Inc.

Window Parts
1919 Blaine Drive RD 4
Hagerstown, MD 21740
301-797-6500

Certainteed

800-782-8777
www.certainteed.com

Clopay

800-2CLOPAY

Craftmaster

Masonite Co.
800-504-1020
www.masonite.com

Crestline

One Wausau Center
P.O. Box 8007
Wausau, WI 54402-8007
800-552-4111

Four Seasons Sun Rooms

800-FOUR-SEASONS

Hopes Landmark Products

P.O. Box 106
Lakewood, NY 14750-0106
716-763-7708

Hurd Millwork

800-2BE-HURD
www.hurd.com

Kolbe and Kolbe

800-955-8177
www.kolbe-kolbe.com

Lincoln Windows

800-777-0551

Marvin Windows & Doors

P.O. Box 100
Warroad, MN 56763
888-537-8253
www.marvin.com

Morgan Mfg.

P.O. Box 2446
Oshkosh, WI 54903
800-766-1992

Norco Windows, Inc.

P.O. Box 140
Hawkins, WI 54530
715-585-6311

Pella Rollscreen Co.

102 Main Street
Pella, IA 50219
800-524-3700

Pella Windows & Doors

800-54-PELLA
www.pella.com

Pozzi

800-257-9663
www.pozzi.com

Premdor

800-663-DOOR
www.premdor.com

Prime-Line Products

P.O. Box 9910
San Bernadino, CA 92407
909-880-8968

Simpson Door Co.

P.O. Box 210
McCleary, WA 98557
206-495-3291

Stanley Door Systems

800-782-6539
www.stanleywork.com

Velux-America, Inc.

P.O. Box 5001
Greenwood, SC 29648
800-283-2831

Vetter Windows

And Patio Doors
715-693-7000
www.vetterwindows.com

Weather Shield
Windows and Doors

One Weather Shield Plaza
Medford, WI 54451
800-477-6808
www.weathersheild.com

Wood, Wood Products, and Wood Flooring

American Hardboard Assoc.

B520 N. Hicks Road
Palatine, IL 60007
708-934-8800

American Plywood Assoc.

Box 11700
Tacoma, WA 98411

Bruce Hardwood Floors

16803 Dallas Parkway
Dallas, TX 75248
800-722-4647

California Redwood Association

888-225-7339
www.calredwood.org

Forest Products Laboratory
Forest Service USDA

One Gifford Pinchot Drive
Madison, WI 53705
608-231-9200

Hardwood Council

www.hardwoodcouncil.com
412-281-4980

Hardwood Manufacturers Association

400 Penn Center Boulevard
Suite 530
Pittsburgh, PA 15235
412-829-0770

Hardwood Plywood & Veneer Association

703-435-2000
www.hpva.org

Harris Tarkett

P.O. Box 300
Johnson City, TN 37605-0300
615-928-3122

Hartco Wood Flooring

900 S. Gay Street Suite 2102
Knoxville, TN 37902
423-544-0767
www.hartcoflooring.com

Maple Flooring Manufacturers Association

847-480-9138
www.maplefloor.com

Minwax Wood Hardener
Minwax High Performance
Wood Filler

800-462-0194

Mr. Mac's Wood Fix
Mr. Mac's Concrete Fix

800-348-3571

National Oak Flooring Manufacturers Association

Box 3009
Memphis, TN 38173
901-526-5016
www.nofma.com

National Wood Flooring Association

1688 Westwoods Business Park
Ellisville, MO
63021-4522

Norton Company
Consumer Products Div.

One New Bond Street
Worcester, MA 01606

Oak Flooring Institute

P.O. Box 3009
Memphis, TN 383173-0009
901-562-5016

Southern Forest Products Association

Box 641700
Kenner, LA 70064
504-443-4464
ww.southernpine.com

Southern Pine Marketing Council

P.O. Box 52468
New Orleans, LA 70152
504-443-4464

Western Wood Products Association

Yeon Building
522 S.W. Fifth Avenue
Portland, OR 97204-2122
503-224-3930
www.wwpa.org

Weyerhaeuser

800-548-5767

Whether you're doing it yourself or hiring professionals to service your home, these checklists help ensure that all important points are covered.

Tear out applicable checklists and make photocopies. You can send a copy to the service company when you arrange service, and/or review the list with the technician at the beginning of the service call.

Mr. Fix-It™

Warm Air Furnace–Homeowner Service Checklist

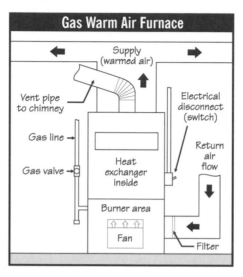

Note: Turn off power to the unit before inspection or maintenance.

☐ Maintain records. Have a professional service the unit yearly. Proper maintenance keeps equipment operating efficiently and ensures safety. Contact the manufacturer of your furnace for specific maintenance requirements. See the References section for contact information.

☐ Change the filter as required—often every other month.

☐ Switch high/low returns at the start and end of the heating season. For complete instructions, check the section on "Heating and Cooling Distribution" in the "Utility Systems—Heating and Air Conditioning" chapter.

☐ Check all flue pipes and vents for rust, water leaks, and loose connections.

☐ Lubricate the fan motor and fan bearing with a few drops of oil twice per year. (This is only required on certain units.)

☐ Check the belt to make sure it's not cracked or loose. (This is only required with belt-driven fans.)

☐ Listen to the furnace operate and follow up on any strange sounds.

☐ Check drain lines to make sure they are clear and draining properly.

☐ Look for water leaks or changes in the system.

_____

_____

_____

Mr. Fix-It

Warm Air Furnace–Professional Service Checklist

Note: Turn off power to the unit before inspection or maintenance.

During a routine service call, the service technician should perform the following general maintenance measures. The technician may perform other checks, too, depending on the type of furnace.

❑   Check and clean burner.

❑   Check flue pipes, draft diverter, heat exchanger, and chimney.

❑   Remove burners to clean burners and heat exchanger if necessary.

❑   Check electrical wiring and connections.

❑   Check and clean circulating fan. Lubricate fan and motor if necessary.

❑   For belt drive fans: check for tension, wear and alignment.

❑   Check supply and returns ducts for air leakage, water stains, rust.

❑   Check and maintain filter.

❑   Perform an operational check of furnace and safety controls.

❑   Test for carbon monoxide in the flue gas and in the air around the furnace.

❑   Check for gas leaks.

❑   Check, clean, and adjust pilot light if necessary.

Gas Warm Air Furnace

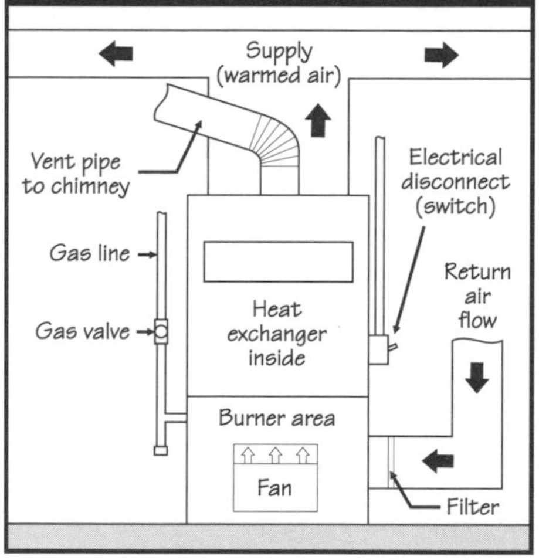

Supply (warmed air)

Vent pipe to chimney

Gas line

Gas valve

Heat exchanger inside

Burner area

Fan

Electrical disconnect (switch)

Return air flow

Filter

For a high-efficiency furnace, the technician should also:

❑   Check for water leaks (condensation from combustion).

❑   Check flue pipes and connections.

❑   Check for condensation on metal pipes and parts.

❑   Check for a clean condensate drain line.

Mr. Fix-It

Hydronic Heating–Homeowner Service Checklist

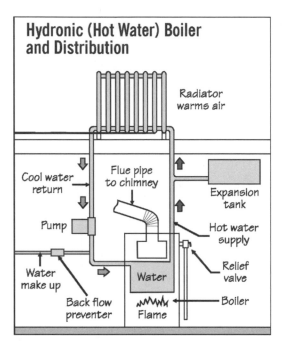

Hydronic (Hot Water) Boiler and Distribution

Note: Turn off power to the unit before inspection or maintenance.

☐ Maintain records, and have a professional service the unit yearly.

☐ Check all flue pipes and vents for rust, water leaks, loose connections.

☐ Listen to the boiler operate, and follow up on any strange noises.

☐ Check drain lines to make sure they are clear and draining properly. (This is required only for high efficiency condensing units.)

☐ Look for water leaks or changes in the system.

☐ Oil the circulating pump twice per year. (Use just a few drops).

☐ Check that the temperature/pressure gauge is in the operating range identified by a professional service technician. Mark the proper range on the gauge.

_____

_____

_____

_____

Mr. Fix-it

Hydronic Heating–Professional Service Checklist

A service technician should perform the following general maintenance measures. The service technician may also perform additional checks, depending on the type of furnace.

❑ Check and clean burner.

❑ Vent the system at the high points as necessary.

❑ Check all flue pipes, draft diverter, boiler housing, and chimney.

❑ Remove burners to clean burners and heat exchanger if necessary.

❑ Check electrical wiring and connections.

❑ Check and lubricate circulating pump(s).

❑ Check for water leaks.

❑ Check temperature and pressure relief valve.

❑ Check water supply system and backflow preventer.

❑ Add backflow preventer if none is present.

❑ Check expansion tank for proper water level.

❑ Perform an operational check of controls for temperature, pressure and safety.

❑ Test for carbon monoxide in the flue gas and in the air around the furnace.

❑ Check for gas leaks.

❑ Check, clean, and (if necessary) adjust pilot light.

Hydronic (Hot Water) Boiler and Distribution

- Radiator warms air
- Cool water return
- Flue pipe to chimney
- Expansion tank
- Pump
- Hot water supply
- Water make up
- Water
- Relief valve
- Back flow preventer
- Flame
- Boiler

Additional checks for a high-efficiency boiler with a draft fan:

❑ Check draft fan for condensation and rust.

❑ Check flue pipe for condensation.

❑ Check condensate drain lines.

Mr. Fix-It

Oil Heating–Homeowner Service Checklist

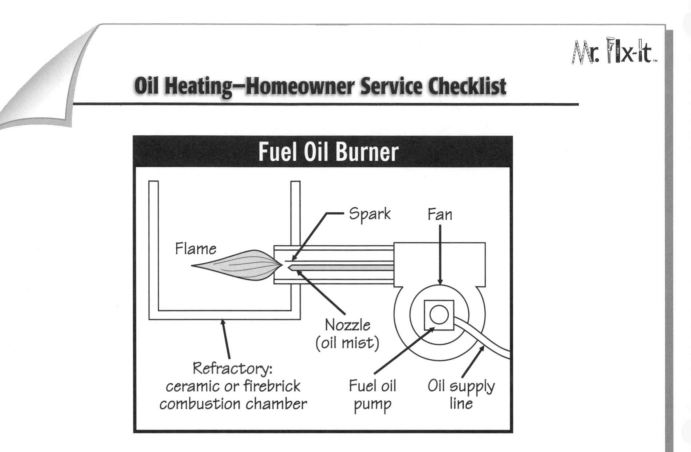

Fuel Oil Burner

Spark   Fan

Flame

Nozzle
(oil mist)

Refractory:
ceramic or firebrick
combustion chamber

Fuel oil
pump

Oil supply
line

Note: **Turn off all power to the unit before attempting inspection or maintenance.**

❑   Follow the maintenance requirements listed on previous pages for warm air or hydronic boiler systems.

❑   Schedule routine maintenance yearly.

❑   Lubricate the burner motor if it has oil ports. (Ask your service technician).

❑   Make sure the system never, never runs out of fuel oil.

_____

_____

_____

_____

_____

_____

_____

_____

Mr. Fix-It™

Oil Heating–Professional Service Checklist

A service technician should perform the following general maintenance measures. The service technician may also perform additional checks, depending on the type of furnace.

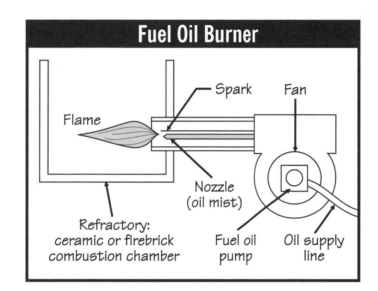

Note: **The first item on this checklist refers to general maintenance requirements found in the checklist for a warm-air furnace, so photocopy the warm air furnace checklist, too, and give both lists to your service technician.**

❏   Follow applicable maintenance requirements listed for a warm air furnace.

❏   Remove and clean burner, clean blower blades, replace or clean filter and/or strainer, replace the nozzle, clean flame and heat sensors, check and clean or replace electrodes.

❏   Lubricate the burner motor.

❏   Check flue and barometric damper.

❏   Check for oil leaks.

❏   Check and clean oil pump.

❏   Clean and test stack control.

❏   Check and adjust draft regulator.

❏   Test for efficiency and make proper adjustments.

Mr. Fix-It.

Steam Heating–Homeowner Service Checklist

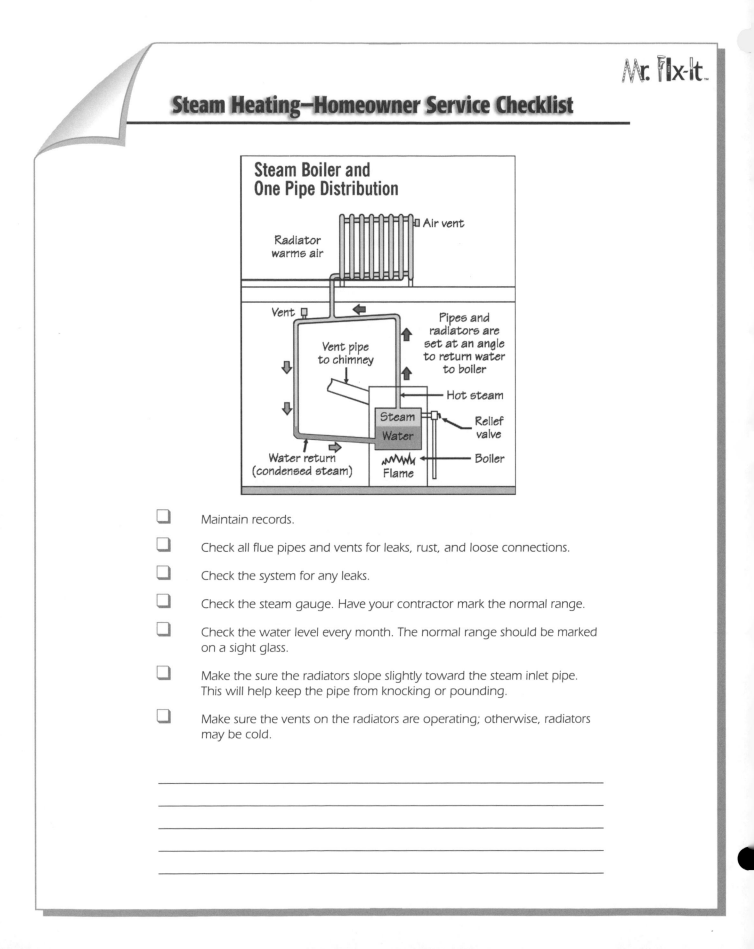

Steam Boiler and One Pipe Distribution

❑   Maintain records.

❑   Check all flue pipes and vents for leaks, rust, and loose connections.

❑   Check the system for any leaks.

❑   Check the steam gauge. Have your contractor mark the normal range.

❑   Check the water level every month. The normal range should be marked on a sight glass.

❑   Make the sure the radiators slope slightly toward the steam inlet pipe. This will help keep the pipe from knocking or pounding.

❑   Make sure the vents on the radiators are operating; otherwise, radiators may be cold.

_____

_____

_____

_____

_____

Mr. Fix-It™

Steam Heating–Professional Service Checklist

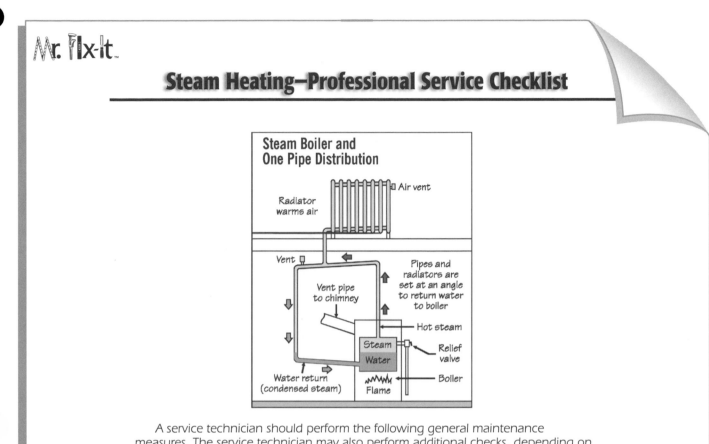

A service technician should perform the following general maintenance measures. The service technician may also perform additional checks, depending on the type of boiler. (For a gas-fired system, see the information on oil burners, which require additional checks.)

❑   Check and clean the burner.

❑   Check all vents on radiators and piping.

❑   Check all flue pipes, draft diverter, boiler housing and chimney.

❑   Remove burners to clean them and the heat exchanger if necessary.

❑   Check electrical wiring and connections.

❑   Check for water or steam leaks.

❑   Check the temperature and pressure relief valve.

❑   Add a backflow preventer if none is present.

❑   Perform an operational check of controls for temperature, pressure and safety.

❑   Test for carbon monoxide in the flue gas and the air around the boiler.

❑   Check for gas leaks.

❑   Check, clean and if necessary adjust the pilot light.

Mr. Fix-It

Central Air Conditioning—Homeowner Service Checklist

Note: **Turn off all power and disconnect switches before performing inspections/maintenance.**

❏ Maintain records, and have a professional service the unit yearly.

❏ Change the filter as often as required (in some cases, every month).

❏ Switch high/low returns (and adjust ductwork if necessary) at the start and end of the cooling season. For complete instructions, check the section on "Heating and Cooling Distribution" in the "Utility Systems—Heating and Air Conditioning" chapter.

❏ Listen to the air conditioner operate, and follow up on any strange noises.

❏ Check drain lines from the furnace to make sure they are clear and draining properly.

❏ Look for water leaks or changes in the system.

❏ Keep plants and obstructions away from the exterior coil and fan. Allow 3 feet of clearance at the air discharge and 1 foot all around the unit.

❏ Keep the exterior coil clean.

❏ Keep the exterior unit level and away from soil or landscape materials.

❏ Make sure that supply and return registers inside your home are not blocked.

Air Conditioning System with Warm Air Furnace

OUTSIDE   INSIDE

— Refrigerant lines

Cool supply

— Cooling coil

— Pan

Condensing unit: coil, fan and compressor

Furnace

Warm return

Condensate drain

Fan

Filter

Floor drain

FALL MAINTENANCE

❏ Disconnect power to the unit to prevent accidental use.

❏ (Optional)—Cover the top of the unit.

SPRING MAINTENANCE

❏ Uncover the unit.

❏ Turn the power on 24 hours before operation. Keep the thermostat off.

❏ Perform the maintenance listed above and arrange for professional service.

_____

_____

_____

_____

_____

_____

_____

_____

Mr. Fix-It

Central Air Conditioning–Professional Service Checklist

Air Conditioning System with Warm Air Furnace

OUTSIDE   INSIDE

Refrigerant lines

Cool supply

Cooling coil

Pan

Warm return

Condensing unit: coil, fan and compressor

Furnace

Condensate drain

Fan

Floor drain

Filter

A service technician should perform the following procedures during a routine service call. The technician may perform additional checks, depending on the type of air conditioner you have.

❑   Check filter and replace as needed.

❑   Check exterior unit for level conditions, a clean coil, clearances, and adequate air flow.

❑   Check interior temperature drop across the cooling coil (15 to 22 degrees F).

❑   Check the condensate drain pan and line.

❑   Check secondary pan and line if unit is located in an attic.

❑   Look for signs of water leaks or excessive air leaks.

❑   Lubricate the fan motor and check the belt if required.

❑   Inspect electrical connections.

❑   Inspect refrigerant lines for signs of leaks.

❑   If performance problems exist, the technician may check for amp draw, clean the coils, check the refrigerant charge, and/or complete general performance tests.

Mr. Fix-it™

Heat Pump—Homeowner Service Checklist

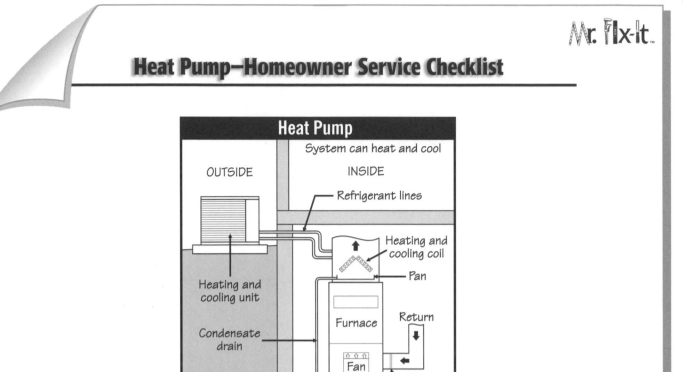

Note: Turn off all power and disconnect switches before performing inspections/maintenance.

❑ Schedule professional service yearly.

❑ Watch for ice forming on the exterior unit. This is a serious problem indicating that the unit needs service.

❑ Follow all the maintenance recommendations for central air conditioning.

_____

_____

_____

_____

_____

_____

_____

_____

Mr. Fix-It.

Heat Pump–Professional Service Checklist

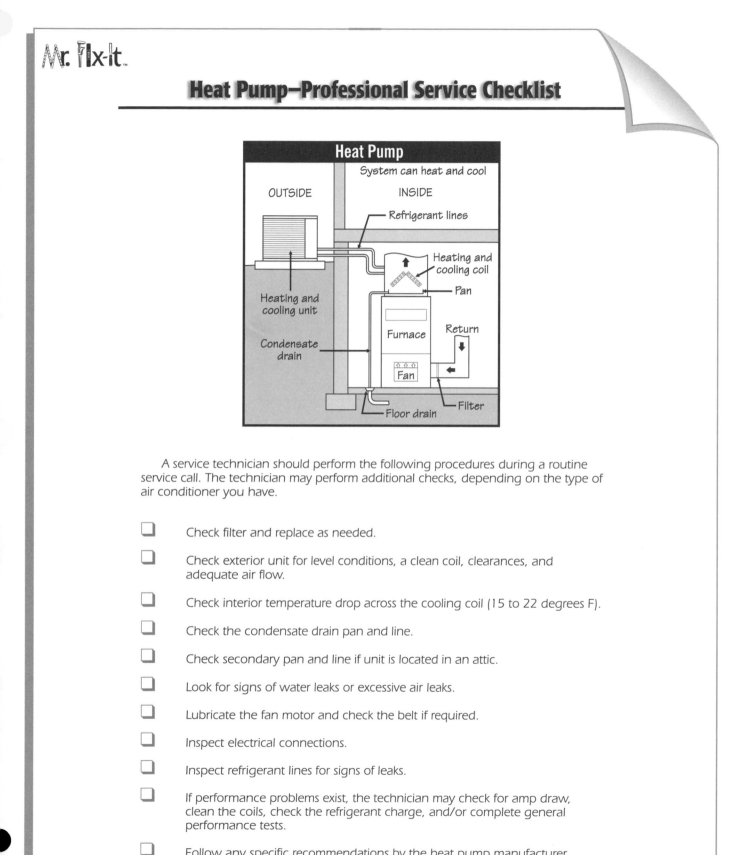

A service technician should perform the following procedures during a routine service call. The technician may perform additional checks, depending on the type of air conditioner you have.

❑   Check filter and replace as needed.

❑   Check exterior unit for level conditions, a clean coil, clearances, and adequate air flow.

❑   Check interior temperature drop across the cooling coil (15 to 22 degrees F).

❑   Check the condensate drain pan and line.

❑   Check secondary pan and line if unit is located in an attic.

❑   Look for signs of water leaks or excessive air leaks.

❑   Lubricate the fan motor and check the belt if required.

❑   Inspect electrical connections.

❑   Inspect refrigerant lines for signs of leaks.

❑   If performance problems exist, the technician may check for amp draw, clean the coils, check the refrigerant charge, and/or complete general performance tests.

❑   Follow any specific recommendations by the heat pump manufacturer.

INDEX

W

Seminars And Keynotes

Tom Feiza - Mr. Fix-It is available for seminars and keynote presentations. Mixing his more than 25 years of engineering experience with "hands-on" home repair expertise, Tom delivers informative and humorous presentations that are perfect for home shows, spouse programs, dinner meetings, seminars, and retail events.

Here's a sampling of Tom's presentations:

Keynote—So You Cut It Twice and It's Still Too Short?

A fun look at home maintenance and repairs. Tom relies on years of experience to relate great stories, humor, and tips with an emphasis on success. Audiences always enjoy the fun, the great tips, and the many free samples and prizes.

Seminar—Just Fix It: The Absolute Best Repair Products

Tom solves the most common fix-it problems using state-of-the-art tools and techniques. Learn to achieve results you never dreamed possible. Enjoy product samples and hot repair tips you can use instantly.

Seminar—Painting Pointers

Toss that roller tray and forget the ladder. Achieve professional results using the proper tools and techniques. Make interior and exterior finishes look and last as if painted by a professional.For more information, contact:

Tom Feiza, Mr. Fix-It, Inc.
P.O. Box 510724
New Berlin WI 53151
Phone: (262) 786-7878 ▪ Fax: (262) 786-7877

E-mail: Tom@misterfix-it.com ▪ Web site: misterfix-it.com or tomfixit.com

ORDERING INFORMATION

Mr. Fix-It books are available through book retailers, Internet book stores, or from Tom Feiza—Mr. Fix-It, Inc:

How To Operate Your Home   ISBN 0-9674759-1-0 $24.95

The ultimate guide for operating your home – just like an owners manual for your car. Answers all those questions about how a home works and how you should be operating your home. Operation and maintenance schedules to keep your home in top shape and to prevent disasters. Service checklists for contractors and much more.........

Just Fix It   ISBN 0-9674759-0-2 $14.94

The absolute best home repairs tips. Hundreds of home repair tips Tom has gathered in over 15 years of his radio and print "how-to" advice. How do you remove that rust stain on the driveway? How do you paint the dark paneling? How do you make your old countertop look like new? And much more.......

Ordering Books From Mr. Fix-It?

To order books from Mr. Fix-It, send the cover price plus $3.00 shipping and handling for the first book and $1.00 shipping and handling for each additional book. Wisconsin residents must add 5% for sales tax.

Send your order and payment (cash, check or money order) with complete return address to:

Tom Feiza, Mr. Fix-It Inc.
P.O. Box 510724
New Berlin WI 53151

You can also contact Tom and find great home repair information at his web site:

www.misterfix-it.com.